EXAMINING *NOSTRA AETATE* AFTER 40 YEARS

EXAMINING NOSTRA AETATE AFTER 40 YEARS

Catholic-Jewish Relations in Our Time

Edited by

Anthony J. Cernera

SACRED HEART UNIVERSITY PRESS
FAIRFIELD, CONNECTICUT
2007

Library of Congress Cataloging-in-Publication Data

Examining Nostra Aetate after 40 Years: Catholic-Jewish Relations in our time / edited by Anthony J. Cernera.
     p. cm.
  Includes bibliographical references and index.
    ISBN 978-1-888112-15-3
  1. Judaism–Relations–Catholic Church. 2. Catholic Church–Relations–Judaism. 3. Vatican Council (2nd: 1962-1965). Declaratio de ecclesiae habitudine ad religiones non-Christianas. I. Cernera, Anthony J., 1950-

BM535. E936 2007
261.2'6–dc22

                          2007026523

Contents

Preface   vii

Nostra Aetate Revisited
    Edward Idris Cardinal Cassidy   1

The Teaching of the Second Vatican
Council on Jews and Judaism
    Lawrence E. Frizzell   35

A Bridge to New Christian-Jewish
Understanding: *Nostra Aetate* at 40
    John T. Pawlikowski   57

Progress in Jewish-Christian Dialogue
    Mordecai Waxman   78

Landmarks and Landmines in
Jewish-Christian Relations
    Judith Hershcopf Banki   95

Catholics and Jews: Twenty
Centuries and Counting
    Eugene Fisher   106

The Center for Christian-Jewish Understanding
of Sacred Heart University: An Example of
Fostering Dialogue and Understanding
    Anthony J. Cernera   143

Nostra Aetate: A Catholic Act of *Metanoia*
    Philip A. Cunningham   160

Are You the One Who Is To Come, or, Is This
the Way It Is? *Nostra Aetate*: What Difference
Is It Making in North America?
    Frans Jozef van Beeck   176

Contributors   213

Index   217

Preface

For those working in the field of Christian-Jewish dialogue, it is difficult to remember what was it like before October 28, 1965, when the Catholic bishops of the world voted to approve the shortest and perhaps most controversial document of Vatican II, *Nostra Aetate*, which addressed the relationship of the Catholic Church to non-Christian religions, especially Jews. Before that time it was not uncommon for Christian churches to discount Judaism as an antiquated religion that had been replaced or superseded by Christianity. Many Christians probably believed that Jews needed to be converted and held an implicit attitude of contempt toward them, believing them to be blind and stubborn to the truth of Jesus. Interfaith marriages were rare and interreligious meetings were exercises in apologetics more than discussion.

The *Nostra Aetate* document was written for Christians, but it signaled to Jews and to the world that the Catholic Church was rethinking its attitudes, teachings, and practices regarding Jews. *Nostra Aetate* is best understood in the context of subsequent statements by the Holy See, the popes, and the conferences of bishops that are trying to implement it. Official Vatican documents such as the *Guidelines and Suggestions for Implementing the Conciliar Declaration, Nostra Aetate* (1974), *Notes on the Correct Way to Present Jews and Judaism in Preaching and Catechesis in the Roman Catholic Church* (1985), *The Catechism of the Catholic Church* (1994), and *We Remember: A Reflection on the Shoah* (1998) all follow the lead of *Nostra Aetate* and deplore all persecutions, hatreds, prejudice, discrimination, and displays of anti-Semitism leveled at any time or from any source.

Nostra Aetate encouraged dialogue and mutual understanding between Christians and Jews by way of "biblical and theological enquiry and friendly discussion." Catholic universities and Jewish institutions have a special responsibility in fostering dialogue and understanding for the sake of discovering truth and promoting peace and justice. Centers and institutes of Jewish-Christian studies and interreligious studies as well as Jewish Studies departments have been established in an increasing number of secular universities. The frequency of workshops and conferences where scholars and students share biblical and theological insights is increasing, and the warmth of that shared wisdom is beginning to bear fruit in excellent collaborative publications by scholars of different faiths. The Center for Christian-Jewish Understanding of Sacred Heart University is proud to be a leader in this most important effort of those who seek the deepest truth of human relations based on God's invitation to work for peace and justice.

The dialogue process of the past forty years initiated by *Nostra Aetate* has challenged many Christian denominations to write significant statements and publish recommendations for future relations with the Jewish people. Similarly, several Jewish organizations and individuals have also published promising statements that attest to their willingness to continue this vital conversation. Of course, there will continue to be disagreements and misunderstandings by all parties, but these can be key parts of rather than impediments to ongoing and productive dialogue.

We are living in extraordinary times and are blessed because people of good will have reached out in trust and friendship. The present volume is intended to be a testament of and contribution to that continuing effort. The papers herein were contributed by prominent leaders in the field of Christian-Jewish understanding whose words and lives play an important part in the *Nostra Aetate* story. Collectively, the essays that follow describe the past, present, and future of that story, calling attention to the pioneers and pivotal events that have paved the way, assessing from various points of view where we are now, and sketching in detail what needs to be done as we move ahead turn the vision of *Nostra Aetate* into a lasting reality.

The volume begins with an essay by Edward Idris Cardinal Cassidy in which he describes *Nostra Aetate* as a document that "left the Catholic Church throughout the world with a binding and irreversible commitment to turn away from almost 2,000 years of hostility towards the Jewish people, and to set out on a new journey of mutual trust and understanding." Cardinal Cassidy focuses on the steps taken in the decades after *Nostra Aetate* to further this mutual trust and understanding, including the formation of commissions and study groups, and the convening of regular international conferences to further the Catholic-Jewish dialogue that had for many years been conspicuous by its absence. This dialogue is still the proverbial "work in progress," and Cardinal Cassidy acknowledges the various difficulties in overcoming "the past spirit of suspicion, resentment and distrust," some of which have surfaced particularly in ongoing dialogue about the Holocaust, and how the *Shoah* should be commemorated. But without minimizing the remaining strains and challenges, Cardinal Cassidy envisions "an exciting future." The essay concludes with a detailed examination of how the spirit of *Nostra Aetate* continues in a variety of recent publications by both Catholic and Jewish scholars that affirm not only mutual respect but the deep commonalities of Christianity and Judaism, and, as one document puts it, their shared "Covenant and Mission."

While Cardinal Cassidy takes us from *Nostra Aetate* to the present, Lawrence E. Frizzell places *Nostra Aetate* in its own historical circumstances, and examines the document in the broad context of the Second Vatican Council's "contribution to Catholic-Jewish relations." While acknowledging that *Nostra Aetate* is indeed a significant breakthrough, Frizzell shows how its spirit and indeed even many of its particulars can be seen in such documents as *The Constitution on the Sacred Liturgy*, *Lumen Gentium*, *Dei Verbum*, *Gaudium et Spes*, and *Dignitatis Humanae*. *Nostra Aetate* is, as it were, not so much a moment as a momentous articulation of an evolving modern tradition.

At the same time, *Nostra Aetate* is certainly a break from an earlier longstanding tradition. In "A Bridge to New Christian-

Jewish Understanding: *Nostra Aetate* at 40," John T. Pawlikowski
highlights ways in which this document may be taken as not only a
new direction in the Catholic understanding and treatment of Jews
but also a document with potentially radical theological consequences,
affecting how Catholics understand Catholicism. Pawlikowski surveys
contemporary scholarship (by Robin Scroggs and others) that
emphasizes how earlier attempts to define Christianity by stressing
its break and differences from Judaism should perhaps give way to a
deeper awareness of the continuing rootedness of Christianity in
Judaism. A number of contributors to this volume pertinently
discuss the ways in which *Nostra Aetate* is a significant step forward
in one faith tradition's understanding and relating to the "Other."
Pawlikowski nicely complements this by reminding the reader of
the extent to which *Nostra Aetate* should also be taken as a critical
opportunity for members of one faith tradition to understand itself.

Mordecai Waxman's essay was originally published in a
Festschrift honoring Cardinal John O'Connor, but fits particularly
well here not only as it acknowledges Cardinal O'Connor's many
contributions to the "revolutionary change of attitude" marked by
Nostra Aetate but also because it provides a behind-the-scenes
narrative of some of the key meetings and events prompted by
Nostra Aetate that initiated, as his title puts it, "Progress in Jewish-
Christian Dialogue." Waxman brings to life the "agenda, discussion,
and character" of international meetings going as far back as 1975,
and we hear first-hand recollections of the negotiations, tensions,
and breakthroughs that are inevitable parts of what is a very
complex conversation and move toward reconciliation. Waxman
focuses particularly on crises surrounding Pope John Paul II's
audience with former U.N. Secretary General Kurt Waldheim,
whose early association with the Nazi party had recently been
revealed, and the controversy that erupted when a group of
Carmelite nuns attempted to turn a building in Auschwitz into a
convent. Waxman tells a fascinating story about how these and
other such potentially divisive events and tensions were overcome,
and in fact came to emblematize the difficult process of dialogue in
which "From the bitter came forth the sweet."

Much like Waxman, Judith Hershcopf Banki surveys the bitter and the sweet in her recollections of "Landmarks and Landmines in Jewish-Christian Relations." In her work with the American Jewish Committee, one of her particular concerns has been examining the contents of Christian teaching material, and the sad fact she documents in this essay is the persistence of anti-Semitism supported by a deeply-ingrained "teaching of contempt." It is embarrassing and painful to recount the details of the continuing tradition of caricatures, slanders, mistreatment, and insensitivity that never seems far from the surface in popular and even institutionalized relations with and conceptions of Jews, Judaism, and the state of Israel, but Banki affirms that if the aim of *Nostra Aetate* is ever to be realized, one key imperative is that "Christians must learn something about the history of Christian anti-Semitism as part of their religious education." She acknowledges that "The progress that has been made since Vatican II is remarkable," but measures this against "the background of estrangement that preceded it" and continues to this day in a variety of misunderstandings, outrages, and missed opportunities. She perhaps speaks for all the contributors to the volume when, guardedly optimistic, she concludes her essay with wise words of assessment, motivation, and hope: "We still have much work to do together."

The "background of estrangement" that Banki speaks of is sketched out in detail in Eugene Fisher's essay, "Catholics and Jews: Twenty Centuries and Counting," which provides a far-ranging overview of Catholic-Jewish relations from the days of Jesus to our own time. Fisher organizes his panoramic treatment around what he labels as "Six Moments of Crisis in Catholic-Jewish History," and even though he presents an abbreviated summary covering over two-thousand years, he attempts to avoid giving a "flattened" view and instead tries to capture some of the complexities of a story that may "open up possibilities for the future." Each of the historical periods he surveys shows the separating of the two religions, a process that Fisher insists was not inevitable—that was in fact not a reflection of but a regrettable deflection from the origins of

Christianity and the spirit of the New Testament. "Separation" turns out to be far too neutral a word: the history that Fisher traces is an ominously accelerating one of triumphalism, exclusion, oppression, and the teaching of contempt, culminating in the "racialist" theories that developed during the so-called "Enlightenment" and took even more monstrous form in the twentieth century. But for Fisher a comprehensive historical view alerts us to not only a shameful series of events that must be repudiated and repented but a glimmer of missed opportunities that must not be missed again. He calls for a return to a kind of Christianity without the accretions that contributed to anti-Semitism, one that again, as in the early days, in the words of the Second Vatican Council, acknowledges and enacts the "sacred bond" between Catholics and Jews, a process that will be furthered as each group comes to learn each others' "language."

Fisher's concluding emphasis on the centrality of dialogue is complemented by my case study of how the spirit of *Nostra Aetate* can be embodied and propagated in a structure such as the Center for Christian-Jewish Understanding (CCJU) of Sacred Heart University, set up to, as the subtitle to the essay notes, foster "Dialogue and Understanding." Like Frizzell and several others in the present volume, I place *Nostra Aetate* in the context of a series of papal documents (including *Dei Verbum, Gaudium et Spes,* and *Notes on the Correct Way to Present Jews and Judaism in Preaching and Catechesis*) that put forth a new agenda for renewal and reconciliation, and make practical suggestions for realizing these goals. I describe how the CCJU promotes interreligious dialogue and understanding through an ambitious program of teacher education, conferences, study tours, awards, and publications. One of the intentions is to help create not just moments but a "culture of dialogue," and in describing the origin and operation of the CCJU, I attempt to provide a blueprint for the development of what one hopes will be many more such centers that facilitate learning with and about the Other, valuable in itself, of course, but also, as many of the essays in this volume reiterate, insofar as it is a vital part of learning about oneself.

Philip A. Cunningham highlights the radical qualities of *Nostra Aetate* as what he calls "A Catholic Act of *Metanoia*," that is, "a total reorientation of attitude or action." Cunningham adds to the contextual study of *Nostra Aetate* undertaken in other essays in this volume by examining its stark contrast with an unfinished encyclical by Pope Pius XI, begun in 1938, that even though it was evidently "intended to condemn racism in the wake of Hitler's rise to power in Germany" was circumscribed by conventional notions of Jews as Christ-killers, perennially separate from all other people. This is a prominent part of the theological landscape that the framers of *Nostra Aetate* had to alter, and worked to do so, Cunningham points out, against sustained opposition that has not disappeared even forty years later. Cunningham's essay focuses on seven key affirmations of *Nostra Aetate*: its repudiation of the charge of deicide; emphasis on the shared legacy of Judaism and Christianity; reiteration of the covenental link of God and the Jews; disavowal of acts of hatred against and persecution of the Jews; call for "accurate biblical interpretation and religious education" as well as further collaboration between Jews and Christians on "biblical and theological enquiry"; and disinclination to attempt to baptize Jews. Besides being a very clear primer on much of the essence of this extraordinary document and the process through which it was forged, Cunningham's essay also implicitly underscores a key instance of how a religion that prides itself on stability and tradition is also quite capable, when circumstances warrant, of dynamic change.

This element of dynamism is on full display in the concluding essay in the volume by Frans Jozef van Beeck, which is animated by his sense that the Great Tradition of Catholicism rests on the possibility—indeed, the inevitability—of change, earth-shattering and optimistic change, and that being a "good Catholic" is no mere matter of holding "enforced truths" and obeying conventional prescribed "rational rules." One of the sub-themes of his far-ranging—and impossible to summarize—meditation on Christian theology and human history is that "Human Openness to Otherness" is at the core of Christianity, and there is a familiar reference point for this thought. If *Nostra Aetate* is radical, it is so by returning us to the fundamental radicalness of Jesus. Neither world nor Church history has remained true to this spirit, and van Beeck surveys many of the mis-steps along the way. But he is ultimately, and persuasively, an optimist, and in his attempt to answer the question posed in his title—"What Difference Is [*Nostra Aetate*] Making in North America?"—he learnedly and rhapsodically suggests that it is part of an urgent call for Jews and Christians to faith and responsibility, to challenges that must—and can—be met daily.

All the contributors to this volume attempt to deepen our understanding and appreciation of *Nostra Aetate* by putting it in one or another context, either personal, social, political, historical, or theological. Van Beeck's essay serves as a fit conclusion to the volume because it adds one more to all of those: he places *Nostra Aetate* ultimately in the context of the *imitatio Christi*, which serves as a stirring inspiration, solid rock, and reminder of the inevitable strains and difficulties as we endeavor, among other tasks, to affirm the unity and connectedness of all humankind and to make the world more fair, just, and loving.

A special word of thanks is due to my dear friend, Rabbi Joseph H. Ehrenkranz, executive director of the Center for Christian-Jewish Understanding (CCJU) of Sacred Heart University, for his tireless and heartfelt efforts to bring Jews and Christians together in peace and understanding—beginning with the two of us. He and his associate, David L. Coppola, have done a great service to both religions by promoting dialogue that has resulted in deep friendships and lasting scholarly collaborations.

I am also grateful to Ann Heekin, director of programs and publications for the CCJU, all those at the Center who assisted with this volume, and Sidney Gottlieb, director of editorial and production work for the Sacred Heart University Press. I am further grateful to Dr. Gottlieb, along with Dr. Coppola, for assistance in writing the prefatory overview to the volume.

Finally, I want to thank all the contributors to this volume, whose ongoing commitment to interreligious dialogue is a declaration of hope for the future, and all those people who for the past forty years had the vision and courage to promote the ideas contained in *Nostra Aetate*. Let us move forward together—without fear and with ever-renewing energy—to bring about God's vision of peace and justice.

Nostra Aetate *Revisited*

EDWARD IDRIS CARDINAL CASSIDY

Introduction

On April 24, 2005, Pope Benedict XVI, during the Mass in St. Peter's Square for the commencement of his pontificate addressed the following words to the Jewish people:

> With great affection I greet also you, my brothers and sisters of the Jewish people, to whom we are joined by a great shared spiritual heritage, one rooted in God's irrevocable promises.

These words, taken together with the presence of an impressive Jewish representation two weeks earlier at the funeral Mass of Pope John Paul II are an eloquent expression of the progress that has been made over the past forty years in Catholic-Jewish relations.[1]

Perhaps we should recall on this anniversary occasion, and with deep gratitude, the remarkable radical change that the Fathers of the Second Vatican Council brought about in this relationship. In N° 4 of the document entitled *Declaration on the Relation of the Church to Non-Christian Religions* (*Nostra Aetate*), which Pope Paul VI and the bishops signed on October 28, 1965, they left the Catholic Church throughout the world with a binding and irreversible commitment to turn away from almost 2,000 years of hostility towards the Jewish people, and to set out on a new journey of mutual trust and understanding.

In that short document, the Catholic Church solemnly declared that "the Jews remain very close to God . . . since God does not take back the gifts he bestowed or the choice he made." The Council recognized, moreover, the debt that the Church owed to the Jewish people:

> The Church cannot forget that she received the revelation of the Old Testament by way of that people with whom God in his inexpressible mercy established the ancient covenant. Nor can she forget that she draws nourishment from the good olive tree onto which the wild olive branches of the Gentiles have been grafted (cf. Rom 11:17-24).

The Council Fathers recalled that the apostles, the pillars on which the Church stands, were of Jewish descent, as were many of the early disciples who proclaimed the Gospel of Christ to the world. St. Paul had written to the early Christians in Rome about his fellow Jews: "They are Israelites, and to them belong the sonship, the glory, the covenants, the giving of the law, the worship, and the promises; to them belong the patriarchs, and of their race according to the flesh, is the Christ" (Rom 9:4-5).

Nostra Aetate N° 4 removed from the Church's teaching the old substitution theory and made it clear that "neither Jews indiscriminately," nor "Jews today can be charged with the crimes committed during Christ's passion." Jews should not therefore be spoken of as rejected or accursed as if this follows from Holy Scripture.

All this indicated a radical change in an era of the Church's relationship with other world religions. The task was then to make these solemn decisions a part of the daily teaching of the Church, and influence accordingly the thought of its members throughout the world.

The First Steps Along the Way

This task was entrusted by Pope Paul VI to the Secretariat for Christian Unity, which was then given with the 1967 reform of the Curia "competence also in questions concerning the Jews under their religious aspect." The Apostolic Constitution *Regimini Ecclesiae* of Pope Paul VI defines the scope of this task and its proper character.[2]

The extent of the challenge posed by this task was indicated by the SPCU President, Cardinal Johannes Willebrands, in his report to the 1972 Plenary of the SPCU, when he stated, "For my part I am astounded to realize how poorly Christians and Jews know each other." He added:

> This is not an obstacle that can be overcome by mere books. A *religious* dialogue is needed here. Catholics will not come to understand what Judaism is, especially in its religious experience, except by meeting Jews who are trying to grasp what is at the heart of Christianity. The converse is obviously true. The task demands that both should be on the same wavelength. Dialogue with Jews appears as a duty within the framework of our mission. It is sustained by that hope which resounds through the biblical texts that Jews and Catholics use in their liturgies.

Cardinal Willebrands pointed out that, with regard to this dialogue, "there is no lack of unknown factors and difficulties." Among those he mentioned, I would underline the following: the difference between Christians and Jews in the way they see the relation of people and religion, with the consequence that "the distinction between the political and religious domains is especially difficult for the Jews"; and the disparity between dialogue among Christians and Christian dialogue with Jews. While the Catholic Church has already been for some time involved in dialogue with other Christians, Catholic-Jewish dialogue "is in its beginnings."[3]

Despite these difficulties, the dialogue soon gained momentum both at the local and the international levels. At the local level, groups of Jews and Catholics were coming together to foster friendship, and mention was made of common action and collaboration between Catholics and Jews. Moreover, on the local level some studies and research were being carried out with the intention of making catechetics more faithful to the principles outlined by the Second Vatican Council. Special commissions had been set up as part of Episcopal conferences in the U.S.A., Canada, France, England, and Holland. Contact had been made between the office in Rome and the Committee on Church and the Jewish People within the "World Mission and Evangelism" division of the World Council of Churches.

The positive response of the Jewish world to the hand of friendship offered by the Second Vatican Council in *Nostra Aetate* N° 4 is often taken for granted today. Yet one could easily have understood a less willing attitude on the part of a people who had suffered so greatly over the centuries, especially at the hands of members of the Church, even those at times in the highest positions. Fortunately, there were some courageous Jewish leaders willing to grasp the hand of friendship. As a result of informal discussions between some of these Jewish leaders and authorities of the Roman Curia, an official meeting in Rome on December 20-23, 1970, took the decision to set up a special International Catholic-Jewish Liaison Committee (ILC) between the Catholic Church and important Jewish organizations.

Taking into account these encouraging developments, Pope Paul VI on October 22, 1974, created within the SPCU a special Commission for Religious Relations with the Jews (CRRJ) "with the scope of promoting and fostering relations of a religious nature between Jews and Catholics." The Commission would be responsible for developing "true and proper relations with Judaism on a worldwide plane" and would be at the disposal of all interested bodies or those concerned with Jewish-Catholic relations, "in order to supply them with information or receive information from them, and in order to help them to pursue their goals in conformity with the directives of the Holy See." It would endeavor to promote "the effective and just realization of the orientations given by the Second Vatican Council, particularly in Section Four of the Declaration *Nostra Aetate*."[4]

It is not possible here to follow in detail the journey from that early situation to the papal ceremonies in St. Peter's Square this year.

I should, however, recall the early teaching documents published by the Roman dicastery: *Guidelines and Suggestions for Implementing the Conciliar Declaration Nostra Aetate N. 4* in 1974,[5] and eleven years later, in 1985, a much more detailed document entitled: *Notes on the Correct Way to Present the Jews and Judaism in Preaching and Catechesis in the Roman Catholic Church* (*Notes*).[6] The document itself explains its purpose:

> Religious teaching, catechesis and preaching should be a preparation not only for objectivity, justice, and tolerance but also for understanding and dialogue. Our two traditions are so related that they cannot ignore each other. Mutual knowledge must be encouraged at every level. There is evident in particular a painful ignorance of the history and traditions of Judaism, of which only negative aspects and often caricature seem to form part of the stock ideas of many Christians.

This is what these notes aim to remedy. This would mean that the Council text and *Guidelines and Suggestions* would be more easily and faithfully put into practice.

International Catholic-Jewish Liaison Committee (ILC)

The International Catholic-Jewish Liaison Committee, which had been set up in December 1970, was to have an all-important positive influence on future Catholic/Jewish relations. This was jointly organized by the International Jewish Committee for Interreligious Consultations (IJCIC) and the Vatican office for Catholic-Jewish Relations. IJCIC had in fact been created specifically for contact with the Catholic Church. There were three original Jewish organizations: the World Jewish Congress with constituents in sixty-five countries; the Synagogue Council of America, acting on behalf of Orthodox, Conservative, and Reform Judaism in the United States; and the American Jewish Committee, which had been active since 1906 in interreligious activities and in the fields of the civil and religious rights of Jews in any part of the world. The meeting in Rome opened up a vast range of questions of common interest and proposed the setting up of joint working groups and study commissions to follow up the discussions. The office for Catholic-Jewish relations noted at the time that "only in a few countries have Christians begun to realize the importance of this question. And even in most countries where Jews and Christians live together almost everything must still be done."[7]

The aim of the Committee was defined as follows: the improvement of mutual understanding between the two religious communities, as well as the exchange of information and possible cooperation in areas of common responsibility and concern. The ILC met for the first time in "an atmosphere of frankness and cordiality" in the Jewish Consistory in Paris on December 14-16, 1971. From the outset it became clear that while it would be desirable in certain fields for a common position to be reached, in other fields the principal aim should be to clarify both similarities and differences with a view to attaining genuine mutual understanding.

Over the next fifteen years, the ILC met almost annually (with the exception of 1980 and 1983) in various European cities and once in Jerusalem.[8] These meetings provided the participants and the organizations they represented with an opportunity of exchanging information regarding matters of shared interest and of discussing questions of common concern. Among other matters, attention was given to anti-Semitism, the situation in the Middle East, human rights, and religious freedom. These ILC gatherings were of special value in developing a spirit of trust at the international level between the Church and the Jewish people.

By the time of the twelfth ILC meeting in Rome in 1985, IJCIC had been enlarged to include among its members the B'nai B'rith Anti-Defamation League and the Israel Jewish Council for Interreligious Dialogue, in addition to the three original members.

At that meeting, both Pope John Paul II and Cardinal Johannes Willebrands similarly looked forward to the future with confidence. The Pope spoke of the "rich, varied and frank relationship" that had been achieved within the ILC over the fifteen years of its existence, "despite the normal difficulties and some occasional tensions," and gave the following advice:

> In order to follow along the same path, under the eyes of God and with his all-healing blessing, I am sure you will work with ever greater dedication for constantly deeper mutual knowledge, for ever greater interest in legitimate concerns of each other and especially for collaboration in the many fields where our faith in one God and our common respect for his image in all men and women invite our witness and commitment.[9]

Cardinal Johannes Willebrands also spoke in encouraging terms, referring to the "link" or "bond" that for the Catholic Church flows from her identity as church.

While the dialogue was achieving good results, Catholic participants were experiencing a certain frustration at not being able to enter into serious discussions on questions of faith of particular interest to both sides. *Nostra Aetate* had stated: "Since the spiritual patrimony common to Christians and Jews is so great, this sacred synod wants to foster and recommend that mutual understanding and respect which is the fruit, above all, of biblical and theological studies as well as of fraternal dialogue." Orthodox Jews, however, were not open to "biblical and theological studies," and other members of the ILC were not willing to go against this opposition, being happy just to concentrate on fraternal dialogue with a view to responding to practical concerns and improving relationships.

Certain events towards the end of the 1980s interrupted this good progress. The beatification of Edith Stein on May 1, 1987, followed closely by the announcement that the recently elected President of Austria, Kurt Waldheim, was to be received in official Audience by the Pope on June 25 of that same year brought a strong protest from Jewish leaders. The personal intervention of Pope John Paul II, first in Rome and then in a meeting with Jewish representatives in Miami in 1987, helped to get the dialogue back on track. In was in these circumstances that the Pope promised the Jewish community an official document on the *Shoah*.[10]

Before that could happen, however, a new dark cloud had already appeared on the horizon. It had suddenly come to the notice of the Jewish people that a cloistered Carmelite convent had been established within the precincts of the extermination camp at Auschwitz. For the Jewish world, this was seen as an attempt to move the emphasis away from the place of Auschwitz within the *Shoah*, and turn it into a place of suffering and death for the Christian victims of Nazism. The large cross in the convent grounds was considered particularly offensive to Jews. The problem was eventually resolved again through the personal intervention of Pope John Paul II and the transfer of the Sisters to a new convent in 1995.

After a break of five years, in September 1990 the ILC was able to resume its work at Prague in Czechoslovakia, which had for centuries been the home of a large and influential Jewish community. The Prague meeting of the ILC proved to be a remarkable success, keeping in mind the background situation of the preceding years. On September 6, 1990, after many hours of discussion and hard work, the meeting approved a remarkably positive statement.[11] It "acknowledged the monumental role of the Declaration of the Second Vatican Council Declaration *Nostra Aetate*, as well as of later efforts by the Popes and Church officials, to bring about a substantive improvement in Catholic Jewish relations." The delegates present in Prague called for a "deepening of this spirit in Catholic-Jewish relations, a spirit that emphasizes cooperation, mutual understanding and reconciliation; goodwill and common goals to replace the past spirit of suspicion, resentment and distrust." The statement concludes with the following hopeful vision of the future:

> After two millennia of estrangement and hostility we have a sacred duty as Catholics and Jews to strive to create a genuine culture of mutual esteem and reciprocal caring. Catholic-Jewish dialogue can become a sign of hope and inspiration to other religions, races and ethnic groups to

turn away from contempt, toward realizing authentic human fraternity. The new spirit of friendship and caring for one another may be the most important symbol that we have to offer to our troubled world.

The ILC has since continued to meet regularly almost every second year.

Another major event that was to prove extremely beneficial for this relationship was the establishment, on December 30, 1993, of diplomatic relations between the State of Israel and the Holy See. As has been already mentioned, the implementation of *Nostra Aetate* had been impeded to some extent by the lack of such formal official relations. The preamble to the *Fundamental Agreement between the Holy See and the State of Israel*[12] makes specific reference to the "unique nature of the relations between the Catholic Church and the Jewish people, the historical process of reconciliation and understanding and the growing mutual friendship between Catholics and Jews."[13]

We Remember: A Reflection on the *Shoah*

On March 16, 1998 the CRRJ published the document on the *Shoah* that had been promised by Pope John Paul II in 1987 and had been eagerly awaited by the Jewish world community. The statement *We Remember* is addressed to "our brothers and sisters of the Catholic Church throughout the world."[14] At the same time it asks "all Christians to join us in meditating on the catastrophe which befell the Jewish people." Towards the end, the appeal is made to "all men and women of good-will to reflect deeply on the significance of the *Shoah*," stating that "the victims from their graves, and the survivors through the vivid testimony of what they have suffered, have become a loud voice calling the attention of all of humanity. To remember this terrible experience is to become fully conscious of the salutary warning it entails: the spoiled seeds of anti-Judaism and anti-Semitism must never again be allowed to take root in any human heart."

We Remember makes clear that, while no one can remain indifferent to the "unspeakable tragedy" of the attempt of the Nazi regime to exterminate the Jewish people for the sole reason that they were Jews, the Church has a special obligation to reflect on this "horrible genocide," "by reason of her very close bonds of spiritual kinship with the Jewish people and her remembrance of the injustices of the past" (I). Moreover, "the Shoah took place in Europe, that is, in countries of long-standing Christian civilization" (II).

This raises the question of the relation between the Nazi persecution and the attitudes down through the centuries of Christians towards Jews. In such a short document, it was not possible to dwell at any length on the history of these relations, but the text admits clearly the prevalence over many centuries of anti-Judaism in the attitude of the Church towards the Jewish people. It acknowledges the "erroneous and unjust interpretations of the New Testament regarding the Jewish people and their alleged culpability," a "generalized discrimination" in their regard, "which ended at times in expulsions or attempts at forced conversions," attitudes of suspicion and mistrust, while in times of crisis "such as famine, war, pestilence or social tensions, the Jewish minority was sometimes taken as the scapegoat and became the victim of violence, looting, even massacres" (III).

While lamenting this anti-Judaism, the document makes a distinction between this and the anti-Semitism of the nineteenth and twentieth centuries, based on racism and extreme forms of nationalism, "theories contrary to the constant teaching of the Church on the unity of the human race and on the equal dignity of all races and peoples." The anti-Semitism of the Nazis was the fruit of a thoroughly neo-pagan regime, with its roots outside of Christianity and, in pursuing its aims, it did not hesitate to oppose the Church and persecute its members also. The Nazi regime intended "to exterminate the Jewish people . . . for the sole reason of their Jewish origin" (IV).

No attempt is made in the document to deny that "the Jewish people have suffered much at different times and in many places while bearing their unique witness to the Holy One of Israel and to the *Torah*" (II). But the *Shoah* was certainly the worst suffering of all. The inhumanity with which the Jews were persecuted and massacred during this century is beyond the capacity of words to convey. "All this was done to them for the sole reason that they were Jews" (II).

We Remember does not seek to deny that the Nazi persecution of the Jews was made easier by anti-Jewish prejudices embedded in some Christian minds and hearts. This is clear in the document, which asks, however, that before making accusations against people as a whole or individuals, one should know what precisely motivated those people in their particular situation. There were members of the Church who did everything in their power to save Jewish lives, even to the point of placing their own lives in danger. Many did not. Some were afraid for themselves and those near to them; some took advantage of the situation; and still others were moved by envy. The document makes this central point clear:

> As Pope John Paul II has recognized, alongside such courageous men and women (those who did their best to help), the spiritual resistance and concrete action of other Christians was not that which might have been expected from Christ's followers. We cannot know how many Christians in countries occupied or ruled by the Nazi powers or their allies were horrified at the disappearance of their Jewish neighbors and yet not strong enough to raise their voices in protest. For Christians, this heavy burden of conscience of their brothers and sisters during the Second World War must be a call to penitence. We deeply regret the errors and failures of those sons and daughters of the Church. (IV)

We Remember calls on Catholics to renew their awareness of the Hebrew roots of their faith, and of the fact that the Jews are their dearly beloved brothers, and in a certain sense their elder brothers. It then expresses regret by way of the following act of repentance:

> At the end of this Millennium the Catholic Church desires to express her deep sorrow for the failures of her sons and daughters in every age. This is an act of repentance (*teshuvah*), since, as members of the Church, we are linked to the sins as well as to the merits of all her children.

While remembering the past, the Vatican document looks to a new future in relations between Jews and Christians. It closes with the prayer "that our sorrow for the tragedy which the Jewish people have suffered in our century will lead to a new relationship with the Jewish people. We wish to turn awareness of past sins into a firm resolve to build a new future in which there will be no more anti-Judaism among Christians or anti-Christian sentiment among Jews, but rather a shared mutual respect, as befits those who adore the one Creator and Lord and have a common father in faith, Abraham" (V).

Pope John Paul II and Catholic-Jewish Relations

The significant progress made in the years 1978-2005 in Catholic Jewish relations owes much to the personal contribution of Pope John Paul II. Apart from the unfailing support that His Holiness gave to those engaged in his name in this great task, he himself intervened with outstanding success in promoting this relationship. During his many travels to countries throughout the world, Pope John Paul II never missed an opportunity to meet with Jewish representatives and encourage dialogue. In the early nineties, some of the Papal visits took His Holiness to countries that had been for many years under Soviet domination, and mostly unaware of what had happened in the field of Catholic-Jewish relations during the previous twenty years. The visit to Lithuania on July 11, 1992, was such an example.[15] The Pope also showed himself always ready to receive Jewish delegations that might come on a visit to Rome.[16]

During his pontificate, Pope John Paul II frequently expressed the belief that actions are more effective than words in getting a message across to the modern day world. A perfect example of this was the historic visit that the Pope paid, on April 13, 1986, to the Synagogue of Rome. Even though the Synagogue is only a couple of kilometers from the Vatican, no pope is known ever to have set foot there. Pope John XXIII did stop his car to bless Jewish worshippers leaving the Synagogue one Sabbath, but John Paul II took an initiative that was to contribute greatly to better worldwide Jewish-Catholic relations.[17]

Another significant initiative of Pope John Paul II was the concert held in the *Aula Paolo VI* within Vatican City to commemorate the *Shoah* on April 7, 1994.[18] The Royal Philharmonic Orchestra, conducted by Maestro Gilbert Levine, performed a moving program that included Max Bruch's *Kol Nidrei* and Leonard Bernstein's Symphony N° 3, *Kaddish*, narrated by Richard Dreyfuss.

The final, and perhaps the most significant, of Pope John Paul's interventions in Catholic-Jewish relations came during the Jubilee Year 2000. At his General Audience on April 28, 1999, Pope John Paul II spoke on Jewish-Christian dialogue in the context of preparations for the Jubilee Year, and expressed the hope that "at the dawn of the third millennium sincere dialogue between Christians and Jews will help create a new civilization founded on the one, holy and merciful God and fostering a humanity reconciled in love."[19]

This theme of conversion and reconciliation, which permeated the celebration of the Jubilee Year 2000, brought forth two very special events that would radically change Catholic-Jewish relations. On March 12, 2000, Pope John Paul II called for and presided over a special penitential service in St. Peter's Basilica, a "day of pardon" to ask forgiveness from the Lord "for the sins, past and present, of the sons and daughters of the Church."[20] One of the seven requests for pardon referred to "Sins against the People of Israel." Pope John Paul II had on several previous occasions expressed sorrow for sins committed by the sons and daughters of the Church against the people of Israel, most notably in the document *We Remember*. But now, in the name of the Catholic Church throughout the world, the Pope offered the following prayer to God:

God of our fathers, you chose Abraham
To bring your name to the nations:
We are deeply saddened by the behavior of those who in
the course of history
Have caused these children of yours to suffer,
And asking your forgiveness
We wish to commit ourselves to genuine brotherhood
With the people of the covenant.

The introduction to this prayer recalled the sufferings endured by the people of Israel throughout history, and asked that Christians might purify their hearts by acknowledging the sins committed against the people of the Covenant.[21]

Two weeks later, Pope John Paul II was finally able to make the long desired visit to Israel, from March 21-26.[22] There were several events of deep significance for Christians and Jews during those days. Indeed, the very visit itself was seen by the Jewish community as an important contribution to Catholic-Jewish relations.

Of the various events that merit special mention the most memorable is undoubtedly that of March 26, 2000, when the Pope and his entourage stood before the Western Wall of the Temple, a most sacred place for the Jewish World. After silent prayer, Pope John Paul II placed in the Wall a personally signed copy of the prayer that he had offered just two weeks earlier in St. Peter's Basilica, expressing sorrow for the suffering of the Jewish people at the hands of Christians down through the centuries and asking forgiveness from God.

On March 23, His Holiness had visited the Yad Vashem Holocaust Memorial, rekindled the flame that recalls the six million victims of the *Shoah*, and laid a wreath of yellow and white daisies over the place where the ashes of many death camp victims are interred. In continuation, as it were, of the prayer offered in St. Peter's, the Pope stated during that moving ceremony in Jerusalem:

Here as at Auschwitz and many other places in Europe, we are overcome by the echo of the heart-rending laments of so many. Men, women and children cry out to us from the depths of the horror that they knew. How can we fail to hear their cry? No one can forget or ignore what happened. No one can diminish its scale. We wish to remember. But we wish to remember for a purpose—namely, to ensure that never again will evil prevail, as it did for the millions of innocent victims of Nazism.[23]

Towards a New and Lasting Future

I have sought to travel briefly over the past forty years of our Jewish-Catholic journey so as to justify the hope that I have for the future of this relationship, " a future based on mutual esteem and reciprocal caring," as the Prague meeting of the ILC described this "sacred duty." The first years of the new Millennium in the Christian calendar has given sound grounds for such a hope being fulfilled.

Already in 2001 the Seventeenth ILC meeting, which was held in New York, from April 30 to May 4, 2001,[24] departed from its former refusal to discuss questions of faith and took as its theme "Repentance and Reconciliation." This subject had been chosen to respond to the frustration on the Catholic side that even after many years of dialogue it had not been possible to enter into theological discussions with the Jewish partner, even though both CRRJ and IJCIC represented faith communities.

In fact, the New York gathering covered ground that previously had been "off limits" for the Jewish representatives. Two documents were discussed and approved. The first was a practical statement on a matter that had been a constant concern of ILC for a number of years: "A Recommendation on Education in Catholic and Jewish Seminaries and Schools of Theology." The other was a statement on "Protecting Religious Freedom and Holy Sites," which concluded:

We stand together as representatives of the Catholic and Jewish communities of faith in calling on men and women of all faiths to honor religious liberty and to treat the holy places of others with respect. We call on all people to reject attacks on religious liberty and violence against holy places as legitimate forms of political expression.

We look forward, prayerfully, to the time when all people shall enjoy the right to lead their religious lives unmolested and in peace. We long for the time when the holy places and all religious traditions will be secure and when all people treat one another's holy places with respect.[25]

As already mentioned, the main theme of the meeting was "Repentance and Reconciliation."

In the jointly agreed Communiqué at the close of the meeting, the participants stated clearly that their partnership is secure and that the vital work of the ILC will continue to flourish in the years ahead. As official representatives of their organized religious communities, they expressed their determination "to engage our leadership and laity in dialogue and cooperation."

The ILC met for the eighteenth time in Buenos Aires, from July 5-8, 2004, with the theme *"Zedeq and Zesaqah (Justice and Charity)*: Facing the Challenges of the Future; Jewish and Catholic Relations in the Twenty-first Century."[26]

The Pontifical Biblical Commission

Another contribution to this fascinating study of the relationship between the two Covenants came from a document published in 2001 by the Pontifical Biblical Commission, which is closely linked to the Congregation for the Doctrine of the Faith: *The Jewish People and Their Scriptures in the Christian Bible.*[27] It seeks to address from a scriptural basis a problem that has haunted Jews and Christians for centuries, namely the real and binding connection between these two faiths. In his introduction, Cardinal Ratzinger quotes from N° 84 of the document, which states:

Without the Old Testament, the New Testament would be an unintelligible book, a plant deprived of its roots and destined to dry up and wither.

The Second Vatican Council, in *Nostra Aetate N° 4*, had suggested that better mutual understanding and appreciation between Christians and Jews could be obtained by way of biblical and theological enquiry, and the present document has been composed in this spirit. This is not the place to dwell at length on this statement of the Pontifical Biblical Commission. I shall just quote what seem to be among the most significant affirmations made by the Commission.

> The New Testament recognizes the divine authority of the Jewish Scriptures and supports itself on this authority. When the New Testament speaks of the "Scriptures" and refers to "that which is written," it is to the Jewish Scriptures that it refers. (N° 84)

Again,

> Christians can and ought to admit that the Jewish reading of the Bible is a possible one, in continuity with the Jewish Sacred Scriptures from the Second Temple period, a reading analogous to the Christian reading which developed in a parallel fashion. Both readings are bound up with the vision of their respective faiths, of which the readings are the result and expression. Consequently, both are irreducible. (N° 22)

In clarifying what this twofold reading entails, and in clearing the ground for a "possible" Jewish reading, the Commission states:

> It would be wrong to consider the prophecies of the O.T. as some kind of photographic anticipations of future events. All the texts, including those which later were read as Messianic prophecies, already had an immediate import and meaning for their contemporaries before attaining a fuller meaning for future hearers. The messianship of Jesus has a meaning that is new and original. (N° 21)

And then the Commission makes an important affirmation that I believe Jewish readers would find most welcome:

> Jewish messianic expectation is not in vain. It can become for us Christians a powerful stimulant to keep alive the eschatological dimension of our faith. Like them, we too, live in expectation. The difference is that for us the One who is to come will have the traits of Jesus who has already come and is already present and active among us. (N° 22)

There is of course much more to this document than the few words that I have quoted. Yet, it should be obvious that the Pontifical Commission has made an important contribution to Jewish-Christian relations. At the end of each section of the document there are a number of positive assertions about Judaism and the Jewish people, and in conclusion expresses the hope "that prejudice and misunderstanding be gradually eliminated in favor of a better understanding of (our) common patrimony."

Dialogue with the Great Rabbinate of Jerusalem

A new and promising development in Jewish-Catholic theological reflection has come as a result of the opening of a dialogue with the Great Rabbinate of Jerusalem. This was certainly made possible by the visit in 2000 of Pope John Paul II to Israel, who on that occasion spent quite some time at the Chief Rabbinate in discussion with the two Chief Rabbis of Israel. This event also offered members of the Pope's entourage and a number of Jewish Rabbis the possibility of coming to know one another. Cardinal Walter Kasper followed up these promising contacts with a personal visit to Israel in November 2001.

After a preliminary meeting in Jerusalem on June 5, 2002, high-ranking delegations of the CRRJ and the Chief Rabbinate of Israel met in Villa Cavalletti, Grottaferrata, in the vicinity of Rome from February 23-27, 2003. The Jewish delegation was led by the Chief Rabbi of Haifa, Shar Yishuv Cohen, and the Catholic

Delegation by Cardinal Jorge Mejia, a former Secretary of the CRRJ. The meeting was held in a warm and friendly atmosphere of mutual goodwill, and was characterized by the effort to highlight common aspects of both traditions. Two main issues were raised, namely: the *Sanctity of Life*, and the *Value of the Family*.

A common declaration was signed at the end of the meeting, in which the two delegations rejected any attempt to destroy human life, based on their common religious understanding that the human being is created in the image of God. Every human life is "holy, sacrosanct and inviolable." They stated clearly that it is a profanation of religion to declare oneself a terrorist in the name of God or to do violence to others in his name. They emphasized the need for education of both communities, and particularly the younger generation, in respect for holiness of human life, and agreed that "against the present trend of violence and death in our societies, we should foster our cooperation with believers of all religions and all people of good will in promoting a *culture of life.*"

Similarly, the participants at this gathering saw the institution of the family as stemming from the will of the Almighty. "Marriage," they declared, "in a religious perspective has a great value, because God blessed this union and sanctified it. . . .The family unit is the basis for a wholesome society."[28]

This meeting was a historical breakthrough, as until then it had not been possible to organize an official dialogue between the CRRJ and institutes in Israel. Moreover, for the first time the Church was able to enter into dialogue with all the different forms of Judaism: Orthodox, Conservative, and Reformed.

A second meeting between the Chief Rabbinate of Israel and the CRRJ took place in Jerusalem December 1-3, 2003, to discuss the theme: *The Relevance of Central Teachings in the Holy Scriptures Which We Share for Contemporary Society and the Education of Future Generations.* The Joint Declaration issued on this occasion noted that once again the deliberations had taken place in an atmosphere of mutual respect and amity, and that satisfaction was expressed "regarding the firm foundations that have already been established between the two delegations with great promise for continuity and effective collaboration."

The participants in this second formal meeting continued their reflections on the relation of the family to the Scriptures and declared that "humankind is one family with moral responsibility for one another." They saw that "awareness of this reality leads to the religious and moral duty that may serve as a true charter for human rights and dignity in our modern world and provide a genuine vision for a just society, universal peace and well-being." It was emphasized that "the response to the challenge of promoting religious faith in contemporary society requires us to provide living examples of justice, loving kindness, tolerance and humility," as set forth in the Scriptures.

The meeting stressed the need for religious education to provide hope and direction for positive living in human solidarity and harmony in our complex modern society. The participants called on religious leaders and educators to instruct their communities to pursue the paths of peace and of well-being of society at large. A special appeal was addressed to the family of Abraham and a call made to all believers "to put aside weapons of war and destruction—'to seek peace and pursue it' (Ps 34:15)."[29]

I should just mention a further very encouraging event that took place in New York at the beginning of 2004. A Catholic delegation including eight Cardinals and two Presidents of Bishops' Conferences met with six Chief Rabbis and a contingent of European, American, and Israeli Jews to discuss how to promote peace and to stand together against growing anti-Semitism. The function was hosted at the Museum of Jewish Heritage by Cardinal Jean-Marie Lustiger, Archbishop of Paris, and sponsored by the World Jewish Congress. Participants described the meeting as the highest-level talks in the troubled history of Catholics and Jews. In a statement issued at the end of the two-day meeting, the participants "expressed consternation at continuing expressions of hatred in the world and noted with concern the recent rise of anti-Semitic manifestations."[30] A second meeting of this group took place at the same venue in February 2005.

And finally, there are three documents which have been published in recent years that also provide hope for the future of this relationship, and in my opinion merit special consideration.

Dabru Emet (Proclaim the Truth)

In September 2000, a group of prominent Jewish scholars published a *Jewish Statement on Christians and Christianity: Dabru Emet (Proclaim the Truth)*.[31] The document opens with the statement that "In recent years, there has been a dramatic and unprecedented shift in Jewish and Christian relations," and suggests that the changes made by Christians in this period "merit a thoughtful Jewish response . . . We believe that it is time for Jews to learn about the efforts of Christians to honor Judaism. We believe it is time for Jews to reflect on what Judaism may now say about Christianity." It then offers, as a first step, eight brief Jewish statements aimed at promoting a better relationship with Christians:

> *Jews and Christians worship the same God* . . . the God of Abraham, Isaac, and Jacob, creator of heaven and earth. While Christian worship is not a viable religious choice for Jews, as Jewish theologians we rejoice that, through Christianity, hundreds of millions of people have entered into relationship with the God of Israel.

> *Jews and Christians seek authority from the same book, the Bible.* Turning to it for religious orientation, spiritual enrichment and communal education, we each take away similar lessons: God created and sustains the universe; God established a Covenant with the people Israel; God's revealed word guides Israel to a life of righteousness and God will ultimately redeem Israel and the whole world. While noting that Jews and Christians interpret the Bible differently on many points, the statement insists that such differences must always be respected.

Christians and Jews can respect the claim of the Jewish people upon the land of Israel.

Jews and Christians respect the moral principles of the Torah. Central to the moral principles of Torah is the inalienable sanctity and dignity of every human being. All of us were created in the image of God. This shared moral emphasis can be the basis of an improved relationship between our two communities. It can also be the basis of a powerful witness to all humanity for improving the lives of our fellow human beings and for standing up against the immoralities and idolatries that harm and degrade us.

Nazism was not a Christian phenomenon. Without the long history of Christian anti-Judaism and Christian violence against Jews, Nazi ideology could not have taken hold nor could it have been carried out. Too many Christians participated in, or were sympathetic to, Nazi atrocities against Jews. Other Christians did not protest sufficiently against these atrocities. But Nazism itself was not an inevitable consequence of Christianity. If the Nazi extermination of the Jews had been fully successful, it would have turned its murderous rage more directly to Christians. We recognize with gratitude those Christians who risked or sacrificed their lives to save Jews during the Nazi regime. With that in mind, we encourage the continuation of recent efforts in Christian theology to repudiate unequivocally contempt of Judaism and the Jewish people.

The humanly irreconcilable difference between Jews and Christians will not be settled until God redeems the entire world as promised in the Scripture. Each community knows and serves God through their own tradition. Jews can respect Christians' faithfulness to their revelation just as we expect Christians to respect our faithfulness to our tradition.

A new relationship between Jews and Christians will not weaken Jewish practice.

Jews and Christians must work together for justice and peace.

Dabru Emet goes further than any other Jewish document in acknowledging the close links that bind Jews and Christians together and in calling for closer collaboration in favor of justice, peace, and the preservation of the moral order. The statement on Christianity and Nazism is particularly welcome in Catholic circles, especially in view of some of the criticism leveled at *We Remember*, while the acknowledgement that "the humanly irreconcilable difference between the Jews and Christians will not be settled until God redeems the whole world as promised in Scripture" is a timely reminder that, as Catholics and Jews look to the future, they must not dialogue with the expectation that they will agree on everything.

"Abraham's Heritage—A Christian Gift"

Within a few months of the publication of *Dabru Emet*, an article by Cardinal Joseph Ratzinger contributed further to this new trend in dialogue. Many members of the Jewish community worldwide had read with concern the September 2000 statement of the Vatican Congregation for the Doctrine of the Faith, *Dominus Jesus*.[32] They were worried by the assertion in *Dominus Jesus* to the effect that followers of religions other than Christianity were in a gravely deficient situation in respect of salvation. The short article by Cardinal Ratzinger, which appeared on the front page of *L'Osservatore Romano* on December 29, 2000, entitled "Abraham's Heritage—A Christmas Gift," seemed to be an attempt to dispel that concern. The article proved, however, to be a much more significant document, providing further encouragement for Catholic-Jewish theological dialogue.

"Abraham's Heritage—A Christmas Gift," referring to the very negative Jewish reaction to the document *Dominus Jesus*, affirms: "It is evident that, as Christians, our dialogue with the Jews is situated on a different level than that in which we engage with other religions. The faith witnessed to by the Jewish Bible is not merely another religion to us, but is the foundation of our own faith."

The Cardinal then gives what has been called "a new vision of the relationship with the Jews."[33] After tracing briefly the history of God's dealings with the Jewish people, the Cardinal expresses "our gratitude to our Jewish brothers and sisters who, despite the hardness of their own history, have held on to faith in this God right up to the present and who witness to it in the sight of those peoples who, lacking knowledge of the one God, *dwell in darkness and the shadow of death* (Luke 1:79)." The article then has the following interesting comment on relations between Christians and Jews down through the centuries:

> Certainly from the beginning relations between the infant church and Israel were often marked by conflict. The Church was considered to be a degenerate daughter, while Christians considered their mother to be blind and obstinate. Down through the history of Christianity, already-strained relations deteriorated further, even giving birth to anti-Jewish attitudes that throughout history have led to deplorable acts of violence. Even if the most recent, loathsome experience of the *Shoah* was prepared in the name of an anti-Christian ideology that tried to strike the Christian faith at its Abrahamic roots in the people of Israel, it cannot be denied that a certain insufficient resistance to this atrocity on the part of Christians can be explained by the inherited anti-Judaism in the hearts of not a few Christians.

For the Cardinal, it is perhaps this latest tragedy that has resulted in a new relationship between the Church and Israel, which he defines as "a sincere willingness to overcome every kind of anti-Judaism and to initiate a constructive dialogue based on knowledge of each other and reconciliation." If such a dialogue is to be fruitful, the Cardinal suggests that "it must begin with a prayer to our God first of all that he might grant to us Christians a greater esteem and love for that people, the people of Israel, to whom belong *the adoptions as sons, the glory, the covenants, the giving of the law, the worship and the promises; theirs the patriarchs, and from them, according to the flesh, is the Messiah* (Rom. 9:4-5), and this not only in the past, but still today, *for the gifts and the call of God are irrevocable* (Rom. 11:29)." Cardinal Ratzinger goes on to propose to Christians that they in their turn might pray to God "that he grant also to the children of Israel a deeper knowledge of Jesus of Nazareth, who is their son and the gift they have made to us." His final conclusion reminds us of the sixth statement in *Dabru Emet*: "Since we are both waiting the final redemption, let us pray that the paths we follow may converge."

Reflections on Covenant and Mission

The year 2002 saw the publication of a statement in the United States of America that created great interest in Jews and Catholics involved in theological dialogue. On August 12, 2002, the Ecumenical and Interreligious Affairs Committee of the United States Conference of Catholic Bishops and the National Council of Synagogues USA issued a truly remarkable document entitled *Reflections on Covenant and Mission*.[34] This was the result of discussions between leaders of Jewish and Roman Catholic communities in the United States, who had been meeting twice a year over a period of two decades.

For some time it had seemed to many that the time was ripe for a study on the relationship between the two Covenants that basically describe the nature of the two religious communities, and on the consequences of that for Christian mission. The document *Reflections on Covenant and Mission* is an encouraging response, that, in the words of the Moderator of the United States Bishops' Commission for Catholic-Jewish Relations, "marks a significant step forward in the dialogue between the Catholic Church and the Jewish community" in this country.

The Jewish and Catholic reflections are presented separately in the document, but together affirm important conclusions. The

Catholic reflections describe the growing respect for the Jewish tradition that has unfolded since the Second Vatican Council, and state:

> A deepening Catholic appreciation of the eternal covenant between God and the Jewish people, together with the divinely-given mission to Jews to witness to God's faithful love, lead to the conclusion that campaigns that target Jews for conversion to Christianity are no longer theologically acceptable in the Catholic Church.

The document stresses that evangelization, or mission, in the Church's work cannot be separated from its faith in Jesus Christ, in whom Christians find the kingdom present and fulfilled. But it points out that this evangelizing mission goes far beyond "the invitation to a commitment to faith in Jesus Christ and to entry through baptism into the community of believers that is the Church. It includes the Church's activities of presence and witness; commitment to social development and human liberation; Christian worship, prayer, and contemplation; interreligious dialogue; and proclamation and catechesis."

But given the "utterly unique relationship of Christianity with Judaism" and the many aspects of this spiritual linkage, "the Catholic Church has come to recognize that its mission of preparing for the coming of the kingdom is one that is shared with the Jewish people, even if Jews do not conceive of this task christologically as the Church does." In view of this, the document quotes Prof. Tomaso Federice and Cardinal Walter Kasper to affirm that there should not be in the Church any organization dedicated to the conversion of the Jews. From the Catholic point of view, Judaism is a religion that springs from divine revelation. The quotation from Cardinal Kasper states:

> God's grace, which is the grace of Jesus Christ according to our faith, is available to all. Therefore, the Church believes that Judaism, i.e. the faithful response of the Jewish people

to God's irrevocable covenant, is salvific for them, because God is faithful to his promises.

Since, in Catholic teaching, both the Church and the Jewish people abide in covenant with God, they both therefore have missions before God to undertake in the world. The Church believes that the mission of the Jewish people is not restricted to their historical role as the people of whom Jesus was born "according to the flesh" (Rom 9:5) and from whom the Church's apostles came. It quotes the following statement from Cardinal Ratzinger: "God's providence . . . has obviously given Israel a particular mission in this *time of the Gentiles*." Only the Jewish people themselves can articulate their mission, "in the light of their own religious experience."

The Catholic section of the document concludes with this profound statement:

> With the Jewish people, the Catholic Church, in the words of *Nostra Aetate*, "awaits the day, known to God alone, when all peoples will call on God with one voice and serve him shoulder to shoulder."

The Jewish reflections are given the title: *The Mission of the Jews and the Perfection of the World*. This mission is described as three-fold, rooted in Scripture and developed in later Jewish sources:

> There is, first, the mission of covenant—the ever-formative impetus to Jewish life that results from the covenant between God and the Jews. Second, the mission of witness, whereby the Jews see themselves "and are frequently seen by others" as God's eternal witnesses to His existence and to his redeeming power in the world. And third, the mission of humanity, a mission that understands the Biblical history of the Jews as containing a message to more than the Jews alone. It

presupposes a message and a mission addressed to all human beings.

The document describes the mission of covenant and witness, before dealing at greater length with the mission of humanity, stating that the message of the Bible is a message and a vision not only to Israel but to all of humanity. It then reminds the reader that Isaiah speaks twice of the Jews as a light to peoples, and quotes the experience of Jonah to illustrate that it is a mistake to think that God is concerned only with the Jews:

> The God of the Bible is the God of the world. His visions are visions for all of humanity. His love is a love that extends to every creature . . . Adam and Eve were His first creations and they are created long before the first Jews. They are created in *the image of God*, as are all of their children to eternity. Only the human creation is in the divine image. *Tikun ha-olam*, perfection or repairing of the world, is a joint task of the Jews and all humanity. Though Jews see themselves as living in a world that is as yet unredeemed, God wills His creatures to participate in the world's repair.

Finally, the Jewish reflections point out certain practical conclusions that follow from the three-fold "mission" in classical Judaism, and which suggest a joint agenda for Christians and Jews. The reflection begins with the following statement:

> Although Christians and Jews understand the messianic hope involved in that perfection quite differently, still, whether we are waiting for the messiah—as Jews believe—or for the Messiah's second coming—as Christians believe—we share the belief that we live in an unredeemed world that longs for repair.

Then it asks: "Why not articulate a common agenda? Why not join together our spiritual forces to state and to act upon the values we share in common and that lead to the repair of the unredeemed world?" Looking then to the Talmud, the document draws from that source thoughts about repairing the world, giving details of charity directed to the poor and deeds of kindness to all, the poor and the rich, the living and the dead; creating an economy where people are encouraged to help one another financially as an expression of their common fellowship; obligations to the sick and mourners; and preserving the dignity of the aged. While Jewish law is of course directed at Jews and its primary concern is to encourage the expression of love to the members of the community, it points out that many of these actions are mandatory towards all people, and quotes the Talmud as saying:

> One must provide for the needs of the gentile poor with the Jewish poor. One must visit the gentile sick with the Jewish sick. One must care for the burial of a gentile, just as one must care for the burial of a Jew. [These obligations are universal] because these are the ways of peace.

Not everyone in the two communities will agree with all that is stated in this document. In fact, when these *Reflections* were published, they created a wide-ranging dispute within the Catholic Church in the United States, but also in wider ecumenical and interfaith circles. Most of the argument centered on the question of whether or not Christians should desire and pray for the conversion of Jews. There was no question in this discussion of Church organizations aiming to convert Jews, but leading Church officials expressed the view that it would be absurd to think that the mission given to the Church by Christ is for pagans and not also for Jews, when all of Christ's preaching and his call to conversion was addressed precisely to the Jews. At the same time, Pope John Paul II has on a number of occasions made it clear that the first Covenant has not been revoked and that therefore the Church is called to concentrate on its mission "with" the Jews, rather than "to" the Jews.[35] The national Jewish-Catholic dialogue in the United States has certainly posed a challenge that can and should be fully shared by Christians and Jews.

Conclusion

From these documents and recent dialogue experiences, it seems obvious that new light has been shed on many of the divisive issues that have negatively influenced Catholic-Jewish relations in the past. Bringing the good results of the dialogue to the knowledge of both communities has been a constant concern of those responsible for this relationship. While satisfaction is the predominant feeling as the Church looks back over forty years at *Nostra Aetate* N° 4, the work is certainly not yet completed. Indeed, as is obvious from the preceding reflections, in some ways it can be said to have only just begun. The need for education to continue and have a much greater place in the life of the two communities has been stressed over and over again even in the past few years. Cardinal Johannes Willebrands was astounded at the beginning of his work "to realize how poorly Christians and Jews know each other."[36] In 1992, Dr. Geoffrey Wigoder of the Institute of Contemporary Jewry of the Hebrew University, Jerusalem, reminded the ILC at its meeting in Jerusalem in 1994 "of the abyss of ignorance in both our communities concerning the other, which includes dangerous myths and prejudices."[37]

Such education seems all the more necessary in view of the number of new manifestations of anti-Semitism that are reported. The ongoing conflict and violence in the Holy Land between Israel and the Palestinian population has hardened some hearts once again against the Jewish people, who see such an intimate connection between the land of Israel and their religion.

The world today urgently needs common witness to the truths that God has entrusted to Jews and Christians. At this time it would seem that Jews and Christians are moving farther away from the old mistrust and suspicion to a partnership in the cause of "peace, justice and a more human, fraternal world." While preserving past gains, they are entering on a dialogue as two equal partners seeking together to build a better world. They began their discussions in order to solve problems and promote a new relationship, and now they are being challenged to move their gaze from their bilateral relations to become a common blessing to a wider world.

The Jewish section of the document *Reflections on Covenant and Mission* expressed this challenge well:

> Does not humanity need a common vision of the sacred nature of our human existence that we can teach our children and that we can foster in our communities in order to further the ways of peace? Does not humanity need a commitment of its religious leadership, within each faith and beyond each faith, to join hands and create bonds that will inspire and guide humanity to reach toward its sacred promise? For Jews and Christians who have heard the call of God to be a blessing and a light to the world, the challenge and mission are clear. Nothing less should be our challenge—and that is the true meaning of mission that we all need to share.[38]

In a letter to Cardinal Kasper for the 2002 meeting of European leaders of Judaism and Catholicism, Pope John Paul II stated that "since the Conciliar Declaration *Nostra Aetate*, great progress has been made—and I am very glad of it—towards better mutual understanding and reconciliation between our two communities."[39]

Cardinal Kasper developed this brief statement in an address on November 7, 2002, at Boston College, with which I will bring to a close this attempt to "rediscover" *Nostra Aetate*, forty years after it was promulgated.[40] As he looks to the future, he reminds us that the dialogue should not only deal with religious questions of principle, nor simply seek to clarify the past: "Our common heritage should be profitably made available in response to contemporary challenges: to issues involving the sanctity of life, the protection of the family, justice and peace in the world, the hostages of terrorism, and the integrity of creation, among others."

There can be no doubt that Christian-Jewish relations have changed radically over the past few years and we can now look forward to an exciting future.

Notes

1. *L'Osservatore Romano*, English Weekly edition N. 16-20 April 2005, 6, indicates as members of 'The Delegation of Judaism', the Grand Rabbi of Haifa, Rabbi Shear Yashuv Cohen and the Director of the Grand Rabbinate of Israel; Dr. Oded Wiener; Dr. Riccardo Di Segni, the Chief Rabbi of Rome, and his predecessor Prof. Elio Toaff, together with the Presidents of the Union of Italian Jewish Communities and the Jewish Community of Rome Rabbi Israel Singer, President of the Governing Board of the World Jewish Congress and President of the International Jewish Committee on Interreligious Consultations (IJCIC) with his wife and Mrs. Maram Stern, Vice-General Secretary of the World Jewish Congress; H.E. Shmul Hadas, former Ambassador of Israel to the Holy See; and Rabbi Arthur Schneier, President of the Appeal of Conscience Foundation.

2. Apostolic Constitution *Regimini Ecclesiae* of Pope Paul VI, August 15, 1967, N. 94.

3. Information Service of the Pontifical Council for Promoting Christian Unity (*IS*) N. 17 (1972/II), 11-12.

4. *IS* N. 25 (1974/III), 22.

5. *IS* N. 26 (1975/1), 1-7.

6. *IS* N. 57 (1985/I), 16-21.

7. *IS* N. 14 (1971/II), 11.

8. Antwerp, 4-6 December 1973 – *IS* N. 23 (1974/I) 21-22; Rome, 7-10 January 1974 – *IS* N. 27 (1975/II), 34-37; Jerusalem, 1-3 March 1976 – *IS* N. 31 (1976/II), 17-18; Venice, 28-30 March 1977 – *IS* N. 34 (1977/II), 6-7: Madrid, 5-7 April 1978 – *IS* N. 37 (1978/II), 11-12; Regensburg, 22-25 October 1979 – *IS* N. 41 (1979/IV), 11; London, 31 March-2 April 1981 – *IS* N. 45 (1981/I), 29-30: Milan, 6-8 September 1982 – *IS* N. 51 (1983/I-II), 36, Amsterdam, 27-29 March 1984 – *IS* N. 54 (1984/I), 21-22; Rome, 28-30 October 1985 – *IS* N. 59 (1985/III-IV), 37-39.

9. *IS* N. 59 (1985/III-IV), 37-39

10. *IS* N. 65 (1987/III-IV), 116-120.

11. *IS* N. 75 (1990/IV), 173-178.

12. *Fundamental Agreement between the Holy See and the State of Israel*, Acta Apostolicae Sedis LXXXVI, 5 July 1994, 716-729

13. *IS* N. 88 (1995/I), 38-41.

14. The full text is given in *IS* N. 97, 18-22. It was also published by the Libreria Editrice Vaticana for distribution by the CRRJ.

15. *IS* N. 83 (1993/II), 93.

16. *IS* N. 88, 37: September 29, 1994, representatives of the B'nai B'rith Anti-Defamation League; February 6, 1995, the American Jewish Committee.

17. *IS* N. 60 (1986/I-II), 29-30.

18. *IS* N. 87 (1994/IV), 229-230.

19. *IS* N. 102 (1999/IV), 254-255.

20. *IS* N. 103 (2000/I-II), 53-58.

21. *IS* N 103, 77.

22. *IS* N. 104 (2000/III), 107-111.

23. *IS* N. 104, 108-109.

24. *IS* N. 108 (2001/IV). A full report on this meeting is given on pages 168-77, and unless otherwise indicated, all quotations in this commentary on the meeting will be found there.

25. *IS* N. 108, 171.

26. *IS* N. 116 (2004/III), 139-141.

27. *The Jewish People and their Scriptures in the Christian Bible* (Libreria Editrice Vaticana, 2002).

28. *IS* N. 112 (2003/I), 35-36.

29. *IS* N. 114 (2003/IV), 200.

30. *The Tablet,* 31 January 2004, 29.

31. Institute for Jewish and Christian Studies, National Jewish Scholars Project *Dabru Emet,* 13 September 2000, online at www.icjs.org/what/njps/dabruemet.htm.

32. *Dominus Jesus,* a declaration of the Congregation for the Doctrine of the Faith on the unicity and salvific universality of Jesus Christ and the Church, August 6, 2000. At the 2001 ILC meeting, Dr. David Berger pointed out that Jews were worried by the assertion in this document that followers of religions other than Christianity are in a gravely deficient situation in respect of salvation and that interreligious dialogue is part of the Church's mission to the nations.

33. *CNS Documentary Service*, 30-35 (February 15, 2000), 565-66. Quotations are to be found there.

34. *Reflections on Covenant and Mission*, Communications United States Conference of Catholic Bishops, Washington, August 12, 2002.

35. *The Tablet*, 12 July 2003, 13.

36. *IS* N. 17, 11.

37. A report on this meeting is to be found in *IS* N. 87, 231, but these words of Dr. Wigoder are from the unpublished working papers of the meeting.

38. "Conclusion," *Reflections on Covenant and Mission*, Communications United States Conference of Catholic Bishops, Washington, August 12, 2002.

39. *IS* N. 109 (2002/I-II), 92.

40. *IS* N. 111 (2002/IV), 232-38.

The Teaching of the Second Vatican Council on Jews and Judaism

LAWRENCE E. FRIZZELL

Introduction

At a meeting with Jewish leaders on March 16, 1990, Pope John Paul II suggested that the *Declaration of the Second Vatican Council on Non-Christian Religions* be placed in the context of the other Council documents.[1] The fortieth anniversary of *Nostra Aetate* is indeed an appropriate context for such an evaluation of the entire Council's contribution to Catholic-Jewish relations.

"The Second Vatican Council was perhaps the most profound religious event of the twentieth century."[2] For Catholics this statement can be accepted without qualification. Certainly many Jewish and other scholars would accept this claim for its impact on the development of Jewish-Christian relations. Perhaps many outside the Catholic community would focus attention on *Nostra Aetate* as a high point in the Council's teaching. However, the impact of this Declaration would have been less profound without the important developments that are found in other documents, especially the Constitutions relating to the very heart of the Church's life. Of course, the subsequent texts of the Holy See and various national conferences of bishops have made a significant contribution to its implementation.[3]

Many commentators use the phrase "watershed event" when describing the impact of the Council. Indeed, a number of significant changes in the life of Catholics followed from conciliar decisions. However, it would be unfortunate to underestimate the continuity of the practice of Christian life on all levels. The Council's accomplishments are clearly founded on the work of pioneers in various fields of theology, liturgiology, and pastoral care. The teaching of Pope Pius XII on the nature of the Church (*Mystici Corporis* [1943]), the Sacred Scriptures (*Divino Afflante Spiritu* [1943]), and the liturgy (*Mediator Dei* [1947]) as well as his leadership in other areas effectively guided the entire Church toward many of the achievements of the Council.

The Constitution on the Sacred Liturgy (*Sacrosanctum Concilium*)

Public worship, the celebration of the sacraments, and other forms of prayer constitute the core of the spiritual life for Catholics, both the community and the individual.[4] For this reason, it was most appropriate that the *Constitution on the Sacred Liturgy* was the first document of the Second Vatican Council to be promulgated (December 4, 1963).

Just as the liturgical heritage of the Church constantly draws upon the Word of God in the Sacred Scriptures, so the Council documents echo biblical texts, themes, and images throughout. The "salvation history" model of biblical theology developed by Gerhard von Rad and Oscar Cullmann may be recognized at many points, but with a clear emphasis on the *mystery*, i.e., the divine plan, operative in these events.[5] The activity of God in creation and human history must be appreciated from the perspective of the divine "economy" and the ultimate goal of history (and, therefore, of every human life). For the Church this salvation history is centered on the person and work of Jesus:

> The wonderful works of God among the people of the Old Testament were but a prelude to the work of Christ our Lord in redeeming humankind and giving perfect glory to God. He achieved his task principally by the paschal mystery of his blessed passion, resurrection from the dead and glorious ascension. (*Liturgy #5*).[6]

The marvels of God's presence and guidance of the twelve tribes of Israel over the centuries will be accorded more attention in other documents. Here the perspective of Christian faith in the universal impact of Christ's work is stressed, without necessarily diminished the magnitude of God's prior gifts to the chosen people. At no one moment did these mighty deeds have the same universal effects that Christian faith ascribes to the "paschal mystery," i.e., the suffering, death, resurrection, and ascension of Jesus (see Rom 4:25; 1 Cor 15:3-5). However, the very term "paschal" emphasizes that only in the framework of the Passover-Exodus and Sinai Covenant can the depths of the Christian interpretation of Jesus' accomplishment be elucidated. This will be evident from the first paragraph of *Nostra Aetate* #4. Throughout the New Testament, writers point to the Exodus as the key event in Israel's history, whose symbols are used to enhance Christian understanding of Jesus' death-and-resurrection. The phrase "paschal mystery" draws attention to the Jewish Passover as paradigm for grasping profound dimensions of Jesus' work.

From the first generation of Christianity, "the Church has never failed to come together to celebrate the paschal mystery, reading those things 'which were in all the Scriptures concerning him' (Lk 24:27)" (*Liturgy* #6). The liturgy is the favored context for applying the message of the Scripture to the contemporary needs of the Church, a lesson learned from the synagogue service. This principle, like the use of psalms and other canticles of the Jewish Scriptures, derived from the practices of the Temple and Synagogue. The focus of all Christian worship on the paschal mystery follows the Jewish precedent of rooting all prayer in the "ascending blessing" of thanks-and-praise for what God has done already for his people. From this perspective of gratitude, help is sought for present needs and the community is oriented to the future, when God's plan will be fulfilled.[7]

At the same time as the Church orients the faithful toward the consummation of history in the triumphant return of Christ, she stresses, again with the ancient Jewish liturgy, that we live constantly in God's presence and must strive to make our worship (e.g., in the

Sanctus, drawing on Isa 6:3) and lives (e.g., in the Lord's Prayer) correspond with the activity of the heavenly Court/Temple, the celestial Jerusalem: "In the earthly liturgy we take part in a foretaste of that heavenly liturgy which is celebrated in the Holy City of Jerusalem to which we journey as pilgrims, where Christ is seated at the right hand of God" (#8).

The central place of the liturgy in the Church's life is clear from the following principle: "The liturgy is the summit toward which the activity of the Church is directed; it is also the fount from which all her power flows" (*Liturgy* #10). This centrality of the liturgy to Christian life echoes the Hebrew understanding of '*abodah,* meaning both worship and work (service). This link between the sublime drama of worship and the fabric of the mundane shows the unity of human life, wherein all details of daily activities must be ordered to the service of God and neighbor, with the purpose of bringing all creation closer to its goal.

In several acts of reform the changes that followed the Council have drawn upon biblical and liturgical principles that ideally should have a beneficial effect on Christian-Jewish relations. Of course, the primary purpose of these reforms is to foster the spiritual life of the faithful, but it is indeed felicitous that people have frequent occasions to reflect upon our roots in the biblical and Jewish heritage. Filling a vacuum of ignorance with a positive appreciation of what the Jewish community was in past ages should be a foundation for a Christian sense of solidarity with the Jewish people now and for cooperating with them to overcome anti-Jewish bigotry in the contemporary world. Bringing the faithful to knowledge of God's Word and the people who preserved it is imperative in every part of the world, whether these Christians are in contact with Jewish communities or not. The message of the Council regarding the Jewish people is very important for all the Christian faithful because it is essential to the integrity of the Church's self-definition.

Following the Council's call for "the treasures of the Bible to be opened up more lavishly so that a richer fare may be provided for the faithful" (*Liturgy* #51), a three-year cycle was devised for the Sunday readings and a two year cycle for weekdays. The ancient synagogue in the Holy Land had a three-year cycle for Sabbaths and, already in the decade preceding the Council, scholars were debating its possible impact on New Testament writings. Did the reformers have this background in mind? Archival sources of this work are not yet available to answer this question. At any rate, the selection of passages from the Jewish Scriptures both for Sundays (except after Easter) and weekdays was an important step toward presenting God's Word in its fullness to the faithful. It also made the teaching of "Old Testament" in seminaries much more relevant.

The series of complex prayers at the Offertory of the Mass was replaced by texts that derive from the Jewish meal prayers for bread and wine. Future priests and other teachers should be introduced to the riches of the Jewish prayer books (especially those of the Orthodox tradition) so that they will be alert to such parallels and to this treasury of Jewish spirituality.

The change of January first from the Feast of the Lord's Circumcision to the Solemnity of the Mother of God may have taken away an opportunity to discuss aspects of the fact that Jesus was born under the Law (Gal 4:4); however, the Gospel (Lk 2:16-21) concludes with reference to the circumcision and naming of the Child. The homily should stress the Jewishness of the Holy Family and their observance of the Law. The change of February second from the Purification of Mary to the Presentation of the Lord provides another link with the Law of Moses, but this is not a holy day of obligation.[8]

The reform of the Divine Office (the Psalms and other texts for daily rhythms of prayer) was discussed in chapter IV of the *Constitution* (# 83-101). This was extensive, dividing the Psalms and canticles into a four-week cycle rather than the monastic model of reciting all these prayers each week.[9] Of interest to our topic is the fact that Saturday continues to be called "Sabbath." The "brief reading" for *Compline* on Saturday evening is taken from Deuteronomy 6:4-7, the core of the *Shema*; this is one of several contacts with the Jewish tradition in the texts for Saturday.

Prayers of intercession ("the prayer of the faithful" or bidding prayers), whose presence in the Good Friday liturgy gives evidence of a very ancient practice, were introduced into the Eucharistic liturgy for Sunday and feasts (*Liturgy* #53); they were introduced as well into the Divine Office of Lauds and Vespers. A careful review of the prayers for the Jewish people in these petitions shows that the spirit of the Council's Declaration, *Nostra Aetate*, was not always observed. Perhaps this work of providing new prayers was well underway before the last session of the Council, when *Nostra Aetate* was promulgated. At any rate, this area should be reviewed in coming years.

Long before the Council, John M. Oesterreicher challenged the usual English translation of the Good Friday Liturgy's prayer *pro perfidiis Judaeis*; he argued that the Latin term does not mean "perfidious" but "unbelieving."[10] Pope John XXIII ordered that the adjective be omitted from the announcement of the prayer; in 1966 and 1974 the prayer itself was changed completely.

The Constitution on the Church (*Lumen Gentium*)

In their search for a deeper understanding of the Church's very nature, with the intention of bringing all humanity to the light of Christ, the Council Fathers discussed the Church's relationship to ancient Israel: "Already present in figure at the beginning of the world, this Church was prepared in a marvelous fashion in the history of the people of Israel and in the Old Covenant . . . At the end of time . . . all the just from the time of Adam . . . will be gathered together with the Father in the universal Church" (*Church* #2).

This statement embraces the entire sweep of human history, relating those who believe in Christ to the children of Abraham as the covenanted people. The ultimate experience of redemption will be shared by all who are "just," gathered into unity with God and each other. The title of this chapter, "The Mystery of the Church," conveys the realization that the Church is "a reality imbued with the hidden presence of God."[11] The term "mystery" refers to the divine plan revealed in stages to Abraham and his descendants, coming to fulfillment in the work of Jesus (see Rom 16:25-26). In *Nostra Aetate* the Council Father endeavored to "sound the depths of the mystery which is the Church"; this led to a longer reflection on "the spiritual ties which link the people of the New Covenant to the stock of Abraham" (#4). To appreciate this point of the Declaration of October 28, 1965, it is necessary to study its roots in the *Constitution on the Church*.

Very succinctly numerous aspects of the biblical message are utilized to describe the work of Christ, who did the Father's will by inaugurating the kingdom of heaven on earth (*Church* #3). Matthew's use of a circumlocution to avoid inappropriate familiarity with the divine Name must be kept in mind when reading the phrase "Kingdom of Heaven," as well as the double meaning of the Hebrew term for kingship/kingdom. The royal *authority* (kingship) of God is recognized now by people of faith, whereas the acceptance of divine *rule* (dominion) by all creation will come after evil has been vanquished definitively.[12] The Council document here identifies the Church as "the Kingdom of Christ," a theme developed in *Church* #5. The identification of the Church with "the Kingdom of Christ" was applied to the Byzantine Empire in Asia Minor and Eastern Europe, with unfortunate ramifications in the period before the fall of Constantinople in 1453.

Acknowledgment is made of the rich heritage from the ancient Hebrews: "In the Old Testament the revelation of the kingdom is often made under the forms of symbols" (*Church* #6). Thus, the Church is a sheepfold, a tract of land to be cultivated, the field of God (1 Cor 3:9): "On that land the ancient olive tree grows whose holy roots were the patriarchs and in which the reconciliation of Jews and Gentiles has been brought about and will be brought about again (Rom 11:13-26). That land, like a choice vineyard, has been planted by the heavenly Cultivator (Mt 21:33-43; see Isa 5:1-7). The true vine is Christ who gives life and fruitfulness to the branches, that is, to us (Jn 15:1-5)" (*Church* #6).[13]

These passages go far beyond the context suggested by Paul, who speaks of "one planting, another watering but only God causes growth" (1 Cor 3:7-8) by alluding to prophetic images appropriated by the Gospels. The field seems to be identified with the promised land where Israel had flourished as an olive tree (Hos 14:7) or fruitful vine (Hos 14:8; Ps 80, etc.). This should lead to an extended reflection on the link between people and land in the biblical tradition, with implications for the Jewish attachment to the land of Israel over the centuries.[14] Using the next Pauline image "the building of God," this paragraph then describes the Church as God's Temple, corresponding ideally to that of the heavenly Jerusalem. Although in ages past theologians usurped such "symbols" by denying the continuing meaning of the realities of Land and Temple for the Jewish people, the rules of typology should be followed, as in the works of biblical writers who applied the Exodus experience to explain the return from exile. The reality has a meaning in itself and also points to a theological or spiritual moral application, without eviscerating the meaning and value of the original for the Jewish people.

Chapter II, "The People of God," contains material of great importance both for the Church's self-understanding and for Catholic-Jewish relations.[15] God's plan for humanity constitutes individuals as "a people who acknowledge him and serve him in holiness. He therefore chose the Israelite race to be his own people and established a covenant with it. He gradually instructed this people . . . and made it holy unto himself. All these things, however, happened as a preparation and figure of that new and perfect Covenant which was to be ratified in Christ . . . " (*Church* #9). After quoting the covenantal promise found in Jeremiah 31:31-34, the text continues: "Christ instituted this new covenant, namely the new covenant in his blood; he called a people made up of Jews and Gentiles which would be one, not according to the flesh, but in the Spirit, and this race would be the new People of God" (*Church* #9).

Again *Lumen Gentium* prepares for *Nostra Aetate* and developments in the theology of the Church's relation with the Jewish people and offset misinterpretations of what may seem to be ambiguous statements in the *Constitution on the Church*.[16] "The Church of Christ acknowledges that in God's plan of salvation the beginning of her faith and election is to be found in the patriarchs, Moses and the prophets . . . The Church believes that Christ who is our peace has through his cross reconciled Jews and Gentiles and made them one in himself" (*Nostra Aetate* #4).

The image of the olive tree (Rom 11:13-26), cited in *Lumen Gentium* #6 and in *Nostra Aetate* #4, helps to foster the truth of continuity in the divine plan rather than have readers think that phrases like "new covenant" and "new People of God" imply the abrogation or demise of God's relationship with the People of Israel (now usually designated as the Jewish people). Theories of God's rejection of Israel/the Jewish people must not be part of Catholic thinking; rather the Church ("whose members, as people of faith, are children of Abraham") should recall with gratitude that "she received the revelation of the Old Testament by way of that people with whom God in his inexpressible mercy established the ancient covenant" (*Nostra Aetate* #4).

An emphasis on continuity must be balanced by recognition of Christianity's claim to "newness" in the union of Jew and gentile into one people, achieved in principle through the paschal mystery of Jesus. Thus the Council speaks of "the messianic people," pointing to the role of Jesus as God's Anointed, leading humanity into a communion of life, love and truth" (*Church* #9) that will blossom forth in the *eschaton*.

Focusing on the Hebrew designation of Israel and *qahal*, a convocation (rendered in Greek by *ekklesia*) by God's word for service, *Lumen Gentium* sees the people's wandering after the Exodus as a type of the Church's pilgrimage toward full communion with God:[17] "As Israel according to the flesh which wandered in the desert was already called the Church (*ecclesia*) of God, so too the new Israel, which advances in this present era in search of a future and permanent city, is called also the Church of Christ" (*Church* #9). This typology is Pauline in origin (1 Cor 10:1-11) and was developed in the Letter to the Hebrews; again it rightly alludes to the unique role of Christ. The phrases "new covenant" and "new People of God" have explicit antecedents in the New Testament. In this text the phrase "Israel of the flesh" need not be taken pejoratively (see 1 Cor 10:8) because the Council does not refer to sins of the desert generation nor contrast it with the Christian Church. However, the title "new Israel" (whose only possible New Testament antecedent is "the Israel of God" in Gal 6:16) must be avoided or used very carefully to avoid a judgmental contrast with the Israel that included people who did not acknowledge Jesus to be the Messiah and Son of God. Again *Nostra Aetate* completes the Council's teaching with its quotation of Paul's list of attributes belonging to the Jewish People (#4, citing Rom 9:4-5) as well as the statement that "God does not take back the gifts he bestowed or the choice he made" (#4 citing Rom 11:28-29).

The rich section (#10-12) on participation of the faithful in Christ's three-fold function as king, priest, and prophet and the meaning of the sacraments could be explored for biblical and Jewish roots, but that will be left for another study.

The Church's clear sense of its universal mission, first enunciated in *Liturgy* #1 and #2, is reiterated throughout *Lumen Gentium*: "All human beings are called to belong to the new People of God. This people, therefore, while remaining one and only one, is to be spread throughout the whole world and to all ages in order that the design of God's will may be fulfilled" (#13). The *Declaration on Religious Liberty* provides a basis for tempering zeal with a deep respect for each individual's freedom of conscience.[18]

Already in *Lumen Gentium* this sense of mission is followed by a reflection on the situation of baptized Christians who are not Catholic (#5; see the *Decree on Ecumenism*). A very important interpretation of the ancient dictum "Extra Ecclesiam nulla salus" ("Outside the Church no salvation") has an explicit reference to the Jewish people:

> Those who have not yet received the Gospel are related to the People of God in various ways. There is, first, that people to which the covenants and promises were made, and from which Christ was born according to the flesh (Rom 9:4-5): in view of the divine choice, they are a people

most dear for the sake of the fathers, for God does not repent of the gifts he makes nor of the call he issues (see Rom 11:28-29). (#16).

How do the Jews relate to the Church? Should there be a second question: How does the Church relate to the Jews of our generation? The Council has alluded to the key ideas flowing from the New Testament, but much work remains for the theologians and ecumenists.[19] Of course, this paragraph includes a carefully nuanced section on the divine help given to all who, "through no fault of their own do not know the Gospel of Christ or his Church, but who nevertheless seek God with a sincere heart."

Chapter VIII of *Lumen Gentium* places the Catholic teachings concerning the blessed Mother of God explicitly within the context of the Council's understanding of the Church itself. Although the biblical preparation for the role of the Redeemer's Mother is sketched briefly (#55), there is no allusion to her Jewishness. This fact is mentioned in *Nostra Aetate* #4, but only in passing. Perhaps the reticence is due to the fact that this is a question "which the work of theologians has not yet fully clarified" (#54).[20]

The Constitution on Divine Revelation (*Dei Verbum*)

Preeminent among the gifts which the Church received from the chosen people is the Jewish Bible.[21] The Council's work embodied in the *Constitution on Divine Revelation* is the fruit of a generation of scholarship inspired by the 1943 encyclical of Pope Pius XII entitled *Divino Afflante Spiritu*.

The *Constitution* begins by mentioning that God's Word is heard and proclaimed (#1); this perspective on the primacy of listening (see Rom 10:14-17) places the Scriptures within the liturgy as the heart of the Church's life. Reading and study are necessary as preparation for appreciating the Word as proclaimed and heeded, after attentive, prayerful listening. Thus the Church draws upon the ancient Hebrew and Jewish experience of God's

Word. Uniquely Christian is the relation of this Word to the Word-made-flesh in Jesus Christ (citing Jn 1:2-3).

The Hebrew term *dabhar* means word, thing, and event; this range of meaning should assist the Christian to grasp the profound link between word and sign (or symbolic gesture), between the historical event and its interpretation, between the liturgy of the Word and the liturgy of sacrifice and sacrament:

> The economy of revelation is realized by deeds and words, which are intrinsically bound up with each other. As a result, the works performed by God in the history of salvation show forth and bear out the doctrine and realities signified by the words; the words, for their part, proclaim the works, and bring to light the mystery they contain. (#2)

Lumen Gentium (#9) already spoke of God's choice of Israel and the covenant which made this people his own. A brief sketch of salvation history is given in *Dei Verbum* #3 and #14: "In his own time God called Abraham and made him into a great nation (see Gen 12:2). After the era of the patriarchs, he taught this nation, by Moses and the prophets, to recognize him as the only living and true God, as a provident Father and just judge. He taught them, too, to look for the promised Savior" (#3). The second text mentions the covenant with Abraham, referring to the "pact of the pieces" (Gen 15, which promises offspring and land) and with Israel at Mount Sinai through Moses (see Ex 24:8) as the basis for God's acquisition of a people destined to have their own land wherein to serve God freely (Ex 19:6). There are slight differences in the description of the divine pedagogy, the second text (*Dei Verbum* #14) referring to Israel's mediation of knowledge about God's ways among the nations.

The unique contribution of Jesus to the divine plan of salvation is taught by stating that he completed and perfected revelation by his presence and work on earth: "The Christian economy, therefore, as the new and definitive covenant, will never pass away; and no new public revelation is to be expected before the glorious manifestation of our Lord, Jesus Christ" (*Dei Verbum* #4). The full expression of Christian certitude about the person and work of Jesus must be made clearly, as the Council documents do time and again (see *Dei Verbum* #5). That the new covenant builds upon the old and does not abrogate the election of Israel flowing from the promise to Abraham should also be enunciated just as carefully.

Dei Verbum dedicates a chapter to "The Old Testament" (#14-16). The Council declares that the books of the Jewish Scriptures are the true Word of God; "that is why these books, divinely inspired, remain permanently valuable," quoting Romans 15:4 as a proof-text (#14). Anyone who knows the Church's use of the Psalms and other canticles in her liturgy and who studies the great patristic and medieval commentaries on most parts of the Jewish Scriptures would acknowledge that practice proves the Church's faith in the divine inspiration of the Jewish Scriptures. However, in both liturgy and exegesis, the tendency has been to see these texts primarily as preparation for the fuller revelation in the work of Jesus and in the New Testament writings.

This thrust of the divine message remains a basic Christian conviction, as is shown in the revised lectionary.[22] In addition, however, the Council acknowledges that lessons for every age can be discovered by studying all parts of the Jewish Scriptures *for themselves*, i.e., as revealing aspects of "that truth which God, for the sake of our salvation, wished to see confided to the Sacred Scriptures" (#11). Because the New Testament presupposes the biblical heritage of the Jewish people and because these texts were composed over a relatively short period of time, there are areas of life that its authors treated only fleetingly. The millennial traditions of Israel, and their interpretation by the Jewish community through the ages, can provide us with many insights needed to grapple with problems of our time.[23] "These books, even though they contain matters imperfect and provisional, nevertheless show us authentic divine teaching" (#15). There is a note after this sentence that refers to Pope Pius XI's encyclical *Mit brennender Sorge* (March 14, 1937), which dramatically confronted Nazi ideology and racism:

Christians should accept with veneration these writings which
give expression to a lively sense of God, which are a storehouse
of sublime teaching on God and of sound wisdom on human
life, as well as a wonderful treasury of prayer; in them, too, the
mystery of our salvation is present in a hidden way. (#15)

This last clause leads to a restatement of the central Christian
conviction that our Bible possesses a profound unity, deriving from its
divine origin: "God, the inspirer and author of the books of both
Testaments, in his wisdom has so brought it about that the New
should be hidden in the Old and that the Old should be made
manifest in the New" (#16).[24] Augustine of Hippo is credited with
this felicitous formula which teaches the necessity of a thorough study
of the two Testaments. Jerome expressed the idea in another dictum:
"Ignorance of the Scriptures is ignorance of Christ."[25] The function of
priests as the ministers of God's Word (*Decree on the Ministry and Life
of Priests #4*) makes a thorough education in the Scriptures a necessity
of the highest order (see *Dei Verbum* #23-26). This should include a
special study of Judaism, both in the Second Temple period and in
later times so that the faithful may never be exposed to anti-Jewish
attacks from the pulpit. *Nostra Aetate* addressed this point directly:

It is true that the Church is the new people of God, yet the
Jews should not be spoken of as rejected or accursed as if
this followed from Holy Scripture. Consequently, all must
take care, lest in catechizing or in preaching the Word of
God, they teach anything which is not in accord with the
truth of the Gospel message or the spirit of Christ. (#4)[26]

The Constitution on the Church in the Modern World (*Gaudium et Spes*) and the *Declaration on Religious Liberty* (*Dignitatis Humanae*)

Just as individual Christians find strength and insight by
contemplation of God's Word, so the Council Fathers and their
theologians refreshed themselves at the "pure and lasting fount of

spiritual life" (*Dei Verbum* #21). Coming to know God and divine ways more profoundly, they answered the great philosophical questions about human life (see *Nostra Aetate* #1) and destiny by reiterating the ancient truth that every human being is created in God's image and likeness (Gen 1:26-28).[27]

"The Council lays stress on respect for the human person: everyone should look upon his neighbor (without any exception) as another self, bearing in mind above all his life and the means necessary for living it in a dignified way" (*Gaudium et Spes* #27). This text continues with the challenge to come to the aid of any person in need, especially the least fortunate. Among the crimes against humanity listed are several that have been perpetrated against Jews: murder, genocide, mutilation, physical and mental torture (#27).

Nostra Aetate incorporates this point into its reflection on the Church's relation to the Jewish people:

> The Church reproves every form of persecution against whomever it may be directed . . . she deplores all hatreds, persecutions, displays of anti-Semitism leveled at any time or from any source against the Jews. (#4)

> We cannot truly pray to God the Father of all if we treat any people in other than brotherly fashion, for all human beings are created in God's image . . . There is no basis, therefore, either in theory or in practice, for any discrimination between individual and individual, or between people and people arising either from human dignity or from the rights which flow from it. (#5)

After striving to provide principles of faith that should eliminate prejudice, the Church tries to foster greater human understanding:

> Those also have a claim on our respect and charity who think and act differently from us in social, political and religious matters. In fact, the more deeply we come to understanding their ways of thinking through kindness and

love, the more easily will we be able to enter into dialogue
with them. (*Gaudium et Spes* #28)

The principles for developing authentic dialogue were already
in the Council's *Decree on Ecumenism* (especially #5-12). Although
addressed to the specific needs of uniting the Christian Churches, a
goal which cannot be applied to Catholic-Jewish relations, the
following principles can apply to interfaith dialogue as well:

1. Interior conversion will come to those who enter dialogue
   with a prayerful mind, open to learn and gentle in service
   of others (see #7).

2. Study of Other's teachings and practice will be the basis for
   discussion of specific questions with the Other on an equal
   footing (see #9).

3. Catholic doctrine should be presented so that it in no way
   becomes an obstacle to dialogue, yet it is essential that the
   doctrine be presented clearly, in its entirety (see #11).[28]

When members of the Jewish community become convinced of
the Church's sincerity in rejecting all forms of persecution and
discrimination and when the principles of "dialogue" have been
understood to eliminate all forms of proselytization, then almost all
of the issues presented in *Gaudium et Spes* can be topics for
discussion.[29] In many areas fruitful collaboration is taking place
already on important social issues.

For Jews and other minorities in European and other countries
with a Catholic majority, the touchstone for evaluating the Council's
success is found in the *Declaration on Religious Liberty*. In the past the
principle behind the exercise of authority in these nations had often
been enunciated as follows: "Error has no rights." The Council,
"increasingly conscious of the dignity of the human person . . . searches
the sacred tradition and teaching of the Church, from which it drew
forth new things that are always in harmony with the old" (#1). The

result is the recognition that rights reside in the human person and people have inalienable rights, including the freedom of their conscience. Of course, every right has a concomitant responsibility, including the necessity of seeking the truth and to embrace it (see #1).

The Council Fathers were well aware of the fact that Catholics in some lands were being persecuted for their faith and hoped that principles enunciated in this declaration (like the principles of the United Nations' 1948 Universal Declaration on Human Rights) would penetrate such regimes. By the same token, countries which follow the Church's guidance whole-heartedly would be required to provide freedom of assembly to religious minorities under their jurisdiction (#4).

"Parents have the right to decide in accordance with their own religious beliefs the form of religious upbringing which is to be given to their children" (#5). In the past a Jewish child, baptized because a Catholic thought the person to be in danger of death, could be taken from the parents' care.[30] Such a case would be extremely rare, but its poignancy caused great debates to arise. No longer will the parental right be scorned.

Religious freedom enables the Church to "enjoy in law and in fact those stable conditions which give her the independence necessary for fulfilling her divine mission" (#3). This mission is the subject of the Council's concern from the very beginning and it culminates in a *Decree on the Church's Missionary Activity*. Taking into account the principles enunciated in documents such as the *Decree on Ecumenism and Religious Liberty*, the Council demands that all Catholics, and especially missionaries, to be educated to respect the rights of others and to present the Christian message in candor, truth, and charity. The burden of the past may weigh heavily upon Church at times, but the search for authenticity in loving imitation of God demands this effort. The history of Catholic-Jewish relations does have bright moments and brilliant leaders in the past; in many places ordinary people showed good will towards Jews, but so often the Jewish people were vilified by those professing faith in Jesus the Jew and claiming to honor his Mother. The Council, especially in *Nostra Aetate* but throughout the other documents of its teaching, provides the foundation for a new era in the Church's relationship with the Jews. Much has been accomplished in many parts of the world in the past forty years. This provides a basis for continuing the diligent efforts to honor God and his Son by obtaining a deeper insight into his plan for ourselves and for the children of Abraham.

Notes

An earlier version of this essay was presented to an intra-ecclesial conference organized by the Pontifical Council for Promoting Christian Unity held in Nemi, Italy in August 1990, which was an occasion to celebrate the twenty-fifth anniversary of the Second Vatican Council's Declaration of the Church's bond with the Jewish people (*Nostra Aetate #4*). See my complementary essay, "The Catholic Church and the Jewish People: Evaluating the Results of the Second Vatican Council," in *New Visions: Historical and Theological Perspectives on the Jewish-Christian Dialogue*, ed. Val A. McInnes (New York: Crossroads, 1993), 115-36.

1. Addressing a delegation of the American Jewish Committee on March 16, 1990, Pope John Paul stated: "Although the Catholic teaching concerning Jews and Judaism is summarized in (*Nostra Aetate*) #4, many of its fundamental elements are also present in other documents of the Council . . . Perhaps the time has come, after 25 years to make a systematic study of the Council's teaching on this matter." See Eugene J. Fisher and Leon Klenicki, *Pope John Paul II—Spiritual Pilgrimage: Texts on Jews and Judaism 1978-1995* (New York: Crossroad, 1995), 133-35.

2. Timothy E. O'Connell, ed., *Vatican II and Its Documents: An American Appraisal* (Wilmington: Michael Glazier, 1986), 7 (editor's preface). In my essay, each document will be designated by a key word or words in Latin or in English. Translations are taken from Austin Flannery, ed., *Vatican Council II: The Conciliar and Post Conciliar Documents* (Collegeville: Liturgical Press, 1975), except where accuracy requires another rendering.

3. For the three texts from the Holy See, consult Eugene J. Fisher and Leon Klenicki, ed., *In Our Time: The Flowering of Jewish-Catholic Dialogue* (Mahwah, NJ: Paulist Press, 1990); and *Catholics Remember the Holocaust* (Washington: United States Catholic Conference, 1998).

4. See *Constitution on the Sacred Liturgy* #2.

5. See #16 and 35; Carlo Colombo, "De Mysterio Ecclesiae in Mysterio historiae salutis," *Acta Congressus Internationalis de Theologia Concilii Vaticani II,* ed. Adolfus Schonmetzer) (Rome: Vatican Polyglot Press 1968), 10-20.

6. This summary statement, making the contents of the Jewish Scriptures "but a prelude to the work of Christ" needs to be balanced by the *Constitution on Divine Revelation,* chapter IV. See *Liturgy* #24. On this point, see Charles Miller, *"As It Is Written": The Use of Old Testament References in the Documents of Vatican Council II* (St. Louis: Marianist Communications Center, 1973).

7. The Jewish liturgy, epitomized in the Passover meal, provided this principle: prayer pointing to the past is not only expressing the people's relation to God *now* but is oriented as well to the final days. The symbolism of the "eastward position" of the celebrant and congregation during the Canon of the Roman rite Mass was lost in the liturgical reform. This theological reference to past, present, and future is emphasized, however, in three of the acclamations by the faithful immediately after the consecration of the bread and wine.

8. The hymns for the Office on February second, very respectful of "the Law," were composed by Peter Abelard (1079-1142).

9. See Stanislaus Campbell, *From Breviary to Liturgy of the Hours: The Structural Reform of the Roman Office 1964-1971* (Collegeville: Liturgical Press, 1995).

10. "Pro perfidiis Judaeis," *Theological Studies* 8 (1947): 80-96, and *Cahiers Sioniens* 1 (1947): 85-101. See Kathryn Sullivan, "Pro perfidiis Judaeis," in *The Bridge,* ed. J.M. Oesterreicher, (1956) II: 212-23. For a survey of these questions, see Lawrence E. Frizzell and J. Frank Henderson, "Jews and Judaism in the Medieval Latin Liturgy," in *The Liturgy of the Medieval Church,* ed. Thomas J. Heffernan and E. Ann Matter (Kalamazoo: Medieval Institute Publications, 2001), 167-92.

11. Words of Pope Paul VI in the opening allocution at the second session of the Council (September 29, 1963). The term *mysterion* in Greek renders *raz* in the Book of Daniel and thus refers to the divine plan of salvation; the Latin equivalent is *sacramentum,* applied to the Church in #1. See Aloys Grillmeir in *Commentary on the Documents of Vatican II,* ed. Herbert Vorgrimler (New York and Herder, 1967) I:140; Yves Congar, *Un people messianique: salut et liberation* (Paris: Cerf, 1975), 27-98; A.H.C. van Eijk, "The Church as Sacrament. A Contribution to Ecumenical Understanding," *Bijdragen* 48 (1987): 234-58; and "The Church: Mystery, Sacrament, Sign, Instrument, Symbolic Reality," *Bijdragen* 50 (1989): 178-202.

12. I owe this distinction, crucial to an interpretation of the Synoptic Gospels, to my colleague, Rabbi Asher Finkel.

13. The Latin text "In illo agro crescit antique oliva, cuius radix sancta fuerunt *Patriarchae*" has been mistranslated in Flannery to read "whose holy roots were the *prophets*" (*Vatican Council II*, 353). "Vitis vera Christus est . . ." is rendered "*Yet* the true vine is Christ . . ." "Yet" sets up a contrast that need not be implied from the original. The translation in Walter Abbott, ed., *The Documents of Vatican II* (New York: Corpus Books, 1966), 18-19 is accurate at both places.

14. Just as Christ is the vine with which the Church's members must be united, so Origen identifies him with the kingdom (see Lk 17:21) and the Land. See Annie Jaubert, *Origene: Homélies sur Josué*. Sources Chrétiennes 71 (Paris: Cerf, 1960), 16-62. Since the *Fundamental Accord* between the Holy See and Israel (December 30, 1993) official Church teaching should be developing insights into Christian appreciation of the Jewish bond with the Land of Israel. Related themes are explored in *The Jewish People and Their Sacred Scriptures in the Christian Bible*, a document issued by the Pontifical Biblical Commission in November 2001 (Boston: Pauline Books and Media, 2002).

15. The themes deserve detailed attention beyond the scope of this essay. See Gerard S. Sloyan, "Who Are the People of God?" in *Standing Before God: Studies . . . in Honor of John M. Oesterreicher*, ed. A Finkel and L. Frizzell (New York: Ktav, 1981), 103-14. In his study *Le Concile de Vatican II: son Eglise, Peuple de Dieu et Corps du Christ* (Paris: Beauchesne, 1984), Yves Congar does not consider the Jewish people or the Church's relation to Judaism. See Albert Chapelle, "Israël, son Serviteur (Lc 1:54)," *Nouvelle Revue Théologique* 125 (2003): 177-86.

16. In the aftermath of the Council, see especially the teaching of Pope John Paul II and instructions of the Commission for Religious Relations with Judaism, with an English version for each indicated in note 1 and 3.

17. See *Church* #48-51, and for background my article, "Pilgrimage: A Study of the Biblical Experience," *Jeevadhara* 71 (1982): 358-67.

18. See my article, "A Catholic Theological Reflection on Mission," *Journal of Dharma* 6 (1981): 141-50.

19. See Daniel Harrington, *God's People in Christ: New Testament Perspectives on the Church and Judaism* (Philadelphia: Fortress, 1980); Franz Mussner, *Tractate on the Jews: The Significance of Judaism for Christian Faith* (Philadelphia: Fortress, 1984); A.H.C. van Eijk, "The Jewish People and the Church's Self-Understanding," *Bijdragen* 50 (1989): 373-93. Teachings of Pope John Paul II must be incorporated into the discussion;

for example, in Munich on November 17, 1980, he declared that the Old Covenant was never revoked by God. See Norbert Lohfink, *The Covenant Never Revoked: Biblical Reflections on Christian-Jewish Dialogue* (Mahwah: Paulist Paulist, 1991), and the discussion by Albert Vanhoye, "Salut universal par le Christ et validité de l'Ancienne Alliance, *Nouvelle Revue Théologique* 116 (1994): 815-35; Emmanuelle Main, "Anciennne et nouvelle Alliances dans le desssein de Dieu," 118 (1996): 34-58; and Vincent Martin, "L'ancien et le nouveau," 118 (1996): 59-65.

20. On the developments in Mariology over recent years, see Giuseppe Besutti, *Bibliografia Mariana 1978-1984* (Rome: Marianum, 1988). The work of Aristide Serra delves deeply into Jewish sources; see *E c'era la Madre di Gesu: Saggi di esegesi biblico-mariana* (Rome: Marianum, 1989). The contribution on Judaism by an Israeli scholar in *Maria nell' Ebriasmo e nell' Islam oggi* (Bologna: Dehoniane, 1987) leaves the field open. In *Redemptoris Mater* (#1), Pope John Paul II states that Mary uttered the first *fiat* of the New Covenant. See John McHugh, "Mary's *fiat* as the Commencement of the New Covenant," *Marianum* 50 (1988): 133-37. See also David Flusser, J. Pelikan and J. Lang, *Mary: Images of the Mother of Jesus in Jewish and Christian Perspectives* (Philadelphia: Fortress, 1986); my essays, "Mary and the Biblical Heritage" in *Marian Studies* 46 (1995): 26-40, and "Mary's Magnificat: Sources and Themes" 50 (1999): 38-59; and Marc Ouellet, "Mary and the Future of Ecumenism," *Communio* 30 (2003): 5-25.

21. The problematic designation "Old Testament" cannot for Catholics be replaced by "Hebrew Scriptures"; our canon (see *Dei Verbum* #8 and 22) includes the deutero-canonical books preserved in Greek. The term "Jewish Scriptures" avoids the limitation of language. Use of the word "gift" implies gratitude on the part of the recipient; the Church acquired the Scriptures when it was still a Jewish-Christian community, albeit for the most part in the Greek-speaking world.

22. Aspects of the continuing debate on this theme may be found in Gerard S. Sloyan, "Some Suggestions for a Biblical Three-year Lectionary," *Worship* 63 (1989): 521-35. Another debate is presented by Ignace de la Potterie, "Reading Holy Scripture 'in the Spirit': Is the Patristic Way of Reading the Bible Still Possible Today?" *Communio* 13 (1986): 308-25.

23. For the examples of Torah and ecology, see my articles, "Law at the service of humankind," *SIDIC* 19 (#3-1986): 4-7, and "Humanity and Nature According to the Jewish Scriptures," *SIDIC* 22 (#3-1989): 5-8.

24. See Edmond Jacob, "A propos d'une ancienne formule sur l'unité des deux Testaments," *Bulletin du Centre Protestant d'Etudes* 36 (1984): 20-26.

25. "Ignoratio Scripturarum ignoratio Christi est (In Isa 17B)." See Pierre Jay, *L'exégèse de Saint Jérome d'après son Commentaire sur Isaie* (Paris: Etudes Augustiniennes, 1985), 392.

26. See *Notes on the Correct Way to Present Jews and Judaism in Preaching and Catechesis* (Vatican: Commission for Religious Relations with the Jews, 1985); *Within Context: Guidelines for the Catechetical Presentation of Jews and Judaism in the New Testament* (1986), in Fisher and Klenicki, *In Our Time*, 59-74); and "God's Mercy Endures Forever: Guidelines on the Presentation of Jews and Judaism in Catholic Preaching" (Washington: Bishops' Committee on the Liturgy, 1988).

27. *Gaudium et Spes* #2 asks "What is the human being?"; *Nostra Aetate* #1 poses a long series of questions whose depths have been explored by various spiritual traditions.

28. *Nostra Aetate* encourages the "development of mutual understanding between Jews and Catholics, especially by way of biblical and theological inquiry and through friendly discussions" (#4). Subsequently texts from the Commission on Religious Relations with the Jews and national conferences of bishops have outlined the principles for making these discussions more fruitful. See Helga Croner, ed., *Stepping Stones to Further Jewish-Christian Relations* (New York: Paulist Press, 1977) and *More Stepping Stones to Jewish Christian Relations* (New York: Paulist Press, 1985). See also the document "On Dialogue with Unbelievers" (August 28, 1968), published in Flannery, *Vatican Council II*, 1002-14. Pope John Paul II has discussed the significance of dialogue with Jews: "The first dimension of this dialogue, that is the meeting between the people of God of the Old Covenant, never revoked by God (see Rom 11:29) and that of the New Covenant, is at the same time a dialogue within our Church . . . between the first and second part of her Bible" (Munich, November 17, 1980).

29. See Thomas Federici, "Study Outline on the Mission and Witness of the Church," *More Stepping Stones*, ed. Helga Croner, 37-55.

30. See "Mortara Case," in *Encyclopedia Judaica* 12 (1967), 354-55, and David Kertzer, *The Kidnapping of Edgardo Mortara* (New York: Vintage Books, 1998). Another such problem occurred in World War II. Parents who died in a Nazi concentration camp had entrusted two infant sons to a Catholic; she had them baptized; after the War relatives intervened to raise them. See Edward Flannery, "The Finaly Case," in *The Bridge*, ed. J.M. Oesterreicher, 1 (1955), 292-313.

A Bridge to New Christian-Jewish Understanding: Nostra Aetate *at 40*

John T. Pawlikowski

In a 1986 address to the Catholic Theological Society of America meeting in Chicago the Canadian theologian Gregory Baum argued that chapter four of *Nostra Aetate* represented the most radical change in the ordinary magisterium of the Catholic Church to come out of Vatican II.[1] Baum's perspective is basically substantiated in the work of Dr. Eugene J. Fisher, longtime staff person for Catholic-Jewish relations at the United States Conference of Catholic Bishops. In a paper presented at the 1985 Vatican-Jewish International Dialogue in Rome, Fisher pointed to the uniqueness of chapter four of *Nostra Aetate* in terms of conciliar documents. He maintained that *"Nostra Aetate,* for all practical purposes, begins the Church's teaching concerning a theological or, more precisely, a doctrinal understanding of the relationship between the Church as "People of God" and "God's People Israel."[2] These affirmations assume particular importance today when some in the Church are claiming that the ecumenical and interreligious documents from Vatican II are only "pastoral" in nature without any doctrinal implications. Such a view, in light of what Baum and Fisher have said, completely misrepresents these documents, including *Nostra Aetate.* Certainly one of the continuing challenges facing those whose understanding of the Christian-Jewish relationship has been profoundly transformed by *Nostra Aetate,* and I count myself among them, is to maintain and even deepen its theological significance.

Examining chapter four of *Nostra Aetate,* we find scarcely any reference to the usual sources cited in conciliar documents: the

Church Fathers, papal statements, and previous conciliar statements. Rather the Declaration returns to Romans 9-11, as if to say that the Church is now taking up where Paul left off in his insistence that Jews remain part of the covenant after the Resurrection despite the theological ambiguity involved in such a statement. Without saying it so explicitly, the 2,221 Council members who voted in favor of *Nostra Aetate* were in fact stating that everything that had been said about the Christian-Jewish relationship since Paul moved in a direction they could no longer support.

It is interesting to note that *Nostra Aetate* never makes mention of the several passages in the Letter to the Hebrews where the original covenant with Israel appears to be abrogated after Christ and Jewish law overturned (Heb 7:12, 8:13, and 10:9). In retrospect this may be unfortunate in light of attempts to return to the "authenticity" of these passages as contemporary Catholic teaching by scholars such as Cardinal Avery Dulles.[3] It would have helped if *Nostra Aetate* had more explicitly rejected these passages in Hebrews as a valid starting point for the theology of Christian-Jewish relationship today. But given the interpretive role of a Church Council in the Catholic tradition this omission of the texts from Hebrews is still theologically significant. It indicates that the Council Fathers judged them a theologically inappropriate resource for contemporary thinking about the link between the Church and the Jewish people.

Nostra Aetate has affected the Catholic Church and beyond in many parts of the world. Many Protestant churches took a cue from Vatican II and issued statements on Christian-Jewish relations that sometimes are even bolder in their assertion about the nexus between the church and synagogue. And the document has generated new theological thinking as well as major revampings of Christian educational materials in North America, Europe, Latin America, and Australia/New Zealand. African and Asian Catholic thinking has thus far been only minimally affected by *Nostra Aetate* although scholars such as Peter Phan and John Mbiti have shown genuine interest in the Christian-Jewish question.

Some Christian theologians have insisted on the overall theological implications of *Nostra Aetate*. The German theologian

Johannes-Baptist Metz is one such example. Metz has rightly argued that the implications of *Nostra Aetate* and subsequent Vatican documents on relations with the Jews in 1974 and 1985 go well beyond the parameters of the Christian-Jewish dialogue. Especially after the Holocaust, Metz insists, they involve a "revision of Christian theology itself."[4] Yet, despite Metz's rightful claim, one of the great challenges still remaining after forty years is the incorporation of church statements on Catholic-Jewish relations into the mainstream of Catholic theological thinking. To this end, the International Council of Christians and Jews has recently joined with the World Council of Churches and other Christian-Jewish centers in launching a multi-year consultation of Christian theologians in the hope finally of achieving such a mainstreaming of the insights of *Nostra Aetate* and the scholarly research it has generated. Certainly there is also hope that this process on the Christian side will inspire further consideration of the implications of the revised Christian thinking for Jewish self-understanding. The Jewish document *Dabru Emet* and the volume of theological reflections that accompanies it has inaugurated such rethinking among Jewish scholars.[5]

The Catholic-Jewish dialogue has gone through several phases since the release of *Nostra Aetate*. Phase one can best be described as the "cleansing" phase. It has primarily affected Catholic education. Thanks to the pioneering work of Sister Rose Thering, O.P., recently profiled in the Academy Award nominated documentary, *The Passion of Sister Rose,* whose studies on Catholic religion textbooks at St. Louis University played a significant role in convincing bishops at Vatican II of the need for a statement on the Church's relationship with the Jewish people, the vision of Vatican II regarding the Catholic-Jewish relationship has been widely implemented.[6] Virtually all of the major Catholic textbook publishers undertook substantive revisions of their materials, often with Jewish consultants. Subsequent studies on Catholic teaching materials by Eugene Fisher and Philip Cunningham have confirmed the continuity of these revisions, though Cunningham did detect one somewhat problematical series published by the Ignatius Press.[7]

Since there has not been a comprehensive study since the early nineties it would prove useful, in this fortieth anniversary year of *Nostra Aetate,* if a new analysis of currently used books were undertaken.

If there is a potential problem on the horizon it has to do with the, possible use of the DVD version of Mel Gibson's *The Passion of the Christ,* with its numerous stereotypes of Jews and Judaism, as a resource in Catholic educational programs. Well over a hundred Christian scholars and church leaders have expressed their deep concern about the potential for this film to undercut the advancements in Christian-Jewish understanding realized since Vatican II, and a number of recent volumes have critiqued many elements in *The Passion of the Christ* for a false presentation of the role of Jews in the death of Christ and the theological implications therein.[8] And a communique from the ongoing dialogue between the National Council of Synagogues and the Catholic Bishop's Secretariat on Ecumenical and Interreligious Affairs in May of 2004 warned educators that the perspectives of the Gibson film cannot substitute for the official teachings on the Catholic-Jewish relations promulgated in *Nostra Aetate* and subsequent documents issued from the Vatican as well as the late Pope John Paul II's two volumes of constructive statements on the Church's bonding with Judaism and the Jewish people.[9]

The first phase of the post-Vatican II Jewish-Christian encounter has seen the removal from Catholic educational materials of the principal defamations of Jews and Judaism found in the textbooks analyzed in the St. Louis University studies. These included the charge that Jews collectively were responsible for the death of Jesus, that the Pharisees were the archenemies of Jesus and spiritually soulless, that Jews had been displaced in their covenantal relationship with God as a result of their refusal to accept Jesus as the Messiah, and that the "Old Testament" was totally inferior to the New, being rooted in legalism while Christianity was based on grace. This "cleansing" phase seems substantially completed though ongoing monitoring remains necessary given the current efforts to "reinterpret" Vatican II in ways that would substantially eviscerate it in certain quarters of contemporary Catholicism.

The second phase of the contemporary Jewish-Christian dialogue dates back in some respects beyond *Nostra Aetate*. It involves decidedly new perspectives with regard to the role of the Old Testament or Hebrew Scriptures in Christian faith identity as well as an enhanced appreciation of the importance of understanding the Judaism of Jesus' days in interpreting the New Testament. Gradually an awareness has been building regarding the positive impact of the Scriptures, as Jesus knew the Old Testament, on his basic perspective. As the late Raymond Brown once remarked, prior to this revolution in understanding the Hebrew Scriptures, Christians tended to emphasize primarily the failures of the Jewish people to abide by their covenantal responsibilities. But more and more scholars are now emphasizing that the basic message of Jesus becomes truncated without a clear, positive association with the Hebrew Scriptures. There is a growing recognition of the spiritual values of the Hebrew Scriptures in their own right and not merely as a backdrop or even foil for New Testament teachings.

Disputes still remain between Christian and Jewish scholars, and within both Christian and Jewish scholarship, about whether Christians and Jews draw authority from the same book, as *Dabru Emet* put it. But clearly there has been a sea change in Christian thinking regarding the role of the Hebrew Scriptures in the faith life of the Christians. Certainly there are still areas of improvement that are required. By and large lectionary texts from the Hebrew Scriptures do not often become the basis for preaching during the Eucharistic liturgy. Training preachers in using these texts constructively in sermons is still a goal to be achieved. The Catholic Bishops' Committee on the Liturgy did issue an important set of guidelines on the presentation of Jews and Judaism in Catholic preaching in September 1988, entitled *God's Mercy Endures Forever*.[10] But little has been done to implement these guidelines in a widespread way. Hence they remain largely a secret in liturgical and homilectical circles. In an important address delivered in Mainz, Germany, in 1980, Pope John Paul II linked the renewed understanding of Scripture with the Church's new appreciation of its relationship with the Jewish people, stating that the dialogue, as "the meeting between the people of God of the Old Covenant, never revoked by God, is at the same time a dialogue without our Church, that is to say, a dialogue between the first and second part of the Bible."[11]

Research resulting from the mindset about Christian-Jewish relations generated by *Nostra Aetate* has begun to influence even more profoundly New Testament interpretation. This is true both with respect to the teachings and person of Jesus and the pastoral journeys of St. Paul. Recent years have seen a profound shift in New Testament exegesis with an increasing number of scholars emphasizing that Jesus must be returned to his essentially Jewish context if the Church is to understand his message properly.

Scripture scholars in particular have played a major role in the process of rethinking the Church's relationship with the Jewish people. For the past couple of decades we witnessed a fundamental change of perspective within biblical studies regarding Jesus and Judaism. The emerging new biblical template has in part been stimulated by the about-face in official Catholic teaching generated by *Nostra Aetate*. Earlier scholarship from the hands of influential figures such as Rudolf Bultmann, Ernst Kasemann, Gerhard Kittel, and Martin Noth which undercut any notion of Jesus' concrete ties to, and dependence upon, biblical and Second Temple Judaism and which argued that Jewish history had come to an end with the coming of Jesus who had no role in that history has generally lost its foothold in biblical circles. It is being replaced by the studies of scholars such as James Charlesworth, W.D. Davies, E.P. Sanders, Daniel Harrington, Clemens Thoma, John Meier, Cardinal Carlo Martini, and Robin Scroggs, to name but a few, who have moved New Testament interpretation in the opposite direction to Bultmann, Kittel, and Noth. Cardinal Martini, a biblical scholar who served as Archbishop of Milan, is an excellent representative of this fundamental shift in outlook on the Jesus-Judaism question. He writes: "Without a sincere feeling for the Jewish world, and a direct experience of it, one cannot fully understand Christianity. Jesus is fully Jewish, the apostles are Jewish, and one cannot doubt their attachment to the tradition of their forefathers."[12]

One of the best contemporary summaries of what where we have come in our new understanding of Jesus' relationship to the Jewish community of his day can be found in the writings of Robin Scroggs. His view was accepted by the late Cardinal Joseph Bernardin of Chicago, an episcopal leader in the promotion of authentic Jewish-Christian reconciliation.[13] Scroggs has emphasized the following points in terms of the vision Jesus appears to have left the earliest Christian community with respect to its identity relative to the Judaism of the time: 1) The movement begun by Jesus and continued after his death in Palestine can best be described as a reform movement within Judaism. Little or no evidence exists to suggest a separate sense of identity within the emerging Christian community; 2) Paul understood his mission to the gentiles as fundamentally a mission out of Judaism whose aim was to extend God's original and continuing call to the Jewish people to the gentiles; 3) Prior to the end of the Jewish war with the Romans in 70 C.E., one has difficulty speaking about a separate Christian reality. Followers of Jesus did not seem to understand themselves as part of a separate religion from Judaism. A distinctive Christian identity only began to develop after the Roman-Jewish war.[14]

While not every New Testament scholar would subscribe fully to each and every point made by Scroggs, a consensus is definitely building that the process of church-synagogue separation was longer and more complex than was once believed. This picture definitely challenges how most Christians have previously been taught. They were raised, as was I, with the notion that by the time Jesus died on Calvary the Church was clearly established as a distinct religious body apart from Judaism. This understanding was subsequently expanded, especially by the Church Fathers, into what is known as the *adversos Judaeos* tradition, which had as its theological foundation the belief in a total displacement of the Jewish people from the covenant.[15] But increasingly, due in part to scholars such as Robin Scroggs, we are coming to see that many people in the very early days of Christianity did not see the Jesus movement as launching a new, totally separate religious community that would stand over against Judaism.

There has also been considerable reevaluation of Paul's view of Jews and Judaism. This is especially important for Protestant Christianity where Pauline thought has exercised a somewhat greater influence in defining the Christian-Jewish relationship than is the case in Catholicism. Paul's missionary journeys are now seen by a number of scholars such as the previously mentioned Robin Scroggs as essentially constituting a Jewish mission to the gentiles (Judaism definitely had a missionary orientation in this period) rather than an effort to create a split between church and synagogue. The late Fr. Raymond Brown once remarked that it was his view that if Paul would have had a son he would have circumcised him. What is beginning to emerge is a picture of Paul as still very much a Jew, still quite appreciative of the Torah (he may well have assumed its continued validity for Jewish Christians), and still struggling towards the end of his ministry to balance his understanding of the newness he recognized in Jesus and his message with the continuity of the Jewish covenant. This tension is certainly apparent in the notable chapters 9-11 of Romans on which *Nostra Aetate* built its revolutionary understanding of the Church's relationship to the Jewish people. It is also possible that some of the Pauline writings, especially those which have served as the basis for later Christological thinking in the Church, may have their roots in Paul's personal contact with the Jewish mysticism of his time, though Paul would have added his distinctive interpretation.

From the scholarly evidence now at hand it does not seem that Jesus conveyed to his disciples and initial followers a clear sense that he meant to create a new and distinct religious entity called the Church which was to separate itself totally from Judaism. This sense of a separate Christian identity apart from Judaism only emerged gradually well after his death. We now are aware as a result of the research of scholars such as Robert Wilken, Wayne Meeks, Alan Segal, and Anthony Saldarini that this development took several centuries to mature. Evidence now exists for regular Christian participation in Jewish worship, particularly in the East, during the second and third centuries and, in a few places, even into the fourth and fifth centuries.

The challenge now facing Christianity in light of this new research on the origins of the Church is whether the creation of a totally separate religious community was actually in the mind of Jesus himself. Cardinal Carlo Maria Martini has addressed this question by reintroducing the notion of "schism" into the discussion of the basic theological relationship between Jews and Christians, an idea that first appeared in the early part of the twentieth century. Martini applies the term "schism" to the original separation of the Church and Synagogue. For him the break between Jews and Christians represents the fundamental schism, far more consequential in negative terms than the two subsequent ruptures within Christianity itself. In introducing the notion of schism, Martini has interjected two important notions into the conversation. First, schism should ideally not have occurred and, second, it should be regarded as a temporary situation rather than a permanent reality. So schism, which had been applied previously only to the two disruptions within the body of Christianity, implies a certain mandate to heal the rupture that has ensued.

There is legitimate room for debate as to the appropriateness of the term "schism" in reflecting on the nature of the Christian-Jewish theological relationship today. I myself do not think it will take us too far. But for Cardinal Martini its strength is that it reminds Christians that they cannot forge an authentic self-identity without restoring the profoundly Jewish context of Jesus' teaching. Clearly the Church will not return to an understanding of itself as one of among many Jewish groups. But in light of recent biblical scholarship it needs to reassess how its self-identity remains rooted in Judaism Johannes Metz has rightly argued that "Christians can form and sufficiently understand their identity only in the face of the Jews."[16] For Metz such a vision involves a definite reintegration of Jewish history and Jewish beliefs into Christian theological consciousness and statement. Jewish history is not merely Christian pre-history; rather, it forms an integral, continuing part of ecclesial history.

The third phase of the dialogue is only in its beginning stages. A number of Christian theologians and a few Jewish scholars have attempted to rethink the relationship between the Church and the Jewish people in fundamentally new ways. And a few significant documents have appeared recently, such as the 2002 Jewish document on Christianity, *Dabru Emet*,[17] a two hundred-plus page document from the Pontifical Biblical Commission with a foreword by then-Cardinal Joseph Ratzinger on the Jews and their Scriptures in the New Testament,[18] and *A Sacred Obligation*[19] from a group of Catholic and Protestant scholars who have been jointly studying the Christian-Jewish relationship since 1969. Finally, there is a study document coming from an ongoing Catholic-Jewish dialogue co-sponsored by the National Council of Synagogues and the Catholic Bishops' Secretariat for Ecumenical and Interreligious Affairs called *Reflections on Covenant and Mission*.[20]

The last of these documents has stirred considerable discussion, including a critical assessment by Cardinal Avery Dulles and a response to his criticisms by several of the drafters of that document.[21] Particularly challenging for some Catholics is its claim that Jews need not be the subject of Christian evangelization, an assertion found in a number of the recent writings of Cardinal Walter Kasper.[22] In fact, *Reflections on Covenant and Mission* was a response to the call by Cardinal Kasper as President of the Holy See's Commission for Religious Relations with the Jews, for national churches to produce new theological reflections on the Church's relationship with the Jewish people. Unfortunately, as has already been noted, these documents and scholarly studies thus far have largely remained on the fringes of mainstream Catholic theology. If we are to be true to the bold new vision of *Nostra Aetate*, these statements and studies must begin to penetrate the core of contemporary Catholic theological reflection. The late Pope John Paul II certainly provided leadership in this regard with two published volumes of addresses on the theological linkage between Judaism and Christianity.[23]

As biblical scholars and theologians have begun to probe the implications of this new vision of Jesus as profoundly intertwined with the Jewish community of his time, they began to see the need for recasting the Church's understanding of its relationship with the Jewish people. The first efforts along this line tended to focus on Paul's reflections in Romans 9-11, where he asserts that God remains faithful to the original covenanted people. They argued that "newness" in Christ cannot be stated in a way that invalidates Jewish covenantal inclusion. Some of these pioneering scholars such as Kurt Hruby, Jacques Maritain, Jean Danielou, and Cardinal Augustine Bea were forced to conclude that it is not possible for the Church to go beyond saying what Paul himself had stated, i.e., that reconciliation between an assertion of redemptive "newness" in Christ and the concomitant affirmation of the continued participation of the Jewish people in the ongoing covenant remains a "mystery" presently understandable to God alone. Only at the endtime might we come to see the lack of contradiction in these twin theological statements.

Theologians, however, do not like to stop creative reflection. So as time went on, the initial inclination of the early scholars on Christian-Jewish relations to remain content with the Pauline "mystery" approach began to wane. New proposals began to come to the fore along the lines of what we term the "single" and "double" covenantal perspectives

The first approach is generally called the "single covenant" perspective. It holds that Jews and Christians basically belong to one covenantal tradition that began at Sinai. In this model the coming of Christ represented the decisive moment when the gentiles were able to enter fully into the special relationship with God which the Jews already enjoyed and which they continue. Christians were grafted onto the tree of Judaism, to use a Pauline image. Some holding this viewpoint maintain that the decisive features of the Christ Event have universal application, including to the Jews. The statement on the Jews and their Scriptures in the New Testament from the Pontifical Biblical Commission referred to earlier appears to argue that within historical time Jews await the Messiah through their own covenant. There is no need for Jews to convert to Christianity, a basic point also made in the September 2002 document, *A Sacred Obligation* (#7). But when the Jewish Messiah eventually arrives, he will have some of the characteristics integral to Jesus' messiahship. Thus Jesus' messiahship retains universal significance. Other scholars in this continuing discussion are more inclined to argue that the Christian appropriation and reinterpretation of the original covenantal tradition, in and through Jesus, applies primarily to non-Jews.

The "double covenant" theory begins at the same point as its single covenant counterpart, namely, with a strong affirmation of the continuing bonds between Christians and Jews. But then it prefers to underline the distinctiveness of the two traditions and communities, particularly in terms of their experiences after the final separation of the church and synagogue. Christians associated with this perspective insist on maintaining the view that through the ministry, teachings, and person of Jesus a vision of God emerged that was distinctively new in terms of its central features. Even though they may well have been important groundwork laid for the emergence of this distinctive new vision during the Second or Middle Judaism period, what came to be understood regarding the divine-human relationship as a result of Jesus' coming has to be regarded as a quantum leap.

It is very likely that discussions regarding the best way to reformulate a Christian covenantal theology will continue in earnest for the foreseeable future. Cardinal Walter Kasper, the President of the Holy See's Commission for Religious Relations with the Jews, has begun to rethink the basic Christian-Jewish relationship in a number of addresses he has given since assuming his role at the Vatican, the two most recent being an address in December 2004 at the Centre for the Study of Jewish-Christian Relations in Cambridge and one in Washington in March 2005 commemorating the fortieth anniversary of *Nostra Aetate.* In these addresses Cardinal Kasper has stressed that the Church's relations with Jews is *sui generis* because Jews have divine revelation from the Christian theological perspective. He has also argued against the need to proselytize Jews because they are already in the covenantal relationship with God. But Cardinal Kasper has not yet offered a comprehensive theological perspective on the Christian-Jewish relationship, which he certainly seems capable of producing, given his stature a one of Europe's most important Catholic theologians. Nor has he indicated his reaction to what appear to be contrary views by another Cardinal-theologian, Avery Dulles, who spoke in a vein that seems to move in an opposite direction from the Cardinal Kasper at the same conference in Washington in March 2005. Given his reappointment as the Holy See's representative to the world Jewish community by Pope Benedict XVI, we can hope that he will have the opportunity to provide the Church with such a comprehensive statement that would solidify and expand his own previous work and integrate the important insights of the late Pope John Paul II on Christianity's intimate bonding with Judaism.[24]

Two developments in contemporary biblical scholarship have important implications for the theology of the Christian-Jewish relationship. The first, brought forth by scholars such as Jacob Neusner, Hayim Perelmuter, and Efraim Shuemli, have emphasized that the Judaism of the first century was far from monolithic. In fact, this period was marked by considerable creativity. New groups were emerging that challenged the viewpoints of traditional Judaism in many areas. What Ellis Rivkin has termed the "Pharisaic Revolution,"[25] a revolution that clearly seeded the perspectives of Jesus and early Christianity as the 1985 Vatican *Notes* on Jews and Judaism insist, was transforming significant aspects of Judaism faith understanding. Many scholars now see the need to speak of "Judaisms," rather than Judaism, at the time of Jesus. This reality makes it much more difficult for Christians to claim that Jesus "fulfilled" Jewish messianic prophesies. And since Christian interpretations of the Jewish-Christian relationship within the single covenant model are often rooted in an ongoing, linear understanding of Judaism, this new understanding of "Judaisms" poses a genuine challenge for the authenticity of such a model. Most advocates of the single covenant approach have not dealt with this new, complex picture of Judaism at the time of Jesus.

The other dimension of recent scholarship has to do with how and when the separation if church and synagogue took place. Most

Christians have been weaned on the idea that the church was basically established as a distinct religious entity by the time Jesus died on Calvary. We now know that such a view is quite simplistic. The late Anthony J. Saldarini made this clear in his 1999 Joseph Cardinal Bernardin Jerusalem lecture in Chicago.[26] Neither the so-called Council of Jerusalem described in Acts nor the claimed expulsion of Christians from the synagogue at the Jewish Synod of Jabneh at the end of the first century completely settled the issue of the Christian-Jewish relationship.

Important Christian and Jewish scholars such as Saldarini are now insisting, based on new documentary evidence, that the actual separation between the Church and Synagogue, while well advanced by the end of the first century, was not completed for several centuries thereafter. These scholars have uncovered evidence of continued Jewish-Christian ties, including joint worship, into the second, third, fourth, and perhaps even the fifth century. Clearly there were Christians who did not see their acceptance of the Way of Jesus as automatically severing their bonds with the Jewish community and there were Jews who obviously were of the same opinion. These Christian Jews continued to believe that their Jewish roots remained integral to their new Christian identity despite the development of the notorious *Adversus Judasos* in the writings of major Church Fathers. We certainly would like to know more about this period, but the documentary evidence is not currently at hand. But the evidence we do have presently still requires a major theological reevaluation from both Christians and Jews of the relationship between them.

As a result of this recent scholarship, a number of scholars have begun developing new images of the Christian-Jewish relationship beyond the ones that first arose in response to *Nostra Aetate*, such as "mother-daughter" religions and "elder and younger brothers." These images depend on an essentially linear development of Christianity out of Judaism which does not stand up anymore in light of the new documentary evidence.

Among the newly emergent images of the Christian-Jewish relationship, the following appear to hold out the most promise.

The first is the "sibling" model advanced by Jewish scholars such as Alan Segal and the late Hayim Perelmuter. This image is rooted in an understanding of the appearance of two new communities within the revolution within Judaism during the Second Temple period. The first of these communities was rabbinic Judaism and the second the Christian Church. Both went beyond former incarnations of Judaism in their basic teachings. While they had some early connections and both retained links with the Jewish Scriptures they eventually split into distinct and separate religious communities. This model has the advantage of stressing continued bonding while also allowing for recognition that Christianity is far more than Judaism for the gentiles.

Another image along the same lines is put forth by Mary Boys in her important volume *Has God Only One Blessing?*[27] She depicts Jews and Christians as "fraternal twins." This image has some of the same advantages as "siblings," although Boys appears to posit a somewhat deeper connection between Jews and Christians than even the "siblings" model. Her model may in fact tilt a bit too much towards the connected rather than the disconnected side of the relationship.

The Protestant theologian Clark Williamson, who has authored important works on the Christian-Jewish relationship, such as *A Guest in the House of Israel,* proposes a relationship model of "partners in waiting."[28] This is a more open-ended image. It lacks the emphasis on inherent bonding contained in the "siblings" and "fraternal twins" models. "Partners," after all, have no basic familial ties, but it does imply some linkage in terms of future hope. There is also a sense of common witness to the world implicit in Williamson's model.

The final model is in the process of being developed by the University of California scholar Daniel Boyarin. In a series of addresses at Catholic Theological Union and the University of Chicago as well as published articles and books, Boyarin has put forth the thesis that what finally resulted from the complex social and religious revolution in Second Temple Judaism were two distinct religious communities known as rabbinic Judaism and Christianity.[29] Thus for Boyarin we should image the Christian-Jewish relationship in terms of "co-emergent religious communities." His perspective accounts fairly well for much of the new historical evidence now at hand in terms of the multiplicity of Judaisms at the time of Jesus and for the gradual process of separation outlined above. But it is weaker than the other images in stressing the continued bonding between Church and Synagogue and thus needs some correction in this regard. This "co-emergence" was a drawn out process, not an instantaneous happening.

As we celebrate the fortieth anniversary of *Nostra Aetate,* we remain in the early stages of the rethinking of the Christian-Jewish relationship launched by that conciliar document. We should note that the newly emerging images are all more parallel than linear in their understanding of the Christian-Jewish relationship. The gradually emerging viewpoint on the relationship has a central motif that we can no longer draw a simple straight line of development from biblical Judaism to rabbinic Judaism to Christianity. Certainly a profound connection remains, but the process is not as linear as once believed, a perspective we continue to maintain in significant ways in the celebration of Christian liturgy. We need now to continue the scholarship and reflection upon it. New models may appear that will capture the complexity of the relationship even better than those we have just examined. For now, my preference is for the "siblings" model. I believe it takes into account the pioneering work of Daniel Boyarin, but leaves us with a better and clearer balance in terms of similarity/distinctiveness. Yet I could move towards the primacy of Boyarin's "co-emergence" model if we were to speak of it as "fraternal co-emergence."

The affirmations of *Nostra Aetate* as well as the new biblical scholarship that it partially generated raise important questions for Christological understanding. Traditional Christological approaches have been significantly rooted in the notion that the Church replaced the Jewish people in the covenant because of their supposed failure to recognize that the coming of Christ marked the fulfillment of Jesus messianic prophecies and the inauguration, in Jesus' lifetime, of the Church as a totally new religious community in opposition to the "old Israel." Such a perspective no longer seems to meet the test of historical accuracy. So Christology will require substantive rethinking as the 2002 statement from the Christian Scholars Group on Christian-Jewish Relations *A Sacred Obligation* makes clear: "Affirming God's Enduring Covenant with the Jewish people has consequences for Christian Understandings of Salvation" (#6).

Because Christology stands at the very nerve center of Christian faith, reevaluations of Christology cannot be done superficially. There is a trend found in some sectors of Christianity, especially in those most open to general interreligious understanding, that tends to depict the Christ Event as one of several authentic revelations with no particular universal aspect. Such a starting point is not acceptable to myself nor to the people who have called for a significant rethinking of the Church's theology of the Jewish people, such as Cardinal Walter Kasper or the scholars associated with *A Sacred Obligation*. We must maintain from the Christian side some understanding that the Christ Event has universal salvific implications. As I have expressed in my major writings on this topic, such as *Christ in the Light of the Christian-Jewish Dialogue*,[30] for me Incarnational Christology has the best possibility for preserving such universalistic dimensions of the Christ Event while opening "authentic theological space in for Judaism," as the late Cardinal Joseph Bernardin termed it.[31]

One potentially productive track has appeared in the writings of the Pope Benedict XVI prior to his election. Then-Cardinal Ratzinger, in a major book as well as in an article, maintained that Jews represent a special case in terms of salvation.[32] Cardinal Ratzinger appeared to exclude Jews from the framework of his controversial document, *Dominus Jesus,* although it would have been immensely helpful if he had said that directly. According to Cardinal Ratzinger, the Jewish community moves to final salvation through its own revealed covenantal tradition. This seems in line with the affirmation found in the Pontifical Biblical Commission's document referred to earlier issued with Cardinal Ratzinger's endorsement that Jewish messianic hopes are not in vain. What is not entirely clear in these works is whether Cardinal Ratzinger would demand explicit recognition of Christ as the Messiah from Jews as a requirement for their salvific confirmation. Hopefully Pope Benedict XVI will use his new position to clarify and enlarge upon the promising start he made in these writings of several years ago.

In rethinking Christology in light of the theological dynamic stimulated by *Nostra Aetate,* there will also be need to take into consideration the implications of the Holocaust for thinking about God and hence for reflection on Christology as well since the two cannot be separated. Both Christian and Jewish scholars, including myself, have addressed this issue.[33] And it will also be necessary, without undercutting the special nature of the Jewish-Christian relationship to pursue the encounter with Islam and beyond that with Buddhists, Hindus, and Jains.

We remain at a very early stage in the process of rethinking the theology of the Christian-Jewish relationship, even after forty years since II Vatican's substantial turnabout on the question. We must remember that it took almost two millennia to forge the negative theology of the relationship which Vatican II abrogated. As Catholics, we will likely never come to a point where our Christological affirmations will lead us to a theology of religious pluralism that will be in total sync with the perspectives of Judaism or other world religions. Nor will the development of new thinking about Christianity exemplified in the Jewish document *Dabru Emet* resolve all Jewish theological concerns about church teachings. But in our globalized world in which interreligious understanding is not merely confined to the realm of theological ideas but directly affects our life together in community, we can ill afford to shrink from this task.

Notes

1. Gregory Baum, "The Social Context of American Catholic Theology," *Proceedings of the Catholic Theological Society of America* 41 (1986): 87.

2. Eugene J. Fisher, "The Evolution of a Tradition: From *Nostra Aetate* to the *Notes.* International Catholic-Jewish Liaison Committee, *Fifteen*

Years of Catholic-Jewish Dialogue: 1970-1985 (Rome: Libreria Editrice Vaticana and Libreria Editrice Lateranense, 1988), 239.

3. Avery Dulles, "Evangelization and the Jews," *America* 187:12 (21 October 2002): 8-16.

4. Johannes Baptist Metz, "Facing the Jews: Christian Theology after Auschwitz," in Elisabeth Schussler-Fiorenza and David Tracy, eds., *The Holocaust as Interruption, Concilium* 175 (Edinburgh: T & T Clark, 1984), 27.

5. The text of *Dabru Emet* can be found in Tikva Frymer-Kensky, David Novak, Peter Ochs, David Fox Sandmel, and Michael A. Singer, eds., *Christianity in Jewish Terms* (Boulder: Westview Press, 2000).

6. I have summarized the St. Louis textbook studies' findings in John T. Pawlikowski, *Catechetics and Prejudice: How Catholic Teaching Materials View Jews, Protestants and Racial Minorities* (New York: Paulist Press, 1973).

7. Eugene J. Fisher, *Faith Without Prejudice: Rebuilding Christian Attitudes Toward Judaism,* revised and expanded ed. (New York: American Interfaith Institute and Crossroad, 1993); Philip A. Cunningham, *Education for Shalom: Religion Textbooks and the Enhancement of the Catholic and Jewish Relationship* (Collegeville, MN: Liturgical Press, 1995).

8. See Philip A. Cunningham, ed., *Pondering the Passion: What's at Stake for Christians and Jews* (Lanham, MD: Rowman and Littlefield, 2004); and Jonathan Burnham, ed., *Perspectives on "The Passion of the Christ": Religious Thinkers and Writers Explore the Issues Raised by the Controversial Movie* (New York: Miramax Books, 2004).

9. See Communique of the Catholic-Jewish Consultation Committee, May 19, 2004, in *Origins* 34/3 (June 3, 2004): 44-45.

10. Bishops' Committee on the Liturgy, National Conference of Catholic Bishops, *God's Mercy Endures Forever: Guidelines on the Presentation of Jews and Judaism in Catholic Preaching* (Washington: United States Catholic Conference Publications, 1988).

11. Bishops' Committee on the Liturgy, *God's Mercy Endures Forever*, 5.

12. Carlo Maria Martini, "Christianity and Judaism: A Historical and Theological Overview," in James H. Charlesworth, ed., *Jews and Christians: Exploring the Past, Present and Future* (New York: Crossroad, 1990), 19.

13. Robin Scroggs, "The Judaizing of the New Testament," *Chicago Theological Seminary Register* 75 (Winter 1986): 1.

14. See Wayne A. Meeks and Robert Wilken, *Jews and Christians in Antioch in the First Four Centuries* (Missoula, MT: Scholars Press, 1978); Robert Wilken, *John Chrysostom and the Jews: Rhetoric and Reality in the*

Late 4th Century (Berkeley and Los Angeles: University of California Press, 1983); Anthony J. Saldarini, "Jews and Christians in the First Two Centuries: The Changing Paradigm," *Shofar 10* (1992): 32-43; and Anthony J. Saldarini, "Christian Anti-Judaism: The First Century Speaks to the Twenty-First Century," *The Joseph Cardinal Bernardin Jerusalem Lecture,* April 14, 1999 (Chicago: The American Jewish Committee, Archdiocese of Chicago and the Jewish United Fund of Metropolitan Chicago, 1999).

15. See Rosemary Ruether, *Faith and Fratricide: The Theological Roots of Anti-Semitism* (New York: Seabury, 1974); and David P. Efroymson, "The Patristic Connection," in Alan T. Davies, ed., *Antisemitism and the Foundations of Christianity* (New York: Paulist Press, 1979), 98-117.

16. Johannes-Baptist Metz, "Facing the Jews," 33; and *The Emergent Church* (New York: Crossroad, 1981).

17. For one Jewish theologian's current thinking, see Irving Greenberg, *For the Sake of Heaven and Earth: The New Encounter between Judaism and Christianity* (Philadelphia: Jewish Publication Society, 2004).

18. Pontifical Biblical Commission, *The Jewish People and Their Sacred Scriptures in the Christian Bible* (Vatican City: Libreria Editrice Vaticana, 2002). For a discussion of the document, see a special issue of *The Bible Today,* May/June 2003.

19. The text of *A Sacred Obligation* can be found in Mary C. Boys, ed., *Seeing Judaism Anew: Christianity's Sacred Obligation* (Lanham, MD: Rowman and Littlefield, 2005), xiii-xvii.

20. "Reflections on Covenant and Mission, by participants in a dialogue between the United States Conference of Catholic Bishops' Committee on Ecumenical and Interreligious Affairs and the National Council of Synagogues," *Origins* 32:13 (September 5, 2002): 218-24.

21. Avery Dulles, "Evangelization and the Jews," with a "Response" by Mary C. Boys, Philip A. Cunningham, and John T. Pawlikowski, *America* 187:12 (October 21, 2002): 8-16.

22. Cardinal Walter Kasper, "The Good Olive Tree," *America* 185:7 (September 17, 2001), and "Christians, Jews and the Thorny Question of Mission," *Origins* 32:28 (December 19, 2002): 464.

23. See Eugene J. Fisher and Leon Klenicki, eds., *Pope John Paul II on Jews and Judaism* (Washington: United States Catholic Conference, 1987); and Eugene J. Fisher and Leon Klenicki, ed., *Spiritual Pilgrimage: Texts on Jews and Judaism 1979-1995—Pope John Paul II* (New York: Crossroads, 1995). Also see Byron L. Sherwin and Harold Kasimow, ed., *John Paul II and Interreligious Dialogue* (Maryknoll, NY: Orbis, 1999).

24. See the works cited in note 24.

25. Ellis Rivkin, *A Hidden Revolution: The Pharisees' Search for the Kingdom Within* (Nashville: Abingdon, 1978).

26. See note 15.

27. Mary Boys, *Has God Only One Blessing?* (New York: Paulist Press, 1999).

28. Clark Williamson, *A Guest in the House of Israel* (Louisville: Westminster/John Knox, 1993).

29. Two of Boyarin's recent books have amplified his theme of "co-emergence": Daniel Boyarin, *Dying for God: Martyrdom and the Making of Christianity and Judaism* (Palo Alto: Stanford University Press, 1999); and *A Radical Jew: Paul and the Politics of Identity* (Berkeley and Los Angeles: University of California Press, 1997).

30. John T. Pawlikowski, *Christ in the Light of Christian-Jewish Dialogue,* new edition (Eugene, OR: Wipf and Stock, 2001).

31. Cardinal Joseph Bernardin, *Cardinal Joseph Bernardin and the Jewish-Christian Dialogue* (Chicago: Liturgy Training Publications, 1996), 78-79.

32. Cardinal Joseph Ratzinger, *Many Religions-One Covenant* (San Francisco: Ignatius Press, 2000); and "The Heritage of Abraham: The Gift of Christmas," *L'Osservatore Romano,* December 29, 2000.

33. John T. Pawlikowski, "God: The Foundational Ethical Question after the Holocaust," in Jack Bemporad, John T. Pawlikowski and Joseph Sievers, eds., *Good and Evil After Auschwitz: Ethical Implications for Today* (Hoboken, NJ: KTAV, 2000), 53-66; and "The Holocaust: Its Challenges for Understanding Human Responsibility," in Judith H. Banki and John T. Pawlikowski, eds., *Ethics in the Shadow of the Holocaust: Christian and Jewish Perspectives* (Chicago: Sheed and Ward, 2001), 261-89.

Progress in Jewish-Christian Dialogue

Mordecai Waxman

In 1991, I was part of a Jewish group that was served a kosher lunch in the Vatican. This may have been the first kosher meal served and eaten there since the days of St. Peter. The event reflected the remarkable change in Catholic Jewish relations in the last thirty years. It came in the context of the biennial meeting between the Catholic Committee on Religious Relations with the Jews and the International Jewish Committee for Interreligious Consultation (IJCIC). These committees and their subsequent meetings were born out of the Second Vatican Council and the *Nostra Aetate* proclamation of Pope John XXIII, which overturned almost 1,900 years of Catholic teachings about Judaism and the Jewish people. Since I have been an active participant in these meetings for the last twenty years, I thought that a recounting of some of the events and results of the encounter between representatives of the Jewish people and the Catholic Church might be of interest in a volume reconsidering the impact of *Nostra Aetate*.

The very first international meeting that I attended was in Venice in 1975. It was held at a Catholic Retreat House and throughout the several days of the meeting, kosher food was served to Catholics and Jews alike. The meeting was characterized by frank and open discussion that seemed an outgrowth of the very cordial relations developed between the participants since the creation of the two committees in 1971.

The Jewish committee consisted of five bodies: the World Jewish Congress and the Synagogue Council, which had been the organizing and founding bodies on the Jewish side; the anti-

Defamation League of B'nai Brith; the American Jewish Committee; and the Israel Interfaith Committee. The key figures on the Jewish side were Dr. Gerhardt Riegner, the Secretary General of the World Jewish Congress, Rabbi Henry Siegman, executive vice-president of the Synagogue Council of America, and the late Rabbi Mark Tanenbaum, who was Director of Interfaith Relations for the American Jewish Committee. The key Catholic figures were Cardinal Willebrands, who headed the Catholic body and continued to do so almost until 1990, and Monsignor Jorge Mejia, who was vice-president of the Catholic Committee on Religious Relations with the Jews.

The discussion in the meetings was far ranging, but it became clear that there were several underlying premises that tended to guide the discussion. One was the general acceptance of the idea that it was necessary to change the perceptions and teachings about the Jewish people. A major step had already been taken in *Nostra Aetate*, which repudiated the attribution of deicide to the Jewish people as a whole and in their various generations and called for new relationships. Another underlying premise that was referred to and clearly affected both Catholics and Jews was that the Holocaust represented a watershed in the history of modern man and a failure of Christian teachings. The implications of this had to be considered and the meaning of the Holocaust and its effects became the central subject of several subsequent meetings. Incidentally, it should be noted that, as years passed, Catholic participants began to use the Hebrew term *Shoah* rather than Holocaust and began to refer to the Hebrew Bible by the Hebrew term *Tanakh* rather than Hebrew Bible and Old Testament.

A third implicit premise that became more and more central to later discussions but was already present in the meeting in 1975 was a recognition that Judaism had not been succeeded and replaced by Christianity but rather that Judaism and Christianity, starting from the same tree, had branched out in different directions and that Judaism had not ended its spiritual history with the Bible but had continued to develop a religious and spiritual culture of which the Church had to be aware and which Catholicism had to study.

In the course of discussion, too, the issue of the diplomatic recognition of Israel by the Church was put on the table. While the Catholic representatives disavowed their right or ability to deal with the subject since, they asserted, they were not empowered to consider political matters, it nonetheless inevitably surfaced as an issue central to Jewish self-perception and was a sometimes formal and sometimes informal agenda item of every subsequent meeting.

While these spoken and unspoken premises did much to shape the agenda, discussion, and character of the meeting, the principal focus of the meeting was the paper of Professor Tomaso Federice. Professor Federice considered the issue of conversion as applied to the Jews and advanced the thesis that any attempt to secure mass conversion of the Jews was unnecessary and undesirable. Basing himself upon the statement of St. Paul in Romans 11:28-29 that God has not revoked his covenant with the Jews, he took the position that the Jews, unlike the gentiles, did not require conversion in order to be "saved." This advocacy of what was, in effect, a two-covenant doctrine, was a revolutionary reversal of Catholic theology. In concert with *Nostra Aetate* it signaled that the Church was prepared to overturn its 1,800 year old theology about Judaism and the Jewish people and to seek a new relationship.

At the same time, the question of the relation of the Catholic Church to another monotheistic faith, Islam, was broached. Catholic representatives made the point that while Christianity must see itself as having a definite relationship with Judaism, it had no such relationship with Islam. Nor did they apply to Islam the "double covenant" doctrine that they were applying to Judaism. They therefore did not mean to apply the new conversion doctrine to Islam.

Some social gestures that were symbolic concluded the meeting. One was the visit of the entire assembled body to the Ghetto and the synagogue, with some attendant ceremonies. The other to which Jewish leaders of the area were invited was the visit paid to the meeting by the Cardinal of Venice, who very soon thereafter became the short-lived Pope John Paul I. Apologizing for the lateness of his arrival because "my gondola was held up in traffic," he made it plain that he agreed with the purpose, the time, and the unspoken premises of the meeting.

I left Venice with the conviction that there was a historic opportunity for our generation, which had already witnessed a revolution in history as a result of the Holocaust and the birth of Israel as a sovereign Jewish state after 1,900 years, to effect a basic change in the relationship between the Catholic Church and the Jewish people and to strike a major blow against anti-Semitism.

Nonetheless, there were limitations on the process that required a great deal of understanding and forbearance on both sides. On the Catholic side there were, as we were warned, elements who were strongly opposed to what were regarded as fundamental changes in Catholic theology: certainly there was more reciprocity to it in the Catholic circles in the United States, who functioned in a pluralistic society, than in the more monolithic European communities. On the other hand, there were cardinals and bishops in Europe who had witnessed the Holocaust at first hand and who felt that the Church had a grave moral responsibility to respond to it and to battle anti-Semitism. In the leadership of this group were Cardinal Willebrands and, when he came to head the Church, Pope John Paul II.

On the Jewish side, there was a limitation on relationships that stemmed largely from the Orthodox component of the Synagogue Council of America. They were in part skeptical of the sincerity of the Church and hesitant to engage in a situation that might result in a discussion of theological issues. A basis for their participation was proposed by the late Rabbi J.B. Soloveitchik, a major Halachist and philosophic mentor to the modern Orthodox group, who proposed that discussion be limited essentially to social issues. The Jewish side was limited by this formula since the Orthodox group was able to veto the participation of the Synagogue Council of America, the overall representative of synagogue and religious Jewry in the committee. Nonetheless, as Rabbi Soloveitchik himself had stated, rabbis and priests inevitably brought a religious outlook to their discussions, and thus a healthy dose of theological and religious thinking invariably found its way into our meetings.

However, it was largely Catholic theology that was under discussion and that needed rethinking on two scores. First, Christianity had to develop a theology about Judaism in order to define itself, and it did so. Judaism had no similar need. Second, the Church has been the oppressor of Jews in the name of its theology. Accordingly, the new approach to Jews and Judaism was followed by the proclamation of guidelines on teaching Judaism to Catholics. Two such guidelines were issued, one in 1975 after consultation with Jews and one, in 1985, that was issued without prior involvement.

The *Guidelines* that appeared in 1975 clearly carried further the themes dealt with in *Nostra Aetate*. Reflecting both papal statements made by Pope Paul VI and discussions between the Jewish and Catholic communities, it proceeded to amplify subjects that had been left vague in *Nostra Aetate*. The value of ongoing dialogue between people who appeared again and again at the meetings of the two committees was demonstrated by increased sensitivity on both sides to the concerns and language of their partners. To cite an example: *Nostra Aetate* makes no mention of the post-biblical religious and cultural tradition of Judaism. In the *Guidelines* in 1975, the statement is made that the history of Judaism did not end with the destruction of Jerusalem, but went on to develop a religious tradition. The notes in 1985 have a section on Judaism and Christianity in history; they refer to the permanence of Israel as a sign to be interpreted within God's design and go on to speak of "the continuous spiritual fecundity by Judaism in the rabbinical period, in the Middle Ages and in modern time." In this regard, it is interesting to note that when the committees met in Rome in 1990, the pope, who in his address had previously quoted only from the Bible, made it a point to quote from the Talmud. Monsignor Francesco Fumagalli, who was then serving as Secretary of the Catholic Committee made it a point to call my attention to it as a special gesture.

However, despite the progress of the dialogue, the Jewish Committee was upset by some of the statements in the 1985 notes and by some of the things that were not said. This document, unlike the 1975 *Guidelines*, was not submitted to Jewish evaluation prior to its appearance.

These notes contained many positive statements. Among them was the declaration of Pope John Paul II that the covenant between God and Jewish people "has never been revoked." Furthermore, the notes elaborated on the Jewish roots of Christianity, emphasizing that "Jesus was always and remained a Jew." They also called attention to interpret hostile statements in the New Testament to early historical circumstances and called on clergy to take account of this in Lenten sermons. They went on to give a more favorable definition of Pharisees and condemned anti-Semitism. Reference for the first time was made to the Holocaust and to the state of Israel. Both references were deemed inadequate by the Jewish body.

While appreciating the positive thrusts of the notes, the Jewish Committee felt that some elements were lacking from the declaration and that some statements reflected a Christian triumphalism. Specifically, it was felt that the universal meaning of the Holocaust was ignored, that the religious significance of Israel was denied, that there seemed to be a new emphasis on "typology" and interpretation of the Hebrew Bible as a preparation for Jesus.

At that time, I was the chairman of IJCIC and I was in touch with Cardinal Willebrands to indicate that we wanted a serious discussion of the notes. The whole matter was, indeed, discussed at our biennial meeting in October. Explanations and interpretations of the text were offered by Monsignor Mejia and Dr. Eugene Fischer, and several critiques from the Jewish side were set forth by Dr. Riegner, Dr. Geoffrey Wigoder, and Rabbi Leon Klenicki. The Christian explanation was basically twofold. First, that the document was entitled: *Notes on the Correct Way to Present Jews and Judaism in Preaching and Catachesis in the Roman Catholic Church.* It was, therefore, couched in theological language that had meaning for Catholics and sought to clarify and set new approaches to Judaism within the context of traditional Catholic theology. The other approach was to point out the progress that had been made and reflected in the *Notes* in the twenty years since *Nostra Aetate*.

There was much validity in both points and the IJCIC participants were, I believe, convinced of the good will of our Catholic fellows and also felt that there was increasing sensitivity to the Jewish position. However, I raised the point in my address to the pope that language which needed a great deal of interpretation and which was defended as a private Catholic theological language was undesirable in an era when communication was to the world at large.

Nonetheless, several major ideas emerged from our confrontation. One was an acceptance of the idea that the Jewish body ought to be consulted before any major pronouncement bearing upon Judaism was made. The second, which had far-reaching consequences, was the increasing recognition of the idea that Jews and Judaism ought to be seen as they see themselves. The imperative emerging from the acceptance of this notion was that Catholics needed to study post-biblical Judaism and to be sensitive to the central concerns of the Jewish people.

Two incidents may make it clear how important recognition of these ideas was, and is. The first was my experience in speaking to the faculty and students of a Catholic college in Minnesota. After my lecture, a group of nuns approached me to say that as devotional literature they were reading the writings of Abraham Joshua Heschel on the grounds that it spoke to their spiritual needs more profoundly than anything in contemporary Catholic devotional literature. The second incident, far more significant, is what emerged at a meeting of our two committees that was held in Amsterdam in. Dutch Jewry had refused to meet with the pope on his visit to Holland. The Dutch Jews who were present at our meeting made it plain why they had rejected the invitation. They spoke of the fact that there had been more than 125,000 highly integrated Jews in Holland prior to the second World War and that there were now only 25,000 who had survived. They complained of the fact that despite the horrors of the Holocaust, the Catholic Church refused to acknowledge and act upon what was a central element in the life and thought of the surviving Jews, the state of Israel. Cardinal Willebrands, presiding at the meeting, and himself a Dutch man, was visibly moved at the intensity of feeling that was displayed and promised to convey the message to the Vatican.

This sense of a need to see the Jewish people and Judaism as they see themselves and to understand that the Jewish community was prepared to be forthright and aggressive in stating its position was central to the controversy that developed in 1987. It broke forth at a time when I was chairman of IJCIC and, as a result, I had a significant share in the developments and in the resolution of the matter. Moreover, it was a watershed in the relations between the two faiths, a central event that has had ongoing consequences.

The whole matter started with a proposed papal visit to the United States during which the pope proposed to engage, as had been his habit, with Jewish leadership. From the Jewish side, it was decided that American Jewry should be represented by the four groups who played a role in interfaith relations, the Synagogue Council of America, the American Jewish Committee, the American Jewish Congress, and the B'nai Brith Anti-Defamation League. It was agreed that a formal meeting would be held in Miami in a hall which seated 196 people and that to it would be invited major figures of the American Catholic Church and of Jewish organizational leadership. The pope was to speak and a representative of American Jewry was to speak. I advocated that the Jewish spokesman should be the president of the Synagogue Council of America, the representative body of religious Jewry and an organization of which I had previously been president. The suggestion was accepted and Rabbi Gilbert Klapperman, who was then the president of the Synagogue Council and an Orthodox rabbi, was the designated speaker. It was anticipated that this would be a formal meeting in which no new ground would be broken.

However, something notably unexpected occurred. The pope had received Kurt Waldheim in an audience. A former Secretary General of the U.N., Waldheim had been elected president of Austria in a campaign in which it was revealed that he had concealed and lied about his membership in the Nazi party and about his participation in army actions that involved shipping Jews and others to concentration camps. The election campaign evoked anti-Semitic attitudes in Austria and his success profoundly disturbed the World Jewish community. Leaders of Western nations had refused to meet with Waldheim. The papal audience, therefore, aroused great feeling among Jews. While various explanations were offered, the matter was never properly explained. The reaction of the Jewish organizations to the reception of Waldheim was to announce that they would not meet with the pope when he came to America. The confrontation that ensued captured the attention of the press, television, and radio and was widely discussed. As Chairman of IJCIC, I presided at meetings at which the matter was debated and I would descend from the meeting to find television and radio and press teams waiting for a report.

Matters continued in this vein for some weeks while Cardinal Willebrands and I corresponded in search of a solution. Clearly, Catholic-Jewish relations, which had been developed with so much effort, were in danger of being broken off. Finally, Cardinal Willebrands suggested that Bishop Keeler of Harrisburg, who was in charge of the ecumenical elements of the papal visit, and I should be in touch. Bishop Keeler indeed contacted me and advised me that he, Cardinal Casseroli, the Secretary of State of the Holy See, the Papal Nuncio, and Cardinal O'Connor had met on the matter. He told me that Cardinal Casseroli, who was in the States for a two-day visit, would remain an extra day if I and some associates would meet with him at the residence of the Papal Nuncio. I appeared the following day, together with Rabbis Mark Tanenbaum, Wolfe Kelman, and Henry Michelman.

Our meeting was frank and cordial. We expressed our anger at the Waldheim meeting and indicated that we felt that the Church had to confront its role in relation to the Holocaust and to anti-Semitism in general. I went on to say that the limitations that were placed upon the Catholic committee—that they could deal only with religious matters and that political matters were beyond their competence—were unacceptable to us, since the political and religious aspects of Israel and the Holocaust could not be separated. Cardinal Casseroli expressed appreciation of the nature of the discussion, said that this was the first time that he had met with a group of rabbis, and that he had to get back to Rome "to talk with the boss."

The American Catholics who were eager that we meet with the pope were not very hopeful that much would result from our meeting. Bishop Keeler felt that the best we could hope for was a statement by the pope deploring the Holocaust. In point of fact, some ten days later I heard from Cardinal Willebrands inviting me to come to Rome with four others and to meet with his committee, which would now include a representative of the Secretary of State, to meet with Cardinal Casseroli in the Vatican, and to meet with Pope John Paul II informally in his summer residence in Castel Gandolfo. It was an unexpected but welcome invitation and we set a date for the meeting in late August. I then took off on vacation to Europe and Israel.

We gathered later that Cardinal Casseroli had been impressed by the direction of the exchange that had occurred with a small group and sought to repeat the discussion in the meeting with the pope. Ultimately, other Jewish organizations asserted their claim to participate and we ended up with nine members, a number I had to negotiate from Jerusalem with Cardinal Willebrands. Nonetheless, the meeting with the pope was informal, although there was less of interchange than there might have been with a smaller group. It did, however, conclude with all of us standing around and making casual talk, during which the pope reminisced about his boyhood and also expressed a desire to visit the Holy Land.

Once in Rome, we were entertained at their home by the American Ambassador and Mrs. Raab, who were tremendously interested in the meeting. Dr. Gerhardt Riegner, who, as always, was an indispensable part of the process and who had remained in touch with the Vatican authorities throughout, and I met with Cardinal Willebrands. We agreed on several propositions, among them that there would be representation of the Holy See on the Catholic committee.

However, there were two major elements in the agreement. The first was that the Catholics stated that there were no theological objections to the existence of a sovereign Jewish state and that the issues were political. They thus disputed the widely held belief among Jews and Christians that there were theological reservations. This, it seems to me, laid the groundwork for mutual recognition between Israel and the Holy See, which came some years later.

The second major statement was the proposal advanced by Cardinal Willebrands, in line with previous discussions, that a major Catholic statement would be developed and, ultimately, issued, assessing the role of the Church in the growth of anti-Semitism from the Lateran Council (thirteenth century) on and the role of the Church in relation to the Holocaust.

The communiqué setting forth the results of our meetings was presented at a press conference that involved Bishop Pierre Duprey, vice-president of the Catholic body, and me, and which was widely reported and featured on Italian television. As a result of these meetings, IJCIC and the American bodies involved decided to restore the meeting with the pope ten days later in Miami. However, meanwhile some significant changes took place. The Orthodox bodies in the Synagogue Council resolved not to participate and forbade the Orthodox President of the Synagogue Council, Rabbi Klapperman, from participating. As a result, I returned on a boat from Europe several days before the meeting in Miami to learn that I had been designated by the Jewish bodies to deliver the address on behalf of the Jewish communities.

It was a strong statement of our feelings on the Waldheim matter, a review of our relations with the Catholic Church, a statement of what we thought needed to be accomplished, and an expression of hope for the future. It had been somewhat modified, but I felt quite comfortable in delivering it, save for changing one or two words that I felt were no longer appropriate—an action for which I paid a considerable price for several years with some of the Orthodox contingent. The pope, in turn, spoke of the relationship between Jews and Catholics in highly positive terms and spoke movingly of the Holocaust.

The whole event in Miami, given the background of controversy, elicited unusual interest. It was widely reported in the newspapers and pictured on television. The *pièce de résistance* was provided by the *New York Times,* which not only printed both my speech and that of the pope, but had an unexpected picture on the front page, showing me delivering my speech and the pope listening attentively, rather then the more obvious picture of the pope speaking. This picture was widely reprinted abroad and for some months I kept receiving copies of papers from Europe and even from Asia.

There were some other interesting touches to the occasion. One, which I had not appreciated at the time, mentioned to me by Mrs. Wexler, president of the National Conference of Christians and Jews, was that it was unprecedented for the pope and another to sit on the same level.

The second was that when I went over to congratulate the pope on his speech, he said to me that he was worried about his pronunciation. I assumed that he referred to the six Hebrew words that he had used, among them *Shanah Tovah,* since Rosh Hashanah was close. I replied that pronunciation comes from the heart, not from the lips. And the remark was quoted by a reporter who had overheard it, without really being aware of the context.

The whole confrontation of 1987 had positive effects in that it led to a more open and forthright relationship between us, and put Israel and the Catholic role in anti-Semitism squarely on the agenda. These subjects were not followed up as rapidly as they should have been, partly as a result of further Jewish dissatisfaction with some remarks of then-Cardinal Ratzinger that were subsequently explained by the Cardinal. Nonetheless, the meeting held in Prague in 1990 was centered around the Catholic Church and anti-Semitism and there was, further, a major statement of responsibility set forth by the German Bishops in the meeting in Jerusalem in 1994. These statements have been supplemented by major statements of the pope condemning anti-Semitism. We all look forward to a formal statement in the name of the Catholic Church on the whole issue.

One major outcome of all of these events was the development of new and warm relations between the Jewish community and the American Catholics. Bishop Keeler picked up my remarks, that no matter what the outcome of that meeting, American Jews and American Catholics needed to talk and act together. Some few weeks later he called me to propose that a committee of bishops be set up, to supplement the splendid work of Dr. Eugene Fisher and to meet on a regular basis with representatives of the Jewish community. I proposed that the Jewish partner be the Synagogue Council of America. As a result, the two committees were set up and have met twice a year to explore issues of common concern and with agreement on common actions. The role of Bishop Keeler, now Cardinal Keeler, was invaluable in developing the pattern and his involvement and concern rapidly made him the central figure in relations with the Jewish community. His statesmanship and his warmth, of which I have been a grateful beneficiary, have given a special and unique tone to Jewish-Catholic relations.

The impact of the relationship has been felt in Catholic seminaries, in changes in Catholic textbooks, in the teaching in Catholic schools, in public statements of the Church, and in the ease of relationships between Catholic and Jewish representatives. The strength of the relationship has been tested on issues in which there was potential disagreement, as there was in the position on the Middle East mandated by the National Conference of Catholic Bishops and drafted by a committee consisting of Cardinal O'Connor and Archbishops Keeler and Mahoney. Much attention was given to Jewish input and reaction, with the result that the document presented was essentially acceptable to all and quieted controversy.

A further test of the new relationship between the Jewish World and the Catholic Church came in connection with Auschwitz. A group of Carmelite nuns had taken over a building in Auschwitz as a convent, with the intention of offering prayers and memorials for the 1½ million people who had been killed there. This evoked a strong reaction among Jews, led by European survivors. Jews felt that Auschwitz-Birkenau was, essentially, a Jewish cemetery of 1½ million souls, although non-Jews had died there too, and that it should not be preempted by any religious group. Various Catholic dignitaries, both in Europe and in America, agreed and agreed that the nuns ought to be moved to a location outside the camp. Several

European Cardinals met with Jewish representatives and agreed to raise the money to provide a convent and educational facilities outside the camp. Everyone was agreed except the nuns and, as a result, the matter dragged on for several years with much delay and consequent bitterness. By now, the matter is largely, though not totally, concluded. However, there was a very unpleasant interlude and it required the intervention of the pope to get the nuns out.

In an attempt to bring matters to a head, Rabbi Avi Weiss, a convinced activist, started to climb the fence around the convent within Auschwitz. He was attacked by Polish workers at the site and the whole event was much publicized. It led to a rise of anti-Semitic feeling in Poland, a country in which only six thousand Jews remain of the 3½ million whose history in Poland dated back for almost a thousand years. This, in turn, led to a homily by the Primate of Poland, Cardinal Glemp, which he later contended was designed to quiet the anti-Semitism outburst, but which was widely regarded as a highly anti-Semitic statement. As a result, when Cardinal Glemp proposed a visit to the United States to meet the very considerable Polish element in the country, the Catholic authorities in American dissuaded him for fear of evoking very hostile reactions in this country. However, a year later he raised the issue of a trip again and this time the Catholic hierarchy here agreed, on the condition that he offer an apology/explanation of his remarks. They sought a meeting with representative Jewish bodies. Most of them, however, refused to meet with him.

Several organizations and several individuals who were active figures in interfaith relations, I among them, did assemble for a meeting in Washington. Twelve of us were there together, with members of the Catholic hierarchy including Cardinal Law and Archbishop Keeler, to hear Cardinal Glemp indeed offer an apology and explanation of his motives. In the course of his comments, he pointed out that he had been born in a small mining town in 1930 and did not know any Jews, since he was only nine when Poland was conquered by the Germans. I suggested that this might explain why he did not understand how odious his remarks were to Jews and further suggested that he add to his statement that what he had said about Jews had been based upon misinformation. He agreed and, indeed, said the same at the press conference that followed. The whole incident was so unusual and unprecedented that I remarked at the press conference that the distance we had travelled in Catholic-Jewish relations could be measured by the fact that, in the past, a Jew would not have met a cardinal, would not have dared to be critical of him, and would certainly never have received an apology.

"From the bitter there came forth the sweet." The result of the whole matter was that Cardinal Glemp invited us to come to Poland, and to bring lecturers on Judaism and Jewish history to Catholic theological schools and universities. The lectures have, indeed, been undertaken by the American Jewish Committee Interfaith Department under the admirable leadership of Rabbi James Rudin. A group of five Jews, of whom I was one, did visit Poland and met the Catholic hierarchy. We were received by Cardinal Glemp with a very positive statement about the role of Jews in Poland and very cordially by Cardinal Franciszek Macharski in Cracow. We were accompanied on the trip by Monsignor Francesco Fumagalli, then serving as the Secretary of the Vatican Committee on Religious Relations with the Jews, who had made all the arrangements for the meetings. Monsignor Fumagalli, it should be noted, was valued by us for the dedication and concern he brought to his role. One unusual element of our relationship is that he had studied at the Hebrew University and was fluent in Hebrew. We frequently talked in that language.

We were accompanied throughout by Bishop Muszynski (now Archbishop), who had undertaken the role of ecumenical relations with the Jews and who discharged it with great warmth and concern. Younger than Cardinal Glemp, he had never encountered Jews until he met the few remnants after the war and had to learn about the Holocaust and its enormity when he undertook his role. The conclusion of our visit to Poland was a visit to Auschwitz-Birkenau, with all its chilling impact, heightened by the fact that we were there in the middle of February. But almost equally chilling was the site of the razed ghetto in Warsaw and the monument at the place from which Jews had been shipped. It consisted of two great tablets and they were inscribed with representative Jewish and Hebrew names, according to the letters of the alphabet, a few lines for each letter. All the names were there, including my own name, that of my wife, and those of our children.

The same trip took us briefly to Czechoslovakia and for several days to Hungary, where we met with the cardinals and other important elements of the Catholic hierarchy to discuss Jewish-Catholic relations. The message was clear. The Vatican was interested and the relationship between the Church and the Jewish people was undergoing a revolution.

I would be delinquent if I failed to mention the vital role that Cardinal O'Connor has played in this revolutionary process. As the Archbishop of the city that has the largest Jewish community in the world, he has been sensitive to Jewish thinking and, more than that, has been sympathetic to it and given it expression. Thus, to a gathering of Arab Ambassadors, Jewish representatives, of whom I was one, and Catholics, held at his residence in connection with the Catholic position paper on the Middle East, he stated that he believed that the Catholic Church ought to recognize Israel. At the same time he resorted to Catholic theology to express his sentiments about the Holocaust and Israel, and said that he regarded the Holocaust as the crucifixion of the Jewish people and the state of Israel as symbolizing the resurrection of the Jewish people. He conveyed the same sentiments to Rome and was an active figure in urging the recognition of Israel.

The same candor was evident in his remarks to Cardinal Glemp just prior to his return to Poland. In the presence of assembled Jews and Catholics, he said to Cardinal Glemp that American Catholics indeed regarded Auschwitz as a Jewish cemetery and urged him to seek the removal of the nuns. Moreover, he suggested that it would be very appropriate, given what had happened to the Jews of Poland and what Israel meant in Jewish life, if a Polish cardinal would urge a Polish pope to recognize Israel.

My involvement in a historic revolution of attitudes and relations between the Catholic Church and the Jewish people has certainly been a high point in my own life. But it would be idle to pretend that that revolution has yet been achieved. It is in process and it may take three generations if it is to continue to bear its full fruit. The prospect has been greeted with skepticism by many Jews and has run counter to long held attitudes of many Catholics. But there is a possibility that it will help to change the world and substitute understanding for prejudice and friendship for hatred. And there is reason to hope that another generation will build upon the achievements of this generation and transform possibility into reality. It would be nice to believe that our greatest songs are still unsung.

Landmarks and Landmines
in Jewish-Christian Relations

JUDITH HERSHCOPF BANKI

In the past fifty years—about the span of time I've worked in the field of Jewish-Christian relations—there have been significant landmarks, virtual turning points, to advance mutual understanding and respect between Jews and Christians, and there have also been landmines: explosive issues just under the surface that, when triggered, threatened to derail years of progress, or even the dialogue itself. Both the landmarks and the landmines must be viewed against the state of Jewish-Christian relations some fifty years ago, and I must tell that story by sharing my own experience.

I came to the American Jewish Committee (AJC) in late 1959, before the Second Vatican Council and many of the landmark developments that preceded and followed it. At the time, I was assigned an intriguing task: to assess, summarize, and circulate the findings of self-studies of Protestant, Catholic, and Jewish religious textbooks stimulated by the AJC. That Jews should be concerned about how Christians depicted them should not surprise anyone. Jews were convinced that a certain tradition of Christian teaching and preaching represented one of the primary sources of anti-Semitism across the centuries.

The devastating reality of the Holocaust—the destruction of half the Jews of Europe and one-third of the Jews in the world—made the task of confronting the roots of this pathology of hatred inescapable, particularly its religious and theological roots. For obvious reasons, namely, the history of persecution, expulsion, and massacre of Jews at the hands of Christians, we were particularly concerned about the content of the Christian teaching materials. Still, it should be stressed that these were *self* studies, in which the religious education materials of a particular religious community were examined by a scholar from within that community and faithful to its values and vision.

When I first began reading the raw data from the Protestant and Catholic textbooks, I was astonished both at the degree of hostility to Jews and Judaism, and at the extent of group libel I found in many of the excerpts. In the light of progress made in recent years, it is somewhat embarrassing to recall some of these statements. But they remind us of the dimensions of the problems we uncovered. Thus, from a Protestant lesson:

> When Jesus was in the Temple for the last time a few days before his Passion, he asked the Jews, "What think ye of Christ?" Their answer was a great disappointment to Him, but on Good Friday they showed what they thought of Him. Their hearts were so filled with hatred toward Him that they shouted themselves hoarse, crying, "Crucify Him." That was the thanks he received for coming into this world to save and bless them.

And from another Protestant lesson:

> The fruit of Israel as a fig tree was bitter and corrupt instead of sweet and good. Israel rejected their Messiah when he came and because of their failure they withered away. This has been Israel's condition as a nation for centuries; she has been dried up with no national symbols, such as a land, a king, a flag.

It should be noted that this latter comment was published in 1962, fourteen years after the emergence of the modern state of Israel. It is a striking instance of reality trumped by theology.

From several Roman Catholic textbooks:

His prophecy was partially fulfilled in the destruction of Jerusalem and more fully in the rejection by God of the chosen people.

Christ, by his miracles and preaching, tried to conquer the obstinacy of the Jews and to bring them to repentance. The Jews, on the contrary, by the bad influence of their hypocrisy and pride, hindered the spread of the knowledge of God among other nations.

The Jews as a nation refused to accept Christ, and since his time they have been wanderers on the earth without a temple, or a sacrifice, and without a Messiah.

These were not the only kinds of references to Jews and Judaism in the textbooks. There were fair or neutral statements as well. But what struck me about the examples I have cited was the vehemence, the intensity with which any sense of continuing mission for Judaism, any meaningful witness for the Jewish people (except witnessing to the superior truth of Christianity), any validity in Jewish terms for the re-creation of a Jewish commonwealth in Israel, were dismissed *a priori*. A few years later, Claire Huchet Bishop, the brilliant French Catholic disciple of Jules Isaac, introduced us to his writings and the brilliantly coined phrase that has since served to characterize this tradition of hostility: *the teaching of contempt.*

It is important to recall the cluster of themes that defined this negative tradition, because some of them are very much with us, and they take both religious and secular forms.

First, there is the theme of a degenerate Judaism, already spiritually exhausted by the time Jesus appeared. I must confess I was baffled by Isaac's defining this position as a teaching of contempt, until I realized that if the Judaism of Jesus' time is seen only as a formalistic creed, empty of values and vitality, then he could not possibly "owe" it anything, or have been nurtured in it, or by it. (As late as 1972, Gerald Strober, who conducted a follow up study of Protestant teaching materials noted that the Protestant materials he studied tended to "isolate Jesus and his closest followers from their Jewish contemporaries" and convey the impression that they are somehow not Jews: "They are made to look like a new kind of group thrust into the midst of first-century Jewish life, without roots in, or sympathy for, Jewish history, tradition, or religious values.") Textbook commentaries on the miracle at Cana, he noted, provided a frequent opportunity for caricature of Judaism, and I would add, for displacement theologizing as well.

Then there is the theme of Jews as a carnal people, incapable of understanding their own scriptures—or anything else—except in a grossly sensual way, a theme that still carries weight in secularized forms of anti-Semitism. Nazi cartoons always characterized Jews as fat, fleshy, ugly, and greedy—caricatures, I note with regret, now found throughout the Arab world. Further, the theme of a people who willfully and deliberately blinded themselves to the significance of Jesus' mission; the theme, most murderous of all, of a deicide—God-killing people—and the corollary themes that accompany that horrendous teaching that Jews have been rejected and accursed by God and their dispersion, their loss of nation, their suffering and persecution over the centuries are evidence of providential punishment for this terrible crime.

The findings of the Catholic textbook studies which illustrated these themes, supplemented by examples from French, Spanish, and Italian language materials, were integrated into an initiative on behalf of an authoritative statement from the Second Vatican Council repudiating these teachings of contempt and condemning anti-Semitism. What finally emerged from the Council as *Nostra Aetate,* after many delays and a bitter struggle, was indeed a milestone. Looking back at *Nostra Aetate* forty years later, it is easy to take that achievement for granted. But at the time, it was a cliffhanger! The outright anti-Semitism expressed by some of its opponents, the attempts to scuttle the document—some of them truly subversive—played out as a daily drama. It was passed on the final day of the Council, in the final minutes: a flawed, compromised document, but still a landmark.

Since the promulgation of *Nostra Aetate,* statements by national bishops' conferences (United States, Dutch, Belgian, French, Swiss,

German, and Brazilian), guidelines issued by the Vatican's Commission for Religious Relations with the Jews, and various papal statements have gone far beyond the Declaration itself. Such authoritative documents have:

> called for "a frank and honest treatment of Christian anti-Semitism in our history books, courses, and curricula and an acknowledgement of the living and complex reality of Judaism after Christ and the permanent election of Israel" (*Guidelines for Catholic-Jewish Relations,* [U.S.] National Conference of Catholic Bishops' Subcommittee for Catholic-Jewish Relations, 1967);

> stressed that "the points on which Jesus took issue with the Judaism of his time are fewer than those in which He found himself in agreement with it" (Vatican study paper, 1969); stated that "the Jewish people is the true relative of the Church, not her rival or a minority to be assimilated" (study paper, National Catholic Commission for Relations with the Jews, Belgium, 1973);

> called it "most urgent that Christians cease to represent the Jews according to clichés forged by the hostility of centuries" (French Bishops' Committee for Relations with Jews, 1973);

> regretted "that an often faulty and hard-hearted presentation of Judaism led to a wrong attitude of Christians toward Jews; hence great care must be taken in religious instruction, liturgical services, adult education and theological training, to offer a correct interpretation of Jewish self-understanding" (Swiss Bishops' statement, 1974);

> urged Christians "to strive to learn by what essential traits the Jews define themselves in the light of their own religious experience" and emphasized that information

regarding the Jewishness of Jesus, the similarity of his
teaching methods to those employed by the rabbis of his
time, the repudiation of Jewish collective guilt for the trial
and death of Jesus and the continuing development of
Judaism after the emergence of Christianity "is important at
all levels of Christian instruction and education," including
"the thorough formation of instructors and educators in
training schools, seminaries and universities" (Vatican
Commission for Religious Relations with the Jews, 1975);

asserted that Jews are "a still living reality," whose
permanence in history, "accompanied by a continuous,
spiritual fecundity," is "a sign to be interpreted within
God's design." (*Notes on the Correct Way to Present the Jews
and Judaism in Preaching and Catechesis in the Catholic
Church*, 1985)[1]

I emphasize that not all of these recommendations have been
formally adopted. Some study documents remained just that. Still,
they stand as landmarks, pointing the Church in a new direction.

The question is: How thoroughly have these exemplary
guidelines and suggestions been implemented at the parish level,
and to what extent has the Church's new policy of respect and
friendship for Jews and Judaism been reflected in textbooks,
classroom teaching, religious information and public worship?

Here there is much good news and some bad news. Recent
materials do note the Jewishness of Jesus, and the better ones show
the continuity of Jesus' teachings with the teachings of his Pharisaic
contemporaries. Still, the image of Jesus as a faithful Jew is a very
hard pill for some Christians to swallow, and I suspect it is hardest
in those cultures which have had very little experience of religious
pluralism, and where national identity is linked to one particular
religious identity. A Polish woman I met at a conference in Eastern
Europe told me: "Polish Catholics have terrible difficulty accepting
Jesus Christ as Jewish. Some are beginning to believe that Jesus
really was a Jew. But Mary, never!"

Christian educators have made a conscious effort to remove the most poisonous teachings of contempt from textbooks and classrooms. To the best of my knowledge, the deicide charge—specifically, that the Jews are a people of Christ-killers—is gone from Christian education materials, although other vestiges of the anti-Jewish polemic still abound. Yet that image is so pervasive in Western culture—what was called, in another time, Christendom—so close to the surface and so accessible in moments of tension or conflict, that it remains a potent vehicle for knee-jerk anti-Semites. Two examples: In May 1987, during the conflict over the revelation that Austrian Chancellor Kurt Waldheim had been a high-ranking Nazi officer during Word War II—there were protests against him by some Jewish organizations—the deputy mayor of the Austrian city of Linz wrote to the head of a well-known Jewish organization: "You Jews got Christ, but you're not going to get Waldheim the same way" (*New York Times*, October 9, 1987). Here in the United States on the *Today Show*, a discussion on the Jewish community's objections to the papal audience granted Kurt Waldheim featured the Roman Catholic participant preaching to his rabbinical counterpart as follows: "Well, the problem is that ours is a religion of forgiveness and yours is a religion of vengeance." Similar comments were heard at the time of President Reagan's unfortunate visit to the cemetery at Bitburg, and such false contrasts were rampant at the time of the Eichmann trial, perhaps because of who was conducting the trial and where it was conducted. Neither the Nuremberg trials of war criminals in the 1940s nor the trial of Klaus Barbie in Paris in the 1980s evoked any reference to the *lex talionis*, but the Eichmann trial did engender Christian press references to "an eye for an eye." And the fact that "the Jews" were conducting a trial in Jerusalem seemed too rich a coincidence for some commentators to pass up.

The tendency to see Jews in terms of Christian theological categories takes on a special form when it comes to Israel. On the one hand there are some who see Israel as a prime player in an end-of-days scenario with apocalyptic overtones. They are pro-Israel politically, but they support the ingathering of Jews in Israel largely as prelude to their mass conversion and the Second Coming—that is, for the sake of Christian eschatology, not Jewish survival.

On the other hand, there are Christians who are hostile to Israel for theological reasons—recognized or unrecognized—of vastly different kinds. One perspective dismisses in advance any possible religious or moral significance in the rebirth of Israel on grounds that the Church is the new Israel and all the promises have been fulfilled in Jesus. Israel is thus seen as illegitimate on religious grounds, but the attitude carries over into political judgments: if Israel's very existence is theologically illegitimate, that state can do nothing right. This is what I might call an anti-Israel position as an extension of traditional Christian supersessionism.

Similarly, hostility to Israel is often expressed by invoking traditional teachings of contempt for political purposes. For example: the Palestinian Christian liberation theologian Naim Ateek accuses Israel of "crucifying" the Palestinians. What is he trying to achieve with this usage? What images is he invoking with this quite deliberate resort to a 2,000-year-old Roman form of execution that has served to vilify Jews for centuries?

The other side of that coin is hostility to Israel based on what we might call philosemitism run amok: *viz.,* Judaism does have a mission, but it is universal and prophetic, not tied to a piece of real estate. The inevitable fall out of national sovereignty: concern with security, military preparedness, budgets, social problems, imperfect solutions to real problems—in short, all the nitty-gritty of normality—is seen as somehow demeaning to the universal calling of Judaism. What follows is that Israel is judged against a standard of perfection while her adversaries are judged more realistically. Failure to achieve this perfection is seen as proof of inherent corruption.

What these positions have in common is that they view Israel—and to a certain extent, Judaism and the Jewish people—abstractly and through theological lenses. Christians rarely comment on Israel with an awareness of history, particularly Jewish history.

Contemporary Christians are not guilty of the dismal record of Christian hostility to Jews and Judaism, nor are contemporary churches guilty for the fact that non-Christian—even anti-Christian—anti-Semites have appropriated labels and libels that originated with Christian anti-Judaism for their own purposes. But two caveats. One, Christians must learn something about the history of Christian anti-Semitism as part of their religious education. Fr. Edward Flannery noted that Christians have torn from their history books the pages the Jews have memorized. Church history materials must put some of these pages back: not to make Christian students feel guilty, but to help them behave responsibly. Christians who don't know that it was the church that confined Jews to ghettos, made them wear special clothing and denied them access to universities and professions, are like Americans who move into race relations without having learned about slavery.

Second, the situation of the contemporary church community *vis-à-vis* the paranoid fantasies spawned by earlier Christians recalls the dilemma of Dr. Frankenstein when the monster he created broke out and ran wild. It was another Christianity that created the monster: the myth of the "synagogue of Satan," of the Jewish world conspiracy, of blood libels and well-poisonings. Contemporary Christianity rejects and repudiates these myths. But as with Dr. Frankenstein, it is not enough to disown the destructive creation: the churches must help to overcome it. That means not only standing with Jews against secular anti-Semitism in all its manifestations, but looking inward to its Christian roots. That means not only issuing documents, but engaging in a systematic effort to remove the vestiges of the teachings of contempt from Christian teaching and preaching.

The landmarks in Jewish-Christian relations consist of both words and actions. The documents cited above signify an affirmation of Jews and Judaism as fellow-believers whose covenant with God has never been revoked. Actions which have punctuated this relationship have been particularly welcomed within the Jewish community: Pope John Paul II's visit to the synagogue of Rome—the first Pope to visit a synagogue—his visit to Auschwitz, perhaps above all, his visit to Israel and the Western Wall in Jerusalem, in which he inserted a prayer asking for forgiveness for the suffering of Jews at the hands of Christians: these were concrete demonstrations of kinship and sensitivity. The signing of diplomatic accords between the state of Israel and the Holy See was a major landmark, because it put to rest a suspicion in the Jewish community that an anti-Jewish theology had prevented the Church from full diplomatic recognition of Israel.

Awareness of history and a concern for Israel also proved to be landmines. The Carmelite convent at Auschwitz became a source of serious tension between significant numbers of the Catholic and Jewish communities. Many Christians could not see what the fuss was all about: what is more natural than to dedicate a place to worship God in a site of such horror and inhumanity? Most Jews felt the convent, established within the confines of the camp that served as the primary center of the murder of European Jewry was not only insensitive, but worse, an attempt to appropriate and "Christianize" the Holocaust. It was a powerful landmine, and anti-Semitism surfaced as the conflict played out. (It took the intervention of Pope John Paul II for the convent to be moved outside the walls of the death camp.) Not as serious, but landmines nonetheless, were the Pope's meeting with Kurt Waldheim after the latter's Nazi past had been revealed, and his granting of an audience to Yassir Arafat.

I would cite the latter as a missed opportunity as much as a landmine. Apparently, Arafat greeted the Pope by announcing: "I am a Palestinian. Like Jesus." It would have betrayed no Catholic doctrine for the Pope to reply that Jesus was a Jew. He did not do so. An opportunity missed.

Another was during the Pope's visit to Syria, when both Syria's president and foreign minister assailed Jews, the foreign minister calling Jews "the enemies of God." The Pope could have responded that, according to current Catholic teaching, Jews are not the "enemies of God" but beloved of God and respected elder brothers. Another opportunity missed.

One does not expect an adversarial tradition of almost two millennia, marred by persecution of Jewry and mutual hostility, to be overturned in a few decades. The progress that has been made since Vatican II is remarkable against the background of estrangement that preceded it. We still have much work to do together.

Notes

This article, while original, is drawn from presentations and papers by the author delivered on several occasions, including the International Liaison Committee Meeting of the Pontifical Commission for Religious Relations with the Jews, and the International Jewish Committee for Interreligious Consultations, May 1992, Baltimore, Maryland.

1. Despite many constructive aspects, *Notes* drew sharp criticism from leading Jewish organizations. For a discussion of positive and regressive aspects of the document, see Judith Banki and Alan Mittleman, "Jews and Catholics: Taking Stock," *Commonweal*, September 6, 1985.

Catholics and Jews:
Twenty Centuries and Counting

EUGENE FISHER

In order to understand *Nostra Aetate,* both when it was written and how it challenges us still today, forty years later, at least the general outlines of the long and very complex history that brought us to the brink of the *Shoah* must be sketched. I am going to do this in terms of what I call the six stages of the relationship. What I want you to think about in this process is that these stages didn't just happen. These weren't inevitabilities. These were decisions of real people in real times in real places. I will speak mostly in terms of the decisions made by my own Catholic-Christian tradition over the centuries and in various settings. The reason I want to put it in these terms is that we tend to think of Jewish-Christian history as somewhat flat, as if Jews were treated in Christendom through all ages as they were, say, by the end of the medieval period, and in all places the same way.

This is really not the case. I think we need to break some of this historically "flattened" memory down into its parts, to realize its peaks as well as its valleys. This more complex view of Jewish-Christian history, I believe, is necessary in order to open up the possibilities for the future because we live in an age when new decisions are all of a sudden possible. A set of decisions, of crises if you will in the Greek sense of "opportunity for change," as Rabbi Leon Klenicki reminds us, faces us today as perhaps in no previous generation. After the *Shoah* and after the Second Vatican Council, we have broken away from a lot of the evils of the past and are privileged for the first time in virtually two millennia with the possibility of remaking, of resetting the entire relationship between the Church and the Jewish people.

Six Moments of Crisis in Catholic-Jewish History

The first stage of Jewish-Christian relations was the briefest. It encompassed the period from Jesus' ministry to the destruction of the Jerusalem temple by the Romans in the year 70 of the Common Era. In this period the earliest Christians were practicing Jews who observed Jewish law and worshiped with Jewish rituals. In other words, their lives, their minds, their spiritualities were framed and forged in the traditions of the Jewish people. One of the earliest tasks these Jews faced was how to embody in their rituals (it is perhaps my own Catholic tradition that leads me to place the liturgical first) what happened to themselves and their world when the death and resurrection of Jesus occurred. Out of these liturgical decisions would come the later theology which would explain what the rituals meant. They faced the task of expressing in rituals what they were experiencing of the risen Christ in their lives. They did this quite naturally the only way they could, as Jews, in and through the rituals and sacred texts of their people. As Jews, they sought understanding through rereading the Jewish scriptures in the light of the Christ event.

There are a number of good Jewish terms for such reapplication of scriptural texts in changing milieu. Rabbis used a number of techniques similar to those used by Christians in the same and other periods, such as typology and a variety of other approaches to finding new meanings in texts for future generations. Christians thus were acting quite "Jewishly" when they adapted their own Jewish rituals to the sacred significance of the Christ event, which was for them the seminal event in the history of divine/human relations, as well as in the history of the relations between God and the Jewish people. It is not accidental that the Christian Eucharist adapts aspects of a typical synagogue service, the reading of Scripture, the commenting on Scripture, interspersed with prayers drawn heavily from the Psalms. The earliest Christians combined the synagogue service with the ritual of the Passover Seder, which the New Testament saw as the setting of Jesus' Last Supper. One can argue the history of that setting for the Last Supper, but it is clear that in the synoptic gospels Jesus' last meal with his followers was a Passover Seder. It was in order to observe the Passover (Pesach), after all, that Jesus went to Jerusalem. The underlying theology of the temple-sacrifice became even more important for Christians as the years went on. It certainly became a crucial factor for Christianity in the year 70 when the temple was destroyed and the Jewish people had to replace this central sacred institution of worship with something.

Rabbinic tradition did it one way, by replacing animal sacrifice with prayer, good deeds (*mitzvoth*), and study of the Torah. Christians did it another, as can be seen in the Epistle to the Hebrews, which argues that Jesus' sacrifice more than compensates for the loss of the Temple sacrifice. The sacrifices of the temple are carried on through the Mass, the Eucharist, and the understanding of the Christ event in Christianity. This is very clear in the Catholic tradition. Embedding Christian faith and worship in Jewish ritual and Jewish biblical self-understanding (since the Jewish Bible was the only bible they had) would have significant implications for future decisions of later church leaders, for it made our Christianity always and forever a spiritual entity as well as a sacramental entity with a sacred bond to the faith, history, and life of God's people Israel.

Some people in the Jewish community today tell us in dialogue "I wish you folks would just leave us alone after all these centuries; enough is enough." I respond by pointing out that we Christians can't leave Jews and Judaism alone because we can't explain ourselves except in the context of our relationship as a Church with the Jewish people, Jewish faith, and Jewish history. There is no way we can break what the Second Vatican Council called a sacred bond, a term that for Catholics is a sacramental term. We use it also of the marital bond itself, which for us, as you will recall, is unbreakable. We do not have divorce in Catholic tradition. That kind of a bond, which images the bond between God and the Jewish people (covenant), is permanent. A major reflection of the Church's earliest appreciation of its sacred bond with Judaism can be found in St. Paul's letter to the Romans, chapters 9-11, upon which the Second Vatican Council relied for its reevaluation of Christian understandings of Judaism. This, I think, is ironic to some extent because so many in the Jewish community have traditionally seen St. Paul as the "bad guy" who took Jewish Christianity away from its Jewish roots and Torah observance. Especially since the *Wissenschafte des Judentuums* movement in the nineteenth century, there has been a major trend in Jewish scholarship to view Jesus as a good Jew over against Paul as a bad goy. Why this view is erroneous can be seen in the work of E.P. Sanders, among others.

But to return to the Council, *Nostra Aetate* reevaluated the entire biblical tradition through the lens of a new, more positive understanding of Romans 9-11. That crucial passage is the only one in which Paul I think consciously reflects on the relationship between the Church, the Jewish people, and God. Most of his writing, for example in Galatians, represents a different argument entirely. There, he is arguing with his fellow Jewish Christians that gentiles coming into the Church don't need to observe all the commandments of the Torah. Faith in Christ (along with a moral life, of course) suffices through the sacrament of baptism. But in Romans 9-11, Paul does take a direct look at the continuing role of Judaism in God's plan of salvation, alongside the Church.

The Council saw that while Paul successfully argues elsewhere for the inclusion of gentiles into the Christian communities without the prerequisite of first converting to Judaism, in Romans 9-11 he argues (albeit somewhat ambiguously) that God's covenant with the Jewish people is "irrevocable." Paul's argument in Galatians was another fateful decision because it meant the "gentile-ization" of the Church and its de-Judaization as more and more gentiles came in over the centuries. The same apostle's views of the irrevocable nature of the covenant between God and the Jewish people enabled a more positive theology of Judaism to develop in the Church today after two millennia when the Second Vatican Council decided to draw on it, rather than the anti-Jewish polemics of the Church Fathers, as the basis for Catholic doctrine on God's covenant with the Jewish people.

The first stage thus goes through St. Paul and the early strata of the gospels. The second stage, which many call "the parting of the ways," began with the destruction of the Temple in 70 C.E. and the radically different implications that Jewish-Christians and other Jews drew from that common catastrophe. That was a complex phenomenon, taking place over several centuries, a gradual development. It did not reach maturity and definitiveness until around the middle of the fourth century, when other decisions were made. These decisions centered on the liturgical calendar and were hotly debated over a long period. One involved not moving the Sabbath, but moving the observance of the Sabbath from Saturday to Sunday, the "Lord's Day." In the Romance languages, such as that spoken in the Diocese of Rome, what happened is more clear than in our Teutonic English. "Sabato" remained the "Sabbath," the last day of the week, while Sunday, the first day, the day of the Resurrection of the Lord ("Domenica") became central to Christianity. This was an indication that the split, that parting of the ways had taken place. This new movement was no longer tied so directly to the Jewish life of prayer or to its liturgical cycle.

The Christian liturgical calendar is based on the Jewish liturgical calendar. Christianity's central feast, like Judaism's, is Passover ("Pesach" in Hebrew, "Easter" in English, "Pascua/Pesach" in Italian). Even in English one can see the rootedness of Easter in Jewish Pesach (Passover) in such phrases as "Paschal Lamb" and "Paschal candle." On the fiftieth day we Christians observe Pentecost, just as Jews observe Shavuoth (the Feast of Sevens). We Christians, however, no longer observe the High Holy Days in the Fall. That is because the theological significance of the High Holy Days (repentance and atonement) takes place in the Easter Triduum celebrating Jesus' death and resurrection. For Christians, Yom Kippur (the Day of Atonement) became liturgically redundant to Good Friday and Easter. That is when we do ritually what Judaism does in the Fall. We do it in the Spring, attached to Passover. Splitting the Christian calendar away from the Jewish calendar, i.e., when we celebrate Easter/Passover away from when Jews celebrate Passover, was highly debated in the Christian tradition for many reasons. For example, it would signify a theological parting of the way that many Christians did not want to make. Other Christians, though, did not want to have to go to the Rabbis to have the date of Easter determined, so it was a very controversial issue.

I am simplifying everything, but the sense of this is important. One has in this second stage both a statement of continuity in the first century and a gradual sense of discontinuity reflected in new ways of celebrating and understanding the newness of Jesus and the newness of our Christian understanding of the one God of Israel that flowed from our understanding of Jesus. During this period one also has the beginnings of things that would have darker implications as the centuries passed. In the Epistle to the Hebrews (which is not by Paul, but dated by most scholars to the period after the destruction of the temple) there is a vision of the sacrificial death of Jesus not only replacing the temple sacrifice but being much better, not only "fulfilling" but replacing and perfecting it. That is a statement of a replacement, or supersessionist theology *vis-à-vis* a central Jewish practice. It is important to note, however, that Hebrews is narrowly focused on the sacrifice of the Temple. So it really doesn't say much about Rabbinic Judaism (in any of its forms) because they don't depend on the Temple for salvation, as we saw above. Hebrews answers the question of why we Christians significantly changed our liturgy from its Jewish roots. But Hebrews neither asks nor answers how Jews would continue to observe God's commandments (Torah) to them as their continuing obligation to God's eternal covenant with them; that was for the rabbis to decide.

During this second stage many of the New Testament and patristic polemical themes against Judaism were developed, such as the negative portrait of the Pharisees in Matthew. Ironically, Matthew is the most Torah/Law observant author of the four Evangelists. At the same time as he developed his negative portrait of the Pharisees (by which he really meant the developing Rabbinic movement of his own time), he also taught great respect for the Pharisees/Rabbis. The basic message in Matthew is that Christians should be even more scrupulous in our observance of the Law than the Pharisees themselves, a sort of "ultra-orthodox" position if one were to use modern categories. Pharisees are his basic model, even with all the nasty things he says about them (e.g., Mt 23). They also, in Matthew as in the other gospels, have absolutely no role in the death of Jesus. All the gospels agree on this; the Pharisees had no part to play in the death of Jesus, only "the chief priests, the scribes, and the elders." Indeed, in Luke, Pharisees try to warn Jesus of the plot against his life if he goes to Jerusalem. Pharisees are counted among his followers (e.g., Nicodemus, Joseph of Arimathea), and the Pharisee Gamaliel is depicted in the Book of Acts as saving the lives of all the Apostles and thus the very existence of the early Church.

In the second century Justin Martyr's misnamed *Dialogue with Trypho* was really an apologetic sliding into polemic. In some cases early Church documents reflect theological differences with fellow Jews, but do not yet reflect what we came to understand much later as "the teaching of contempt." They do not depend on the collective guilt charge (that Jews as a people were and are guilty of the death of Jesus). Certainly there is no basis for the collective guilt canard in the New Testament. But as time moved forward, more and more negatives were added. For example, as Christians, like other Jews, reflected on the destruction of the Temple, they blamed it on the sins of the People of God. But as the centuries went on and Christians no longer identified themselves as Jews, Christians began to blame the Jews as "others" rather than seeing a self-indictment in the acknowledgment of sin.

That made a fateful turn so that the destroyed Temple was seen as proof of divine punishment for Jewish sin. What Jewish sin? Well obviously the sin of killing Jesus. Why would God be angry with the Jews for killing another Jew? Because Jesus was the Son of God. The destroyed Temple became kind of an inverted (some might say perverted) proof of Jesus' divinity. God would not have been so angry with the Jews for killing Jesus if Jesus weren't intimately connected with God. This is the beginning of what Jules Isaac would in our century call "the teaching of contempt," but it took several centuries for that to develop. It was not an inevitable outcome of the New Testament. One cannot go directly from the New Testament, even from John's gospel, which talks collectively about "the Jews," to the developed teaching of contempt that Jules Isaac described in 1960 so devastatingly that Pope John XXIII commissioned Cardinal Bea to include the issue in the agenda of the Second Vatican Council.

The Second Vatican Council thus took a fresh look at the New Testament to see what it really said without the layers of patristic interpretation that had been imposed on the text (eisegesis) rather than drawn out of it (exegesis). One great decision of this second stage for Christians was about how far to part with Judaism. We saw above how this worked itself out in liturgical innovations and continuities because the link was still there with Passover in the preservation of Holy Thursday. Today as a memory of Jesus' Passover with his disciples it is still central to the Church's self understanding.

In the second century, Marcion of Pontus proposed a radical break with Judaism. He took the logic of discontinuity, if you will, to its logical conclusion, and said, "We have the New Testament. We don't need the Hebrew Scriptures anymore. They teach a different God, a god of vengeance and justice, not the New Testament God of love and mercy." Deeply influenced by agnostic dualism, Marcion wanted to get rid of the Hebrew Bible so he could get rid of the God of Israel. Even much of the New Testament, such as the Gospel of Matthew, was too "Jewish," so Marcion sought to get rid of it, too. By the time he was through, he was left with the Gospel of Luke and expurgated parts of the Epistles of Paul. The Church thought otherwise and declared that his teaching was heretical. Marcion has the dubious distinction of being one of the first defined heretics in Church history. In this decision, Christianity decided not to make too radical a break with Judaism but to maintain the relationship because the New Testament makes no sense except as imbedded in and as a midrash on, if you will, the Hebrew Bible, which is and remains God's word. The God that the New Testament teaches is no other than the God of Israel.

The "pre-Christ" history of the Christian people is no other than the history of the Jewish people as reflected in the Bible. Now that did not answer the question of God's relationship with Jews post-Christum who did not accept the Church's proclamation about Jesus. That was a separate question handled a bit later in the next stage. The point I want to make is that while Marcion's vision was declared heretical, some of his categories, e.g., comparing "old" versus "new," the God of justice versus the God of mercy, etc., stuck in the catechetical language of the teaching of the Church. Many negative effects even to this day go back to Marcionism. The 1974 Vatican *Notes* thus have to make a clear point that one can't place a God of love over against a God of justice. It is the same God in both Testaments. The reason they had to make that point was that too many Catholics were laboring under a misperception that was very similar to Marcion's: that there are two Gods and that the Old Testament teaches vengeance while the New Testament teaches mercy. Some of us grew up hearing those kinds of things in the past. Hopefully, fewer Catholics will hear them in the future.

The third stage begins at the end of the fourth century and the beginning of the fifth with the establishment of Christianity first as a licit religion, which Judaism already was, then as the official religion of the Roman Empire. The transition to power in the Church's history leads to a very serious temptation to triumphalism, theologically as well as politically. The earlier apologetical and polemical language of the Church had been developed while it was a persecuted minority. Now the Church gained immense power. In a famous vignette of the period, St. Ambrose forces an emperor to go down on his knees. Ironically, the emperor wanted the people of Milan to rebuild a synagogue that had been burned by Christians in a riot. Ambrose did not want them to and bent the emperor to his will. The rejection of Marcion now became a part of the next decision faced by the Church, what to do with a large portion of the Jewish community that did not see itself fulfilled in the risen Christ or the Christian interpretation of what was increasingly known as the Old Testament (not a term that the New Testament authors would have ever used in their lives).

During the following centuries the Church was to use both the force of secular authorities and of religious persuasion to suppress every religious tradition that existed in Europe in the beginning of the fourth century. These were gone. Look, for example, at the Pantheon. They just wiped them all out in one way or another. That was their express goal and they achieved it. There was only one exception to the universal intolerance of Christianity for other religions, and that was Judaism. Only Judaism survived this period in Europe and maintained its position, albeit a limited position, in the Christianized Roman Empire. Why?

Part of the reason can be seen in the framing of the theology of St. Augustine of Hippo. The negative part of his thinking toward Jews is often talked about, but the positive part of his theology is often forgotten. Augustine argued that since the Church's proclamation of the gospel required its continuity with the Hebrew Scriptures, the people who wrote and therefore bore witness to the sacredness of the Bible had to be preserved, since their witness was valid. Since they witness to the sacredness of the Bible, they were to be preserved, but since they resisted its fulfillment he wanted to keep them down a bit, because he didn't want them witnessing too spectacularly to that fact that they didn't feel the need for or have the question to which Jesus is the answer. Since Judaism was very attractive to potential converts to Christianity, laws were enacted to keep Jews from becoming too visibly prosperous or having authority over Christians. It was illegal for Jews to own slaves, hold certain positions of authority, or have occupations that were too prominent.

Gregory the Great, who was elected to the papacy in 590, embedded Augustinian theory in canonical legal principles that held, where papal teaching was followed, throughout the Middle Ages and were reconfirmed from pope to pope. Gregory prohibited any attempts at forced conversion of the Jews, since this might lead to insincerity in conversion, he argued, and therefore the state of their souls would be worse than if they remained faithful Jews. That became the canon law of the Church for centuries, in some places honored only in the breach. But Jews could and did appeal to those canon laws and appeal to the popes to enforce them. Judaism thus was allowed to survive in Christendom and even in some places and times to thrive. Jews were not physically kept from

leaving Christian Europe; they did not want to. They didn't see a
better future anywhere else, which is something I think we need to
deal with as well.

The fourth stage, and here I have not a general but an exact date,
began in 1096, with the mass violence perpetrated against the helpless
Jewish communities of the Rhineland by marauding crusaders.
Robert Chazan's wonderful book on that first crusade shows that it
was not the first wave or the second wave of crusaders who committed
the massacres.[1] Rather, it was the third wave, the dregs of the followers
who were pretty much uncontrolled and virtually leaderless who got
the idea that they didn't need to go all the way to the Holy Land to
kill infidels. They could just do it right in their backyard, because they
had the Jews there to do it to. It's a very tricky story. The local bishops
tried to protect the Jews, but in vain. In one case, the Jews were given
refuge in the home of the local bishop. The crusaders stormed the
palace, overwhelmed its defenders, and slaughtered the Jews. A
martyrology developed in Judaism—an interesting one from a Jewish
point of view, in that period.

In the second crusade, the pope commissioned St. Bernard of
Clairvaux to travel around preaching against any attacks on the Jews
as being against Church teaching and as being irrelevant to the
point of the crusades, which was to free Jerusalem from the
Muslims. He was reasonably successful, but not all subsequent
crusades followed this example. The year 1096 represents the first
massive blood letting in Christian history. Remember that a
millennium had passed before it took place. Violence was not and
is not an inevitable part of Jewish-Christian relations. It was in
1096, as in our own century, the result of real decisions made by real
people who consciously chose evil over good.

After 1096 the theology of contempt against the Jews escalated
dramatically. It came to be very different than it had been in early
centuries, where the concern was with Judaism being too attractive
to Christians. We have records of bishops of the ninth and tenth
centuries trying to ban Christians from going to rabbis to have their
fields and children blessed, which indicates that a reasonably good
relationship prevailed. One does not ban a practice if it's not fairly

common. In the twelfth century the situation deteriorates in historical terms relatively rapidly. I would argue that the increase of negative theology is really part of a rationalization for the murders of Jews by crusaders: "Yes, Jews were killed, but that's because they deserved it." This is my own theory. Someone else will have to do the doctoral dissertation, hopefully at Catholic University, to prove or disprove it. But the fact of the escalation of theological anti-Jewish rhetoric is quite startling, and is, I think, quite obvious in this period.

It is in this period of the twelfth, thirteenth, fourteenth, and fifteenth centuries when so much of that which we consider endemic to Christianity is first introduced; it didn't exist before. This is when the ghetto started. This is when the blood libel was invented in Britain, and perfected in the Rhineland area of what is now Germany. It was only then that the Jews were really demonized. One can see a dramatic change in terms of portraiture. For example, on the cathedral of Strassbourg in France at the end of the latter period, there is a theological apologetic on the portals. Two statues depicting two beautiful women stand, one being the Church and one the synagogue. The Church is resplendent, triumphant, and in glory. The other beautiful woman is the synagogue and she is poignant, with the staff of the Law broken and the tablets of the Law falling out of her hands. That's a statement of theological triumphalism. But there's not an ounce of the racism we today connect with anti-Semitism.

Compare this with a cathedral in Regensburg, Germany, from some time later. There is a carving of something I was told was once fairly common in Germany: the Judensau (Jew sow). There you can recognize the Jews by the typical hats that they were by this time forced to wear. This identifying mark of the Fourth Lateran Council and Innocent III showed stone images of Jews suckling at the teats of a sow. That is very crude, and is a different sort of image from that in Strassbourg. The attempt is to dehumanize the Jews. That was a meaning and an intention not present a couple of centuries earlier on the cathedral of Strassbourg. What was going on in the minds of the people who did that sculpture?

This period saw the beginning of the Passion play. The earliest one dates from the thirteenth century in the Benedictine monastery in Germany, from which we have the manuscripts of the *Carmina Burana* folk songs. But it dates to that period in which the Jews are depicted as a "bloodthirsty race," for killing Jesus and by implication Christians as well. The enforced ghettoization of the Jews began in Italy, where the Jewish area of Venice, which had been called ghetto ("factory") for quite a while, was moved to a new site. One still sees on tourist maps "Ghetto Vecchio" and "Ghetto Nuovo" ("old" and "new" Ghetto). Ghetto Nuovo was an island with one bridge; it had a gate on the bridge and the Jews were expected to be back there at night and stay there. Sometimes that was for their own protection, especially around Good Friday, when Christians might come out of churches and do harm to the Jews, having misunderstood the gospel message of the day as blaming Jews for Jesus' death rather than placing responsibility on sinners. Jesus, the gospel teaches, died for *our* sins. To the extent that we Christians try to off-load our responsibility for the death of Christ, evading our guilt by blaming Jews for Jesus' death, we remove ourselves from participating in his Resurrection.

Beginning in twelfth century England and culminating in 1492 (Spain) and 1496 (Portugal), the Jews were expelled from virtually all of the Western Europe. This was rationalized by the blood libel charge that had been invented before that. Some Jewish families found refuge in Italy, which did not expel its Jews. Still, Italy did not really have much of the apparatus of the practice of contempt. It did have the ghettoization and other restrictive laws, but if you were a Jew living almost anytime during Christian history in Italy, you weren't in much physical danger most of the time. There were certain things that the Italian system required you to do, but if you did those you could survive and even prosper. So a number of the refugees from the Spanish expulsion of 1492 ended up in Italy. There still exists the beautiful sephardi synagogues in Venice, for example, built by these refugees. Its beauty is all inside. The outside is nondescript and that was part of the accommodation of the time. But there, Jews were allowed to have a beautiful synagogue and a relatively peaceful life in relative prosperity, relative to a lot of the rest of the world. So the situation varied in Catholic countries from one area to another, and it should be noted that Italy is profoundly influenced by Catholic tradition and certainly by papal teaching. Much of Italy, of course, was ruled directly by the popes and therefore the papal decrees were followed throughout the period. Likewise, some Protestant countries like the Netherlands gave refuge and a chance for a relatively normal life to Jews expelled from other countries. By the time of the Enlightenment, the Jewish communities of Europe were decimated and in most places severely oppressed. They were moving into eastern Europe in large numbers.

The fifth stage lasted from the Enlightenment to the eve of World War II. Jews were still considered outsiders by much of European society. Even though they were legally there and could claim various legal privileges and rights, they also had numerous legal inhibitions on them. They couldn't own horses, couldn't be in most of the trades, and so participated in only a few minor areas of commerce. They went into areas such as money lending and the jewelry business, I think, because these were good businesses to be in if you were likely to be expelled. You could take your assets with you in a little sack as you jumped out the back window while people banged on the front door.

Simultaneously, this period (the eighteenth and nineteenth centuries) saw the development of a pseudo-scientific racism. This was the dark side of the Enlightenment. According to Arthur Hertzberg, Voltaire, for example, says that the Jews cannot be assimilated into Western society.[2] They are different; they are qualitatively different from and inferior to the rest of Europeans. They cannot be assimilated no matter what they do. They will still have these negative characteristics. That's a racial theory that was developing, whereas the Church's idea was to love the Jews for conversion and facilitate that in anyway reasonably possible. This "enlightened" theory is different. The Jews cannot be assimilated. For the Church the Jews could be baptized and become full Christians.

The racialist theories were developed to some extent to justify what Europeans were doing in Latin America and North America to

Native Americans, what they were doing in Africa in developing the slave trade, and what they were doing in Asia and the Middle East. Racialism was a handy way of justifying that "if these folks aren't fully human you can do to them anything you want." If one looks around Europe, however, the significant group of "outsiders" are the Jews, so these same racial theories were applied to the Jews of Europe. And then came Chamberlain and Wagner and others. Jews, for them, were subhumans, little more than dangerous animals, "vermin." Nazism perfected this system of subdividing humanity into separate species, with only Aryans (Germans, Dutch, Danes, Austrians, British, etc.) being fully human. Italians, Greeks, Poles, and other Slavs were a little less human and the list went down until it reached the Jews, Gypsies, and Africans at the very bottom. These, of course, were not really human at all, so Europe needed to be cleansed of these unhuman things. People can do this because "they" are not human beings. One can justify the Holocaust as a purification of Europe for the "Millennial Rule" of the Third Reich.

Now that's a quick view of two thousand years. But I think it is more important to note that you don't get there directly from the Gospel of John. It doesn't work. You can't get from the Gospel of John to the mid-twentieth century without taking into account a lot of different complexities. It didn't always happen the same way everywhere. There was essentially the same teaching by the Roman Catholic Church in Austria as there was in Italy. But the results were very different in terms of the treatment and understanding of their fellow citizens in Italy than they were in Austria. Eighty-five percent of Italian Jews survived and almost any Jew that could get her or himself into the hands of the Italian army survived. The Italian army would not give up Jews to Germans even when the Nazis demanded it. That's an untold story in many ways but a very real one; so the record shows that Catholics acted very differently depending on where they were.

It's a very complex story. Take just the country of France and one can see various groups of Catholics raised essentially the same in terms of the faith, but some becoming Vichyites, others becoming resisters, and some dying trying to save Jews. World War II provides a very complex set of stories. We have to work on reconciling Jewish and Catholic historical memory. This is, of course, the sixth stage. It is the one we are in now. It began with the opening of the death camps and the discovery of what went on in them, of coming to terms with what was done to the Jews of Europe. Two out of every three Jews who were alive in Europe in 1940 were dead by the time the camps were liberated. That's astounding. It's incomprehensible. But the process to begin to comprehend it had to begin. The Second Vatican Council was our first step, as Catholics, toward an answer, but we are just in the beginning of that stage of answering it. This is where the question of youth comes in, because the lesson of this history is that if one is not very careful with one's decisions generation to generation, they can come back to bite one very deeply.

A Personal Reflection on *Nostra Aetate*

The fourth section of the *Declaration on Non-Christian Religions* dealt with the Church's understanding of and its attitude toward Jews and Judaism in just fifteen sentences in Latin. It is important to realize that this was the first time any Ecumenical Council of the Church (i.e., a full gathering of the world's bishops in formal assembly) had ever, in fact, asked this question. References in earlier Councils, such as the Fourth Lateran Council (1215 C.E.), were, while negative, merely "disciplinary" in character, and had no doctrinal implications for Church teaching as such. *Nostra Aetate*, distinctively, makes no reference to previous Councils of the Church or writings of the Fathers of the Church. It was a new, fresh look at the question after nearly two millennia of essentially uncontested presumptions, many of them erroneous as Pope John Paul II has noted, going back to second-century polemics against Judaism. Further, *Nostra Aetate* was, in the view of its framers, a conscious attempt to begin the process of discerning the implications of the dogmatic *Constitution on the Church, Lumen Gentium*, whose words *Nostra Aetate* echoes and amplifies. Speaking of those who have not "yet" received the Gospel but who "are "related to" the people of God "in various ways," *Lumen Gentium* states:

> In the first place we must recall the people to whom the testament and the promises were given and from whom Christ was born according to the flesh. On account of their fathers this people remains most dear to God, for God does not repent of the gifts He makes nor of the calls He issues.

This calling, *Lumen Gentium* states, is part of "the plan of salvation."

Nostra Aetate begins by noting that it is when the Council "searches into the mystery of the Church" itself that she encounters the mystery of Israel, acknowledging that the very "beginnings" of the Church's own faith are to be found in the Hebrew Scriptures, and affirms that believers in Christ, far from standing on their own, are rather "Abraham's sons according to the faith and included in the same Patriarch's call." The Church knows no God other than the God of Abraham and Sarah, and no salvation other than that accorded Israel in the Exodus: "The Church, therefore, cannot forget that she received the revelation of the Old Testament through the people with whom God in His inexpressible mercy concluded the Ancient Covenant" and that to this day the Church "draws sustenance from the root of that well-cultivated olive tree onto which have been grafted the wild shoots, the Gentiles."

The Council then goes on to translate (properly from the Greek) a passage many vernacular translations, including, I must admit, that of my own Bishops' Conference, had translated in the past tense, the key passage from Romans 9:4-5, "Theirs [i.e., the Jews'] is the sonship and the glory and the covenants and the law and the worship and the promises." That single, present-tense "is," an accurate translation of Paul's key caveat on all he says in Romans and all of his other epistles, I would argue, was and remains the most revolutionary tense correction in the history of Christian biblical scholarship and official Church teaching. For it throws on its head the entire ancient "teaching of contempt" by which Israel, the Jewish people, was to be considered in the past tense, rejected by God for allegedly rejecting "the time of their deliverance," etc. No, Paul thunders, and the Council nearly two millennia finally repeats. One can bend, one can open God's Law, the divine Path, to admit gentiles. But in so doing one cannot, ever, for a moment, close what God has promised to keep open, the salvation of the Jews on the basis of the covenant God established with them and which neither the Jews nor God have ever revoked.

I have pondered these fifteen sentences now for over three decades, always wondering at their order. Logically, what comes next in the document should have come first. For what comes next is the rejection of any implication of collective guilt of the Jews for the death of Jesus "then or now" despite the involvement of some (the Latin does not state "omnes"; it has no adjective) "Jewish authorities" for the death of Jesus. Should not the great canard, "deicide," the "God-killer" charge, have been cleared away before a theological, indeed doctrinal assessment of God's current and future covenanting with the Jews as a people been approached? Should not one prune away the false detritus of the past before addressing the great hopes of the future? Yet these most elegant fifteen sentences of the Council begin with a huge, doctrinally pregnant, unprecedented (save in St. Paul) affirmation before they go on to rejecting the collective guilt charge and condemning anti-Semitism and mandating radical changes in "catechetical work" and "the preaching of the word of God."

I think they were right. The Jewish people, God's people in their own way no less than God's people in Christ, the Church, need first to be acknowledged as such, human beings, God knows, with flaws and greatnesses, called to be and to continue to be a witness people to all of humanity, and to the Church (as Pope John Paul II said to the Jews of Warsaw in 1987). When this essential fact of salvation history is accepted by Christians, then the involvement of a few Jews and Romans in Jesus' death is put in proper perspective. From a Christian, a Catholic point of view, Jews are the People of God, to whose everlasting witness to the One God and to God's plan of salvation for all humanity we join our voices. That some of Jesus' fellow Jews in the first century collaborate with Rome, as so very many Christians of all persuasions collaborated with Nazism's anti-Jewish and therefore anti-Christian genocidal attack, is a great sin for those who did so. But it is not the guilt, great as it is, then or now that counts. It is the hope for all humanity that our mutual, our joint witness to the One God, the God of salvation for us all, that counts. Is not that what we are about, ultimately, we Jews and Christians: fighting history, sucked into history only to emerge to fight again? Isn't it what God calls us to be, beyond our failing meager selves? Is not that the point?

Contemporary Controversies between Catholics and Jews[3]

Any discussion of the current controversies between Catholics and Jews over issues related to the *Shoah* (and they are many) must be set within the much larger context of the truly astounding progress in Catholic-Jewish relations in the final third of the twentieth and beginning of the twenty-first century. Indeed, I would argue that the current level of high-voltage Jewish criticism of contemporary actions of the Holy See is itself a reflection of that progress. In no previous century since the Church assumed vast political power following the conversion of Constantine have Jews felt secure enough in Christian-dominated societies to speak as freely and frankly as they do today. While the framers of the Second Vatican Council's declaration on the Jews, *Nostra Aetate*, might not have foreseen such a result, this unintended but certainly lively byproduct of the renewal of Catholic teaching on the Church's relationship with the Jewish people is to be welcomed as a sign of a dialogue that is doing what it was intended to do, allow the participants to bare their souls to one another without inhibition or fear of intimidation.

Controversies within recent memory, widely reported in newspapers throughout the world, range from Jewish concerns over who the pope was to meet (Waldheim, Arafat), to where cloistered convents and crosses should be located (Auschwitz, Birkenau), to who the Church should declare saints (Edith Stein, Cardinal

Stepinac, Pope Pius XII). Many Catholics, Jews need to know, are understandably confused as to why some in the Jewish community feel constrained to second guess so many of what are, after all, internal matters in the life of the Church. Catholic confusion is only compounded when we consider that many of these complaints came at a time of rapid progress in the dialogue vigorously lead by a pope, John Paul II, who was deeply committed to it and whose active promotion of Catholic-Jewish relations was unprecedented in the history of the Church. And why beat up on Catholics all the time? Why not go after somebody else once in a while? We don't go around setting up Messianic Jewish "synagogues," or saying that God doesn't hear the prayers of Jews, or opining that the Anti-Christ will be a Jew. Why us? (Many Jews are surprised to learn that there is such a thing as "Catholic paranoia," but there is.)

The answers, on reflection, are not too difficult to discern. First, Roman Catholicism is by far the largest church within the community of the baptized. Its pope, certainly in our time, is thus the most visible single individual within that community. So Jews concerned about what that community might do (and history has taught them all too well that such concerns are not by any means paranoid) will tend to watch very closely, even minutely what the leadership of the Catholic Church does that might affect them. That great pioneer of the dialogue, Msgr. George G. Higgins, once likened the point of view of the Jews in Catholic-Jewish relations to that of a mouse in bed with an elephant. The mouse gets little sleep, watching for any little tremor in the elephant's body that might indicate that it is about to turn over.

Second, in my experience many Jews have a very heightened notion of the power and authority of the papacy. A major Jewish journal not long ago published without comment a letter to the editor that Pope Pius XII could have ended World War II just by telling the troops, most of whom were at least nominally Christian, to lay down their arms and go home. Would that it were so! Popes have not even aspired to that kind of direct political clout over secular authorities and the laity in a long, long time.

Perhaps the single issue underlying all the controversies is memory. How, Jews ask, will the next generation of the world's more than one billion Roman Catholics be taught about Jews and Judaism, about the Holocaust? What is at stake for Jews is not just the past but the remembrance of the past, since they understand very well that how we Catholics define the past for the next generation will deeply influence the fate of future generations of Jews within Western civilization. One great strength of tradition-oriented institutions, like the Church and rabbinic Judaism, lies in their ability to frame the issues of human continuity from generation to generation. Stalin was right: the Catholic Church has no troops. But it has a prodigious memory and a gift (we believe from the Holy Spirit) to interpret for its followers the meaning of human history. It has preachers and teachers. The Jewish community, having lived with and under us for much of the last two millennia, understands quite well the long range significance of Catholic memory. That is why they worry about it so much.

If I were Jewish, I might worry about us, too. Sensitivities on both sides, some spoken, some unspoken, abound in each of the Holocaust-related controversies. Jews for an entire generation hesitated to talk very much even with each other about what had happened to them (two out of every three Jews in Europe murdered, one third of the entire world Jewish population). It was only in the mid-1970s, perhaps in response to the TV miniseries, *Holocaust*, that survivors felt able to talk to their children and to other Jews. And when they did, Holocaust "revisionists" popped up in colleges and on the media to deny that it ever really happened. So began the period of building Holocaust museums and pushing for Holocaust education in public and private schools, twin efforts that have greatly enriched the educational and moral environment of the last remaining superpower (and thus potential world bully). As Pope John Paul II has said, the Jewish witness to the *Shoah* is "a saving warning for all humanity, which shows [them] to be still the heirs of the Prophets."

Yet even though the Holy See's Commission for Religious Relations with the Jews and the U.S. Conference of Catholic

Bishops (among others) have on numerous occasions condemned Holocaust denial for the "great lie" that it is, still Jews worry. Now, Jewish worry manifests itself a little differently than does Catholic worry. On the one hand, the spokespeople for the worriers tend to have grown up in New York City, which is not as sensitivity-conscious in its public discourse as, say, Virginia, or Michigan, or even California. On the other hand, many of the spokespersons are rabbinically trained, and if not, nonetheless profoundly influenced by the rabbinical style of discourse. Anyone who has read even a few chunks of the Talmud will realize quickly that it is quite a different genre of religious literature than either the protracted ruminations of Augustine or the clipped logical framework of Aquinas. It is argumentative, not only among rabbis ("But, Rabbi X said . . .") but also with the biblical text itself. "How," the argument raged among rabbis over the centuries, "could Joseph have been so morally callous? He knew for all those years of his opulent living in Egypt that his father mourned his death. Yet he could spare not one messenger to tell his grieving father that he lived and prospered? What a breach of the commandment to honor your father and mother!" I know of no Christian preacher who has ever raised this question. Yet arguing with the texts and with the most revered of Jewish ancestors is typical of rabbinic discourse.

So when Jews look at a Vatican text which they take seriously, they probe it for weaknesses, dissecting its logical and moral vulnerabilities. Here again they have done us Catholics a great service. The Jewish reception of every one of the statements of the Holy See, beginning with *Nostra Aetate* itself (which none other than Abraham Joshua Heschel panned as too little and too late), has been negative and even fractious. It is what Jews do to their own texts. It is an honor, perhaps oddly enough, when they do it to ours. The service is to hold our feet to the fire; to temper thereby our dross metal statements into solid steel capable of serving the ages. Consequently, one can discern in official Church statements over the years a steady progress in Catholic teaching about Jews and Judaism. Since getting this teaching right has everything to do with authentic Catholic teaching (Vatican II noted wisely that it is when searching her own mystery that the Church encounters the mystery of Israel), we should, despite the often fractious format in which it is presented to us, be grateful for the honor Jews pay us in disputing on their own terms with us.

Yet dispute is not dialogue. Dialogue seeks to know what is hurtful to the Other and to avoid it. For dialogue is not debate. Its goal is not winning but understanding. It would, therefore, be helpful if our Jewish partners in dialogue would learn that utilizing the level of rhetoric on Catholics that is common within the Jewish community can block understanding as often as it communicates to us legitimate Jewish concerns. This is especially true, I would submit, when the subject is the papacy.

Until quite recently, the history of Catholics, like the history of Jews in the U.S., was one, by and large, of immigration and discrimination, of being excluded from the "better" neighborhoods, schools, jobs, and social clubs. Entire political movements were formed whose primary purpose was to keep Catholic immigrants out, first out of the country and then, failing that, out of the established economic and social system. We were numerous and unsavory. We would swamp and bring down social and educational standards, polluting American culture. Above all, we were dangerous, subjects of blind obedience to the "whore of Babylon," the pope, and thus at once un-Christian and un-democratic, of uncertain loyalty to the American experiment.

The pope: symbol of what was really wrong with the poor, huddled, teeming, "ethnic" masses of "papists" who swarmed into America, threatening all that was good and sacred about the great "city set on a hill." If only Catholics would give up the pope, the mantra went, they could be socialized, Americanized, Christianized, sanitized, and made fit for respectable company. But we wouldn't and, by and large, we didn't, holding back our assimilation and acceptance in this country for generations for the sin of holding on to the papacy.

The papacy, as the viciously anti-Catholic political cartoons of Conde Nast and his cohort constantly reminded us, was the symbol of what was wrong with us, what was unassimilable. So the papacy, then and even now when the great century-long wave of nativist, No-Nothing bigotry has subsided to a trickle, remains for Catholics a symbol of who we are as Americans, and what it cost our parents and grandparents to remain Catholic in a land of legal equality and ethno-religious discrimination.

So when Jewish leaders criticize the pope, whether Pius XII or John Paul II, even many of the "progressives" (whatever that actually means) among us find ourselves a bit disoriented, with sensitivities triggered that we may not have known that we had. For Catholics with a historical memory, Jews are fellow immigrants who suffered from much the same set of discriminatory attitudes and systemic exclusions. It is not at all accidental that the names of the leaders of the labor movement tend to be "ethnic," Jewish and Catholic. Nor is it accidental that Catholics and Jews tended, again until recently, to cluster in the same urban ghettos. So how is it, we ask, when we recognize our American story in the Jewish-American story, that so many Jews seem to miss the, to us, deeply obvious point that to attack the papacy (never mind that we criticize the pope, he is *our* pope to criticize, after all, just as Israel is the Jewish community's prerogative to criticize) is to raise up for us the specter of the nativist bigotry we thought had been left behind after John F. Kennedy's campaign for the presidency (when he had to go to Texas to swear loyalty to America).

In jumping all over the popes, many Jews do not seem to realize that they are by no means "speaking truth to power," as they themselves, I feel, sincerely believe. They are triggering the half-buried paranoias of the grandchildren of unwelcomed immigrants. If Jews are to communicate with American Catholics what should be real concerns for both communities, there will need to be a softening of the rhetoric until the volume is turned down enough so that we Catholics can hear what they are saying. Right now, the discourse is too loud to be comprehensible.

The difficulty of communication, of course, is very much two-sided here. If Jewish discourse tends to Catholic ears to be too disputatious, pointed, and at times judgmental, Catholic discourse (especially that of Rome) can strike Jewish ears as too soft, nuanced,

and hesitant on what are, for them, the big issues, especially the
Holocaust. The recent statement of the Holy See, *We Remember: A
Reflection on the Shoah* is a case in point. As the Jewish responses
(mostly emanating from the headquarters in New York of national
Jewish groups) were, understandably, written in "Jewish," so the
Vatican document, emanating from Rome and addressing at once
all of the world's one billion Catholics, was decidedly written in
"Catholic" (or, more precisely, "Vaticanese," a sub-dialect that many
American Catholics have difficulty comprehending sometimes).
One of the characteristics of "Vaticanese," in certain circumstances
(not so in others but that is another story) is its desire not to say
more than it actually wants to say. This can result in a plethora of
caveats and distinctions, a habit with which anyone familiar with
medieval scholasticism will find themselves at home, but which in
the larger world is, shall we say, an acquired taste.

As I read the document the first time (on a charter bus going
into Rome from the airport after a flight from Jerusalem with a
distinguished group of U.S. bishops and their rabbinical
counterparts from around the country), I could see that what made
eminent sense to me was in a number of key areas going to cause my
rabbi friends no end of difficulty. In retrospect, I think I
underestimated the difficulty, but was not surprised by its intensity.

The points at issue in the Vatican text are essentially related to
its perhaps too-brief summary of the history of Jewish-Christian
relations in only a few paragraphs. Naturally, things were left out
which, from a Jewish point of view, needed to be said, but which the
authors may have felt were implicit in the text and thus did not need
to be spelled out.

Two key distinctions illustrate both this dynamic and the need
for further dialogue. The first is the distinction in the text between
"the Church as such," which is held blameless for the Holocaust and
what lead up to it, and "the sons and daughters" of the Church, for
whose teachings, actions, and inactions over the centuries and
especially during the Holocaust the Church as a whole is called
upon by the document to repent. This language struck many Jews
as less than straightforward. In fact, it is traditional. Although it is

not the most fashionable ecclesiology in certain academic theological circles today, it cannot be said (as some Jews feared) that it was invented just to get the Church off the hook with regard to its evident historical responsibility for setting the stage for the *Shoah*. Indeed, to the authors of the document, which was after all essentially a ringing statement of repentance for past Catholic sins, the Church's acknowledgment of responsibility was obvious in the statement's structure and very existence. How and why repent if there was no sin?

Cardinal Cassidy, who signed the document as President of the Commission that authorized it, has explained on various occasions that the distinction is made, traditionally in Roman Catholicism, between the Church as a sacramental, saving institution, the Body of Christ on earth, and the Church as a human institution, which includes all levels of "the sons and daughters" of the Church, from popes to newly baptized infants. The latter can indeed be as an institution guilty of sin and therefore needs, constantly to repent ("semper reformanda"). The former sense of "Church," since it refers directly to the actions of Christ in heaven and on earth, and thus to the integrity and validity of the sacraments necessary for salvation, including the sacraments of Eucharist and reconciliation, cannot be said to be "sinful" without impugning the Godhead as sinful and the sacraments as corrupt and ineffective.

So the Church as a human institution and as a whole must repent of its manifold sins against Jews and Judaism, sins which paved the way for something, namely genocide, that the Church at its worst never contemplated as a possibility. This, to me, and taking the validity of the document's distinction into account, is the clear teaching of the Vatican's *We Remember*. Yet in explaining how this is so the document makes a second distinction which again sounded to many Jews as a less than an honest reckoning but which, again, I believe is vital to an accurate historical record of the period and any discussion of the Church's role in it. This is the distinction between anti-Judaism and anti-Semitism.

The distinction as made in the Vatican document has clear, logical merit. The Church's traditional polemic against Judaism, which was aptly named "the teaching of contempt" by Jules Isaac, whose theory was accepted by Pope John XXIII and formed the basis of the Second Vatican Council's declaration, *Nostra Aetate*, was as it manifested itself in the first and second centuries, intended to show Christianity's superiority over the then-equally young Rabbinic interpretation of texts common to Jews and Christians. (In the first century, one should recall, virtually all Christians were Jews, so the New Testament is properly read as an internal Jewish document, an argument by Jews directed to Jews about the most authoritative way to read the Jewish Scriptures, i.e., to understand what Judaism should become after the destruction of the Jerusalem Temple.)

But beginning already in the second century, as the pope trenchantly pointed out in his address to the Anti-Judaism/Anti-Semitism seminar sponsored by the Holy See in November of 1977, the need of Christians (now increasingly gentile) to polemicize against rabbinic Judaism became so strong that a series of "misinterpretations" of the New Testament text were introduced that were, wrongly but ultimately, accepted by subsequent generations of (gentile) Christians as "the gospel truth" about Judaism. These included the nefarious and insidious notion of collective Jewish guilt for the death of Jesus—as if all the Jews spread around the Roman empire in Jesus' time had somehow (through an early yet undiscovered version of an e-mail chatroom?) learned of the trial of Jesus in time to go to Jerusalem to scream, "Crucify him!" And that they could all have fit in Pilate's courtyard.

Absurd, of course, but no more absurd than the Scripture-defying notion that such personal guilt could be handed down, collectively, to succeeding generations of Jews, as a people, by birth. Yet most Christians believed it. Perhaps it was comforting. If a Christian could blame "the Jews" for the death of Jesus, then one would not have to take responsibility for the real culprit, one's own sins. The awesome phrase, "Christ died for *your* sins" could thus be domesticated and put aside (no matter that one thus "put aside" ones only chance for redemption and salvation, which theologically is dependent upon the extent to which one acknowledges one's own responsibility as a sinner for Jesus' death, as the Council of Trent, seemingly in vain, tried to remind Catholics).

Here, however, even more distinctions than are made in the Vatican document become necessary. While the teaching of contempt against Judaism was by the end of the third century so well developed and so widespread as to be uncontested among subsequent Fathers of the Church, it did not (save in far-away outposts such as the Iberian peninsula) result in any large scale violence or even forced conversions of Jews until the eleventh century. In other words, the first millennium of Jewish-Christian relations, despite the accretion of absolute power over Jews by the Church beginning with the conversion of Constantine in the 4th century, did not result in an attempt by the Church to wipe out Judaism. On the contrary, thanks to St. Augustine and to St. Gregory the Great, who as pope instituted Augustinian theory as papal canon law, Judaism alone among the myriad of ancient cults of the Roman empire that pre-dated Christianity was allowed to survive—and accorded legal status (to which it could and did appeal to the popes for protection if and when civil authorities got out of hand.)

So there exists for the first millennium of the Christian era, not an unmitigated "anti-Judaism" (otherwise like paganism it would have been destroyed or absorbed) but a half-anti- and half-philo-Judaism in Catholic theory and practice. It was protected and denigrated at the same time. What word can we give to this highly ambiguous theoretical and practical posture by the Church toward Jews and Judaism? Ambivalent anti-Judaism? Hesitant anti-Judaism? Certainly, a qualifier is needed.

In the eleventh century, however, as I have already discussed earlier in my essay, things took a decided and unequivocal turn for the worse. At the beginning of the century/millennium, apocalyptic fervor seems to have whipped up a rather large-scale "pogrom" against Jews in France (Jews, of course, being blamed for holding back the coming of the true messiah by not acknowledging that he had already come). In 1096, the third wave of the first crusade, being leaderless (the nobility and the clergy having already gone with the first two waves) turned into a mob that massacred thousands of Jews in the Rhineland area of what is now modern Germany. This was over the protests of the pope who had launched the crusade and the local bishop/princes who felt an obligation (going back to Augustine and Gregory) to protect the "ignorant" but theologically significant Jews (since they witnessed to the authenticity of the divine revelation of Sinai, without which the "New Testament" makes little sense).

There are a number of theories to explain why, but what is important here is simply to note that things changed radically after the eleventh century. The "ambivalence" on the popular level faded, replaced by an increasingly negative anti-Judaism that began to take on the tinge of an anti-Jewishness. I have noted above a very telling example of this change: Whereas before, as in the classic French cathedral of Strasbourg, the Church and the Synagogue were depicted as two equally beautiful women, with the former resplendent and triumphant and the latter downcast and defeated, with the tablets of the Law falling from her hands, the Cathedral at Regensburg, Germany, has the infamous "Judensau" carved on its facade, with Jews suckling at its teats. This disgusting image is qualitatively different from the theological triumphalism of the French cathedral. It seeks to dehumanize the Jews, not simply illustrate the superiority of Christianity.

But if this is "anti-Jewishness," a new term needs to be confected for the next step. Here, the Jews are demonized, considered to be collectively guilty for the death of Jesus and therefore justifiably punished (e.g., through the destruction of the Temple, dispersion throughout the world, etc.), but also imagined as bitter and vindictive over Christian persecution of them, and accordingly out to destroy all of "Christian civilization." Jews are in league with the devil. Whereas for Augustine and the Fathers of the Church, the Jews were pitiable in their suffering, they are now seen as a threat to Christian society. As noted above, Passion plays beginning in the fourteenth century thus go well beyond the gospels and even the Fathers of the Church in depicting Jews as part of a cosmic plot, lead by Satan, to destroy Christendom and enslave all humanity.

As I argued in detail earlier in my essay, the Protestant Reformation did not seek to reform this aspect of medieval thinking, and the Enlightenment merely secularized it, the latter taking it to a new and even more insidious stage of development in wedding pseudo-science with greed to create a theory of racialism that supported colonialism and the slave trade. While there were many victims of such theories and practices, within Europe there was one group above all that many in society were predisposed (because of the teaching of contempt) to see as different, inferior and threatening all at once: the Jews. The historical progression is an ominous one: from Voltaire's assertion that the Jews could never assimilate into Western society to the pronouncements of secular Jew-haters such as Chamberlain and Gobineau passing their hatred off as "science" and then to Nazi ideology, casting the now no longer fully human but still demonized Jews in the role of the great polluter of the purity of Teutonic blood lines, destined to rule the world for a thousand years.

The Vatican statement's distinction between the anti-Judaism of the Fathers of the Church and the anti-Semitism that rationalized genocide is thus a quite cogent one. The latter on several grounds rejects theological elements central to Christianity. The one did not simply "slide" into the other. Over a millennium and a half of historical developments intervene between the two. We need, indeed, not fewer distinctions but more to do even basic justice to the complex ambiguities of Western history with regard to the Jewish people. There is patristic anti-Judaism, which is distinct from but related to medieval anti-Jewishness. And centuries later there emerges a distinct new theory (again historically related to its predecessors): modern, racial anti-Semitism, which owes its theoretical essence not to the Christian teaching of contempt, but to the dark underside of an enlightened Europe becoming rich on the slave trade and colonialism.

As Professor Yosef Yerushalmi said a number of years ago, if the logic of Christian anti-Judaism led directly to genocide, that would

have happened many centuries ago when the Church in much of
Europe actually had the political power to carry out the logic of its
beliefs. It didn't. It only happened in our own secularized century,
after the breakdown of the theocentric vision of Christendom, with
the moral restraints that vision imposed. Yet it is unlikely that the
Jews of the twentieth century could have been so easily pinpointed
and scapegoated by Nazi theory were it not for the traditions of
Christian anti-Judaism and anti-Jewishness that preceded the
nineteenth-century invention of racial anti-Semitism. That
Christian tradition of negative teaching about Jews and Judaism is
thus a "necessary cause," Yerushalmi argued for the Holocaust. But
it is not a "sufficient cause," since much more needs to be said to
begin to explain the success of genocidal anti-Semitism in the first
half of the century in Europe.

However one defines the distinctions and causal links, the
Vatican document's call on the whole Church to repent its role
in paving the way for the Holocaust is, at least to this reader,
quite clear:

> At the end of this millennium the Catholic Church desires
> to express her deep sorrow for the failures of her sons and
> daughters in every age. This is an act of repentance
> (*teshuvah*), since as members of the Church we are linked
> to the sins as well as the merits of all her children. The
> Church approaches with deep respect and great compassion
> the experience of extermination, the *Shoah* suffered by the
> Jewish people during World War II. It is not a matter of
> mere words, but indeed of binding commitment . . . We
> wish to turn awareness of past sins into a firm resolve to
> build a new future in which there will be no more anti-
> Judaism among Christians . . . but rather a shared mutual
> respect as befits those who adore the One Creator and Lord
> and have a common father in faith, Abraham.

That is the mandate of the Holy See's statement that Catholics need
to keep firmly in mind.[4]

Toward the Twenty-First Century

This section of the paper will be of necessity the shortest, for study of the past, even in depth, does not really enable one to divine the future with any certainly. Though it can enable us not to repeat old mistakes, it cannot prevent new ones. Nonetheless, I cannot help but be extremely optimistic about Catholic-Jewish relations in the long term, both here in the U.S. and internationally. The "signals" that I discern are all essentially positive and point us toward a renewed sense of trust and, indeed, shared mission in and for the world. What are some of these?

First, I would point to the remarkable progress made in the elimination from Catholic teaching of the ancient teaching of contempt against Jews and Judaism outlined above in part one. When Sister Rose Thering, O.P., in the late 1960s first undertook an analysis of the treatment of Jews and Judaism in Catholic religious education materials, the portrait which emerged was grim, indeed, replete with stereotypes and presumptions of the guilt of all Jews, then and now, for the death of Jesus. My own study, undertaken a decade after the Second Vatican Council, found remarkable progress but still a long way to go. The most recent study, done by Dr. Philip Cunningham, concluded that the teaching of contempt has been "entirely dismantled" and as such is no more in Catholic educational materials, though vestiges, theological and historical, can still be found. This positive picture is the result not only of implementing documents promulgated by the Holy See (1974, 1985, 1998) but also the series of statements on Catholic-Jewish relations made by episcopal conferences throughout the world (the earliest being the 1967 *Guidelines* issued by our own conference here in the U.S.) designed to apply the conciliar vision to particular local realities. The U.S. bishops, for example, issued statements in 1975 and 1988 to implement the Vatican documents of 1974 and 1985, and are beginning the process of working on one for the 1998 statement.

Often when I am speaking, a Jewish participant will say something to the effect that the universal statements of the Holy See are all well and good, but when will it "trickle down" to the grassroots level. In actual fact, it already has, indeed had done so to a surprisingly high level already in the mid 1970s. Stalin may have been right that the Church has no troops. But it has its classrooms and its pulpits, and that is where the battle for future generations is taught. Whether the students have ever heard of *Nostra Aetate* is irrelevant. What they are getting in their textbooks is, in fact, radically different from what previous generations of Catholics, going back to the second century, were getting. Catholicism, like rabbinic Judaism, is a living tradition. Within certain, sure boundaries it can and will change to preserve what is essential to its understanding of revelation.

Necessarily lagging behind the changes in what the Church teaches about Jews and Judaism is Jewish awareness of those changes. Many people in the Jewish community, as I indicated above, seem to think that the Council in fact changed very little, that the portrayal of Jews and Judaism in Catholic classrooms is pretty much the same as one would get, say, out of a sixteenth-century Passion play. This is to underestimate the Church's delivery system, its official teaching, which is measured generationally in its effect (and may take several generations to produce the desired effect, there being over a billion of us now and of all ages and relative involvement in Church life), but does have a cumulative effect. And a lot has happened. The reason for it to become more widely known and appreciated within the Jewish community that Catholic teaching has definitely and permanently turned away from the ancient teaching of contempt is not that we desire gratitude from Jews. When one comes down to it, the Church has mandated these radical changes not simply out of a neighborly sense of fairness to Jews (though that is part of it) but because it came to be seen that the negative polemics against Judaism over the centuries had so encrusted themselves around our understanding of Sacred Scripture that we were consistently misreading the New Testament itself.

One small example may suffice. If one is engaging in an ongoing polemic against Judaism and the "Old Testament," one may well miss the point of Jesus' "Law of Love." That was not a new

"Law" in any sense, but a brilliant coalescing of two crucial passages from the Hebrew Scriptures (Dt 6:5 and Lev 19:18), both of which are not simply cute sayings but the culmination of major biblical passages. Deuteronomy 6:5 is the paradigm by which the biblical author summarizes the inner meaning of the Ten Commandments (Dt 5) as love of God. It is part of a central Jewish prayer, the *Shema*, which is also commanded in the bible to be placed on the doorpost of every Jewish home (the *mezuzah*), and is to this day. Leviticus 19:18 likewise culminates and distills the entire chapter 19 of Leviticus. It is not simply having nice thoughts about one's neighbor, but a concrete and surprisingly practical structure for a just society. By ripping these two passages out of their context (a context which Jesus and his hearers would have automatically filled in at the time, so basic are these passages to Judaism), and calling them "new," Christians for generations deprived themselves of an in-depth understanding of their deep spiritual and social challenge and reduced God's Word to "feel good" psychology. Jesus' teaching is not about helping us feel good about ourselves: it is about how to live life at one with the Creator. It is best and most profoundly understood not as "over against" Judaism, but as a striving for the core of the Torah: God's Teaching, God's Law. The more we allow the Jewishness of Jesus and the evangelists to permeate our own, Christian understanding of the New Testament, the better we will understand it.

The difficulty Jews have in accepting the fact that Catholic teaching has changed for the better is only one side of the problem to be overcome on the Jewish side. The other is the need to be disabused of a number of misunderstandings of what Christianity is and what it teaches in general. The first article I ever published in the field of Jewish-Christian relations was entitled "Typical Jewish Misunderstandings of Christianity."[5] While I was careful to point out that these misunderstandings were by no means equivalent to the systematic contempt of the Christian *contra-Judaeos* tradition of the Church Fathers, they can be quite disconcerting to Christians when confronted with them. In the article, I traced some of the misunderstandings to medieval Jewish apologetics, which were understandably developed by the rabbis to help Jews fend off all-too-persistent Christian missionaries. (Some of these arguments have more recently been recycled to help Jewish youth today fend off the far-from-tender ministrations of such missionizing groups as the so-called "Jews for Jesus," which is hardly a Catholic operation and thus another story than the one I am narrating here.)

Other misunderstandings, including those perpetrated in Martin Buber's one really bad book, *Two Types of Faith*, I traced back to the brilliant nineteenth-century German-Jewish thinkers of the *Wissenschafte des Judentuums* movement. Thinkers such as Leopold Zunz and Abraham Geiger, I argued, themselves intellectually besieged by Christian polemics that were embedded in the works of German philosophers such as Hegel and German biblical scholars such as Wellhausen, crafted *tour de force* responses that to a great extent utilized Catholic anti-Protestant polemics and Protestant anti-Catholic polemics as truly representative of Christianity. Thus, Christianity is portrayed as placing mediators "between" God and humanity so that God cannot be addressed directly in prayer, and even as "deifying Mary" (two Protestant stereotypes of Catholic beliefs). And at the same time Christians were presented as having a quasi-magical religion in which what one did, morally, didn't matter so long as one's faith was pure ("deed" vs. "creed," a Catholic stereotype of the Reformation).

By accepting as true of all Christians what some Christians were saying polemically about each other, generations of Jewish scholars have erected a (mis)understanding of Christianity recognizable to no Christians. I argued in 1973 and repeat the argument today that while this brilliant strategy might have had its place in the nineteenth and first half of the twentieth century, it is less than helpful for Jews to keep it today when what is needed is not apologetics but understanding and the beginnings of trust.

If the first two "signals" of progress have to do with the admittedly asymmetrical jettisoning of the polemical baggage of the past (Christians having vastly more, and more invidious baggage to deal with), the third is the increasing ability of Jews and Catholics as religious people imbued with an ancient, divinely revealed wisdom, to speak together to all humanity about humanity's deepest concerns and needs. One can see innumerable instances of cooperation on the social level all around the U.S., ranging from local parish/synagogue soup kitchens to joint lobbying in Washington for the poor and the needy within the U.S. and around the world.

Likewise, we are developing the ability to speak together about issues of common concern. In the U.S., the National Council of Synagogues (and the old Synagogue Council of America) have issued several joint statements in the last decade, ranging from calling for the teaching of values in public education to condemning Holocaust revisionism and pornography, and to joint reflections on the social and religious implications of the (Christian) Millennium/Jubilee Year 2000. On the international level, the Holy See and the International Jewish Committee for Interreligious Consultations have issued joint statements on the meaning of marriage (and its implications for social policy) and on the environment.

These joint social policy statements and deeds, however, are only the first stage of what I would envision as the possibilities of jointly addressing the world's concerns. Our common goal, *tikkun olam*, calls us to more than that. We need to talk, carefully and non-disputatiously, about what we can say together about humanity's deeper concerns, the meaning of human life, the nature of human history oriented toward a Messianic End, what we are called by God to be and to do in this time of awaiting that End. This latter discussion may one day have fruit in joint reflections on these deeper, yet shared concerns. Both "sides" will be clear that what divides us theologically will always divide us. And yet . . . And yet . . . We should not fear delving a bit into our common biblical heritage to see what we can learn from each other and what we might, in all the integrity of our "otherness" from each other, articulate commonly to a world that needs to hear what I firmly believe God has given us not just to cherish among ourselves but to share with others.

This last task of the dialogue has only just begun, and among individuals, not really systematically by our communities' leaderships as a whole. We here most probably will not live to see its

deepest fruit. But while we cannot finish the task, to paraphrase the
rabbis, we cannot desist from it, I believe. For neither Judaism nor
Christianity were called into being by God just for the sake of
themselves. A larger, redemptive pattern for humanity, both of our
traditions attest about themselves, may be discerned in our
chosenness.

Notes

1. Robert Chazan, *European Jewry and the First Crusade* (Berkeley and
Los Angeles: University of California Press, 1996).

2. Arthur Hertzberg, *French Enlightenment and the Jews: The Origins
of Modern Anti-Semitism* (New York: Columbia University Press, 1968).

3. This section of the paper is a revised version of my essay originally
published as "Catholics and Jews Confront the Holocaust and Each Other,"
America, September 11, 1999.

4. The full text of *We Remember*, along with relevant statements from
European and U.S. hierarchies, and the statement of Cardinal Edward
Cassidy clarifying the intent of the Vatican document, is available in
Catholics Remember the Holocaust, publication no. 5-290 (Washington,
DC: U.S. Catholic Conference, 1999).

5. Eugene Fisher, "Typical Jewish Misunderstandings of Christianity,"
Judaism (spring 1973).

The Center for Christian-Jewish Understanding of Sacred Heart University: An Example of Fostering Dialogue and Understanding

ANTHONY J. CERNERA

Nostra Aetate (Declaration on the Relationship of the Church to Non-Christian Religions, 1965), and subsequent documents, Guidelines and Suggestions (1974), Notes on the Correct Way to Present the Jews and Judaism in Preaching and Catechesis in the Catholic Church (1985), and We Remember: A Reflection on the Shoah (1998), prepared the path for a theological and educational agenda that was both corrective (the purging of anti-Jewish material from textbooks, catechisms, and preaching) and provided an opportunity for renewal, especially in the growth in theological study and dialogue between Christians and Jews.

Since the founding of the first Interfaith Center in 1953, the Institute for Judeo-Christian Studies at Seton Hall University (IJCS), dialogue between Christians and Jews has become an essential priority of Christian churches. Today, there are twenty-seven centers of interreligious dialogue and education operating in the United States. The history of the Center for Christian-Jewish Understanding of Sacred Heart University, Fairfield, Connecticut, provides a good view of the way such centers have engaged in interreligious dialogue and education.

Nostra Aetate in Context

Many Church historians point to a symbolic turning point in Christian-Jewish relations at the 1960 meeting between Pope John XXIII and French Jewish scholar, Jules Isaac. Their friendship would lead the pope to support the reconsideration and reversal of teachings of contempt for Jews and would eventually hold up interreligious relations between Christians and Jews as an important priority of the Church.

A broader study of the texts from the Second Vatican Council (1962-65) points to a renewal movement in Church thinking that was part of the larger consciousness of the Council. For example, *Dei Verbum* (1964), the *Constitution on Divine Revelation*, provided the theological framework for the reversal in Catholic Church teachings on Judaism by affirming God's lasting covenant with the Jewish people. In this way, the sacred books of the Old Testament were acknowledged as the true Word of the One Living God. In rejecting the former substitution theory of the Church, which taught that the New Testament replaced the Old Testament, *Dei Verbum* states:

> Now the economy of salvation, foretold, recounted and explained by the sacred authors appears as the true Word of God in the books of the Old Testament, that is why these books, divinely inspired, preserve a lasting value. For whatever was written in former days was written for our instruction, that by steadfastness and the encouragement of the Scriptures we might have hope. (*Dei Verbum*, 14)

It is within this framework that *Nostra Aetate* marked a critical milestone in the history of Christian-Jewish relations and provided the opportunity to open and sustain a dialogue with non-Christian religions, but in particular, with Jews who share a common spiritual patrimony as people of Revelation and the Word. The document explicitly rejected every form of persecution and discrimination. Its insistence on dialogue opend up profoundly renewed relations between Christians and Jews:

> Since Christians and Jews have such a common spiritual heritage, this sacred Council wishes to encourage and further mutual understanding and appreciation. This can

be obtained, especially, by way of biblical and theological inquiry and through friendly discussions. (*Nostra Aetate*, 4)

Of all the influences that shaped the text of *Nostra Aetate*, the living memory of the *Shoah* prodded the conscience of the Church to begin a self-examination concerning its treatment of Jews over the ages. During the debates over the drafting of *Nostra Aetate*, Boston's Cardinal Richard Cushing made the issue more than a theological case of differences, and turned it into a penitential plea to the council fathers when he asked:

How many [Jews] have suffered in our own time? How many died because Christians were indifferent and kept silent? If in recent years, not many Christian voices were raised against those injustices, at least let ours now be heard in humility.[1]

The Second Vatican Council also called for the Church to be in solidarity with the entire human family in recognizing the communitarian nature of human activity as a response to God working in the world. *Gaudium et Spes* (1965) also emphasized that solidarity cannot be forced or achieved at once, but must be realized through a process of dialogue. Dialogue was identified as the chief means by which the dignity of all people is honored in the common search for the truth of human existence and the shared responsibility to seek solutions to the most pressing social problems of the day. *Gaudium et Spes* further asserted that the conditions of dialogue demand truth and liberty in an exchange that seeks not to obscure differences but to clarify them:

Doctrinal dialogue should be initiated with courage and sincerity, with the greatest freedom and with reference. It focuses on doctrinal questions which are of concern to the parties to dialogue. They have different opinions but by common effort they try to improve mutual understanding, to clarify matters on which they agree, and if possible, to enlarge the areas of agreement. In this way, the parties to dialogue can enrich each other. (*Gaudium et Spes*, 56)

Refining the Stance of Dialogue: The Guidelines *and the* Notes

Nostra Aetate was written for Catholics, but it signaled to Jews and to the world that the Catholic Church was willing to begin anew on a pilgrimage of faith with other religions. With the experience of nine years and many approaches taken in different countries to implementing *Nostra Aetate*, the 1974 document, *Guidelines and Suggestions for Implementing the Conciliar Declaration, Nostra Aetate* (issued by the Vatican Commission for Religious Relations with Jews), proposed some practical applications in areas of the Church's life.

Among the four areas addressed by the *Guidelines*—dialogue, liturgy, education, and social action—it was the document's call for educational reform that was particularly important. The *Guidelines* examined Catholic teaching materials, the formation of educators in schools, seminaries, and universities, and the role of sustained scholarly enquiry in the field of exegesis, theology, history, and sociology. Echoing *Nostra Aetate*, the document also called attention to the special role of Catholic higher education in contributing to deeper study *vis-à-vis* Judaism, and in particular, the promotion of scholarly research and dialogue in collaboration with Jewish scholars.

The 1985 document *Notes on the Correct Way to Present Jews and Judaism in Preaching and Catechesis* (issued by the same Commission) focused more on the correct ways to teach and preach about Jews and Judaism. It provided important educational resources that were needed to continue to remove anti-Jewish material from textbooks and catechisms, including some apologetic approaches used by the clergy for preaching. It also addressed Christian religious education in all forms. The effort was to indicate more clearly the Jewish roots of concepts such as covenant, law, prophets, messiah, manna, Passover, redemption, and testament, to name a few.

Notes addressed the critical issue that truth in dialogue was not possible without truth in teaching and preaching, and stressed that the Church no longer "superseded" or "replaced" an antiquated Judaism but is rooted in Judaism and grafted on the good stock of Israel. Just as Catholics (since 1959) no longer prayed at the Good Friday liturgy for "the perfidious Jews" but "that the Jews will be faithful to the covenant as they hear it," the Church's self-understanding was organically related to understanding the Jewish people in light of their own religious experience. In its special emphasis on correct teachings about Judaism, *Notes* recognized the importance of interreligious education for the entire faith community and the special responsibility of local educators and religious leaders in the overall mission of restoring relations between Catholics and Jews.

Historical Developments Since Vatican II:
Creating a Culture of Dialogue

The founding of the Institute for Judeo-Christian Studies at Seton Hall University preceded the Second Vatican Council, but did not arise out of a vacuum. The theological investigations and social activism of its chief architects, Monsignor John Oesterreicher and Dominican Sister Rose Thering, originated in their personal encounters with anti-Semitism and galvanized their pioneering work. The legacy of the IJCS in the work of restoring relations between Christians and Jews cannot be overestimated. Additionally, the Institute gave form to a sustained interfaith dialogue on both a theoretical and practical level that would lay the foundation for the future of interreligious study both within the academy and independent of it.

The time between the establishment of the first study center at Seton Hall University and the proliferation of new centers that began in earnest in the late 1980s was one of an emerging culture of dialogue between Christians and Jews inspired by the example and ministry of Pope John Paul II. As a public figure, Pope John Paul II never lost an opportunity to express visibly his love for the Jewish people. The most profound examples of this personal witness were the papal pilgrimages to key historical Jewish sites, especially those associated with the *Shoah*, which came to characterize his papacy.

Nearly a decade before Pope John Paul II commissioned the statement, *We Remember: A Reflection on the Shoah*, his mission of reconciliation with the Jews illustrated the educational value of symbolic gestures. Unmistakable acts of good will that recognized the past sufferings and still raw wounds of the Jewish people were shared by Christians not only in remembrance but in repentance. Beginning with his 1979 visit to the Auschwitz-Birkenau Camp, followed by his convening of the first World Day of Prayer for Peace (1986) and leading up to his visiting the Great Synagogue in Rome (1986), Pope John Paul II sought to create a culture of dialogue between Christians and Jews by urging reconciliation as the base from which all true dialogue emerges.

In a 2001 lecture at Sacred Heart University, Cardinal Walter Kasper, president of the Pontifical Council for the Promotion of Christian Unity and the Vatican's Commission for Religious Relations with the Jews, reflected on the work of Pope John Paul II as exemplifying the role of wisdom and witness in the search for the truth. Cardinal Kasper drew an analogy between the ministry of John Paul II, the encounter of witness and wisdom (faith and reason), and the defining role of the Catholic University in the mission of the Church. He described the ministry of Pope John Paul II as an expression and deep synthesis of faith and reason. "When we speak of truth," said the Cardinal, "we are not merely referring to the truth sought by our own intellect, but to that which comes from God through revelation."[2]

The culture of dialogue advanced by Pope John Paul II did not diminish the role of theological enquiry but also insisted on its necessary complement in human experience. As an expression of the search for truth, symbolic gestures witnessed to truth in service of the greatest good, which is the dignity of all life. For the work of a Center dedicated to interreligious dialogue and understanding, this translated into the mutual recognition of the truth of the Other (despite theological differences) as a daughter or son of God. This recognition became a shared work of fostering truth and peace.

The Center for Christian-Jewish Understanding:
An Example of Fostering Dialogue and Understanding

The Center for Christian-Jewish Understanding (CCJU) of Sacred Heart University was established as a research and academic division of the University in 1992. Its structure within the University setting and its dual audience of faculty/students and a broader national/international network of theological scholars followed the example set at Seton Hall University (IJCS). However, the founding of these two centers was separated by about forty years. By the time CCJU opened its doors, Holocaust education and activism had already taken firm root in Centers, schools, and government policy initiatives. In 1992 there were three independent Centers, and four Centers affiliated with a colleges or universities that were primarily local and focused on their respective academic and local public communities. With the growing intensity of dialogue between Christians and Jews evident in documents and statements on the international and national levels, the Center for Christian-Jewish Understanding began to create forums for national and international dialogue that could be shared with wide audiences.

In the same year that CCJU was founded, Pope John Paul II issued the first revised catechism since the sixteenth-century one that followed the Council of Trent. The new *Catechism of the Catholic Church* integrated the current teachings of the Church with respect to Judaism and directed them to a wider audience which included all Catholics. The responsibility for promulgating these teaching layin the hands of pastors.

The culture of dialogue between Christians and Jews that defined *Nostra Aetate* and subsequent documents took a critical turn with the appearance of *We Remember: Reflections on the Shoah* (issued by the Commission for Religious Relations with the Jews). *We Remember* called forth a deeper movement in interreligious dialogue by signaling that intellectual knowledge of the Other was a critical first but not a final step in the restoration of relations between Christians and Jews. This stage in Christian-Jewish understanding was well-prepared by the emergence of Holocaust

Centers, Holocaust studies programs and departments, and Holocaust Museums and Memorials throughout the United States and abroad. Their educational mission was to ensure the accurate memory of the *Shoah* for future generations.

A significant contribution of *We Remember* was to make the critical link between the historical and moral lessons of the *Shoah*. It was not enough to make the historical record accurate and accessible. The Holocaust needed to be understood on the level of morality. The antecedent statements of forgiveness and reconciliation issued by the Catholic bishops from Hungary (1992), Germany (1995), Poland (1995), United States (1995), Switzerland (1997), and France (1998) took on deeper meaning as a new era of friendship and ethical responsibility between Christians and Jews had now begun.

Two years later, in 2000, the Vatican established full diplomatic relations with the state of Israel. By formalizing diplomatic relations, the Vatican opened the doors to deeper political, moral, and theological dialogue between Jews and Christians. In the same year, acknowledging the increasing number of statements from official church bodies (both Roman Catholic and Protestant) that expressed both repentance for the Christian mistreatment of Jews and Judaism and a commitment to reform Christian teaching, numerous prominent Jewish scholars and religious leaders of North America issued the statement, *Dabru Emet: A Jewish Statement on Christians and Christianity.* This statement insisted that the challenges of living in a religiously pluralistic world demanded creative responses from the Jewish community:

> We believe these changes merit a thoughtful Jewish response . . . We believe it is time for Jews to learn about the efforts of Christians to honor Judaism. We believe it is time for Jews to reflect on what Judaism may now say about Christianity.

The mechanism established for Christian-Jewish dialogue in the first years of CCJU was to become a formidable vehicle on both the international and national levels for the promulgation of theological inquiry, scholarship, and education. CCJU combined the academic and research components of the university in a manner modeled on the IJCS prototype. It recognized and addressed the multiple audiences for the interfaith message (scholars, religious leaders, local community). This had been highlighted by some of the early local Centers and their efforts in local educational outreach to schools, churches, and synagogues. The Center also began to elaborate multi-dimensional strategies to accomplish its ambitious goals. The CCJU model was also informed by lessons from the Centers of Holocaust Education that pointed to the importance in bridging the gap between the scholarly community and the general public by making interfaith study and dialogue widely accessible.

Four core values defined the work of CCJU in promoting interreligious dialogue and understanding on a national and international level. It was to be a center for teachers and learners; a center that promoted substantive symbolic gestures; a center for learning in the presence of the Other; and a center for educating leaders.

A core conviction of CCJU is that the development and passing on of theological scholarship requires a process of dialogue that links knowledge with the mutual respect and reconciliation that it seeks to achieve. It attempts to enact a pedagogy built on the educational theory that in interreligious dialogue, all are teachers and learners. Each faith tradition has something to teach about its distinctive beliefs and practices and each has something to learn from the Other. This experience has the potential to enrich each tradition's understanding of the Other, while also deepening its own religious identity. The scholarship needed to sustain interreligious learning recognizes dialogue—and the new relations between Christians and Jews that come from that dialogue—as critical to the ultimate aims of scholarly inquiry.

An early example of implementing this conviction at CCJU was the 1992 program, the New Catechism Conferences. Conferences in major cities across the United States were geared toward priests, bishops, rabbis, and religious leaders and educators. Each conference featured Catholic and Jewish speakers who presented their perspective on the new Catholic Catechism. In the belief that the Catechism was a reference point for how the documents of the

past thirty years concerning Christian-Jewish relations were
embedded in the teachings of the Church, CCJU saw the text as
important both for educating a new generation of Catholics in the
substance and spirit of the Vatican II and as a vehicle for promoting
dialogue between Christians and Jews.

Initiatives at CCJU expanded again in 1995 when it embarked
on a Teacher Education Conference in cooperation with the
German Society for Christian-Jewish Collaboration. In 1996,
CCJU also sponsored a symposium on values in education. The
conference made the connection between reform in values
education and the diminishing of violence through pedagogical
principles that embrace reconciliation. In hindsight, the conference
was a harbinger of ideas promoted in the 1998 document, *We
Remember,* which held up the need for *teshuvah* (a turning away
from wrong and a returning to a right relationship) in Christian-
Jewish relations.

Symbolic Gestures of Substance

In addition to important theological and scholarly work, the
deepening of dialogue between Christians and Jews increasingly
took place through the use of symbolic gestures that raised political
awareness. It also underscored the difficult lesson that knowledge of
the Other must be accompanied by the repentance of past faults in
order that a trusting and fruitful relationship can be established and
sustained. Beginning in the late 1990s, the Center for Christian-
Jewish Understanding embarked on a strategy for making use of
substantive symbolic gestures as a core part of its educational
agenda. CCJU developed programs, conferences, and publications
that educated to a deeper level of reflection by showing the value of
such gestures to inform theologically, challenge morally, and lead to
respectful dialogue.

One such educational and fundraising program began in 1996
with the aim of recognizing examples of Jewish and Christian
leaders who had significantly advanced the cause of interreligious
understanding with its annual *Nostra Aetate* Awards Program. The

first *Nostra Aetate* award recipients were Cardinal John O'Connor of the Archdiocese of New York and Connecticut Senator Joseph Lieberman. Now in its tenth year, the awards program seeks to create national and international awareness for the work of leading figures in interreligious dialogue who symbolize the tenets and the promise of *Nostra Aetate*.

Another effort was a conference sponsored in Auschwitz, on the theme of "Religion and Violence, Religion and Peace." Participants included Jewish, Christian, and Muslim leaders from twelve countries. The conference was a historic first for its inclusion of five Orthodox rabbis in an interfaith discussion Their inclusion overturned the Orthodox prohibition (with its roots in the anti-Semitic aggression of the Inquisition) of participating in interreligious dialogue of a theological nature. Other symbolic gestures that taught theologically as well as morally included the 1998 CCJU visit to the Holy Land to establish a Papal Forest in Nazareth to be shared by surrounding Jewish, Christian, and Muslim communities. CCJU also participated in the Interreligious Assembly for Peace held at the Vatican (1999). Rabbi Joseph Ehrenkranz, executive director of CCJU, was one of twelve Jewish leaders attending.

In all these events, CCJU both initiated and partnered with interreligious organizations, in addition to the Vatican, in teaching the knowledge of the Other through a process of dialogue that embraced both theological reflection and reconciliation. This was executed in the context of highly visible symbolic places, people, and programs that explicitly made the connection between interreligious knowledge of the Other and the transformation that is possible when the mistakes of the past are no longer denied or revised but remembered in order to facilitate repentance.

Using the document *We Remember* as an illustration, the critical link between reflection and repentance may be argued to have been most forcefully made not in 1998 (when the document was issued) but in 2000, when Pope John Paul II made a pilgrimage to the Holy Land. The document called for *teshuvah*, and earlier the pope's 2000 visit symbolically enacted *teshuvah*. The document taught the failings of members of the Church with respect to the *Shoah*, while the papal visit transformed that awareness to a deeper level of reflection and repentance within the worldwide Catholic community.

Leaders of the Center for Christian-Jewish Understanding accompanied John Paul II on this pilgrimage, which included a visit to the Church of the Annunciation in Nazareth coinciding with the Roman Catholic Church's worldwide Feast of the Annunciation, the day of March 25 when Catholics commemorate the Angel Gabriel's announcement of the "good news" to the young Jewish woman, Mary, that she would conceive and bear her son, Jesus. John Paul's visit extended the "good news" to symbolize reconciliation and peace with the Jewish people. Likewise, a visit to the Papal Forest, mentioned above, symbolized the "common ground" from which the growth in Jewish-Christian relations would flourish in the years to come.

The visceral impact of Pope John Paul II's visit to the Western Wall, the holiest site of the Jewish people, and his prayer of forgiveness made on this site was well-described by Israeli Ambassador to the Holy See, Aharon Lopez, when he stated: "By following the Jewish tradition, he won the hearts of Israelis."[3] This historic journey of healing concluded with the visit to the Tent of Remembrance at Yad Vashem, the Holocaust Memorial that bears witness to the six million Jews who perished under Nazi tyranny. Israeli Prime Minister Eliud Barak described the event as the climax of the historic pilgrimage of reconciliation and a moment that held within it 2,000 years of Jewish-Christian history.

Learning With the Other

A key initiative of the Center for showing how to teach about the Other was the five-year series of international conferences on the theme "What Do We Want the Other to Teach About Us?" The conferences held in Jerusalem, Rome, Edmonton (Canada), Bamberg (Germany), and Fairfield, Connecticut (United States) were based on the principle that adequately understanding the

Other must be complemented by the need for the Other to be presented accurately.

In this form of educational engagement, each participant and tradition is able to experience being the "other" to someone else. The result of this dialogical process was an educational method that was both theological and pedagogical in approach. In 2006, CCJU published selected papers from the conferences in a volume titled *What Do We Want the Other to Teach About Us?*, representing the responses of Jewish, Christian, and Muslim scholars to this key question.

Educating Leaders

From the time of its inception, CCJU had focused its teaching on scholars, religious leaders and educators. Programs such as the catechetical and Holocaust teacher education conferences, ongoing lecture series, and publications (including the semi-annual publication, *CCJU Perspective*) enabled the Center to reach a broad national audience of key influencers in educational and pastoral ministries. In this context, CCJU's teaching was directed, at one level, to fostering understanding of Judaism in its work with local educators and religious leaders in schools, churches, and synagogues.

At another level, CCJU's international conferences for advancing theological inquiry and dialogue reached an even greater audience of scholars and religious leaders via publication in a variety of volumes, including *Towards Greater Understanding* (1997), *Religion and Violence, Religion and Peace* (1999), *Religion, Violence and Peace: Continuing Conversations and Study Guide* (2003), and the previously mentioned *What Do We Want the Other To Teach About Us?* (all published by the Sacred Heart University Press).

A third initiative by CCJU to educate leaders is its Annual Institute for Seminarians and Rabbinical Students. Launched in 2000 to introduce Jewish and Christian aspiring clergy to the questions, problems, and opportunities they may encounter in Christian-Jewish relations, the Annual Institute recognized that the education of emerging leaders was essential for future growth in interreligious dialogue. Besides offering students a forum for interreligious dialogue, access to first-class speakers, and materials and resources on Christian-Jewish understanding, the Annual Institute often serves as a springboard for continuing relationships between the future Jewish and Christian religious leaders of the United States. When nearly two hundred seminarians and rabbinical students had participated in the CCJU Institute, an additional program, Colleagues in Dialogue, was established to sustain the study, conversations and relationships begun at the Institute. This program has been reconvening annually since 2005.

The sustained effort by the Center to support young religious leaders was also the inspiration for another program launched in September 2005, the U.S. Bishops Study Tour. During the first study tour, Rabbi Joseph Ehrenkranz, executive director of the Center, and I, in my official capacity as president of Sacred Heart University, led six American bishops and two Orthodox rabbis to Krakow and Rome. The purpose of the study tour was to pilot a program that would help to foster interreligious dialogue among world religious leaders that could become a model for all religious leaders. The goal was for the leaders to learn from each other the theological, historical, and spiritual connections between Jews and Christians and to build bridges of understanding, thus preparing the way for generations to come.

Through a process of immersion, the bishops and rabbis visited the Nazi camps of Auschwitz and Birkenau. This visit formed the basis for an honest dialogue on the meaning of the *Shoah* for Jews and Christians. On the second part of the study tour, in Rome, the group met with leaders of the Vatican's Pontifical Commission for Religious Relations with the Jews to discuss ways of improving dialogue worldwide. At the Great Synagogue of Rome, the city where the Jewish people have the longest continuous history in Europe, participants learned together about prayer and liturgy in the Jewish tradition. Later, the Israeli Ambassador to the Holy See, Oded Ben-Hure, led a discussion on the importance of understanding the state of Israel for restoring world Jewry. The U.S. Bishops Study Tour program will continue with a second group in September 2007.

Summary

The origins and development of the Center for Christian-Jewish Understanding of Sacred Heart University illustrate that the growth and success of this Center is indebted to the visionary work of the Institute for Judeo-Christian Studies at Seton Hall University. Many Centers around the world have together made center-based work the preeminent institutional expression of interreligious dialogue following the Second Vatican Council. There is no one-size-fits-all approach to a Center, since both the content and the audience for such work is broad and diverse. The growth of local centers, either independent or affiliated with the academy, facilitates educational outreach directed at teachers, local Christian and Jewish religious leaders, and the broader community. These Centers will continue to be critical in providing a grassroots orientation to interreligious knowledge and dialogue.

The CCJU model of interreligious dialogue that has emerged over the past fifteen years is distinguished by a national and international presence among religious, educational, and public leaders for the purposes of advancing scholarship and fostering relationships of mutual respect among Christians and Jews. Along with an emphasis on scholarship and intellectual exchange, the history of CCJU also underscores the important human dimension of forging relationships of trust and openness. Based on its past successes, the Center will continue to foster interfaith study and dialogue in the presence of the Other as an ideal model of learning.

Future Challenges

Looking forward to future challenges and opportunities for center-based work in interreligious dialogue, it may be said that more than forty years after *Nostra Aetate*, centers for dialogue and understanding have helped to create a culture of dialogue. They have educated a great number and variety of people to a reinvigorated model of dialogue. Whereas religious dialogue in the not-too-distant past was defined by negotiation, compromise, or correction, the work of the Centers has transformed that process. Today, dialogue assumes an attitude of openness and a respect for the truth of the Other, as well as the freedom to express that truth. Dialogue now places more importance on the act of listening, rather than speaking, to the Other. Dialogue is seen in its role in spiritual/pastoral and intellectual growth, as the deeper understanding of the Other's beliefs, as a means of enriching one's own.

On the immediate horizon of the interreligious study center, four challenges appear:

1) *The violence of some religious groups in acts of terror and aggression that threaten to derail even the most committed attempts at sustained dialogue among Jews, Christians, and Muslims.* Dialogue requires participants to listen before all else and requires finding equal partners on all sides of the divide who are willing to enter into respectful dialogue and come to reconciliation over the errors of past relations.

2) *The promotion of continuing theological scholarship in the field of interreligious study.* The questions that must be asked and answered are "How can the best thinkers among emerging scholars be attracted to the field and how can universities support such scholars and scholarship?"

3) *Bringing the agenda of interreligious understanding into the public square.* "Interreligious" should not mean that only religious leaders or educators are the dialogue partners. National and international public leaders must be more deliberately brought into interreligious conversations promoted by centers.

4) *The quest to sustain momentum.* This is a challenge that every religious movement eventually faces. In the late 1960s, *Nostra Aetate* provided the catalyst for a worldwide renewal in theology and relationships. Private funding for Holocaust education and awareness in the 1980s helped to reeducate generations of Americans on the recorded history and moral lessons of the *Shoah*. From the late 1990s up until his death, Pope John Paul II's letters and symbolic gestures invigorated interreligious dialogue by giving it a dimension that was capable of moving the worldwide Christian

community towards reconciliation with Jews. The work of interreligious education, dialogue, and understanding has from its earliest days rested on the shoulders of great visionaries. As the efforts of interreligious centers continue and expand, the challenge will be one of future leadership. It is my hope that many will take up this noble vocation.

Notes

1. Quoted in Philip A. Cunningham, "Uncharted Waters: The Future of Catholic-Jewish Relations," *Commonweal* 133, no. 13 (July 14, 2006).

2. Walter Cardinal Kasper, "The Role of the Church and a Catholic University in the Contemporary World," *CCJU Perspective* 10, no. 1 (fall 2003), 32.

3. Aharon Lopez, quoted in David L. Coppola, "A Pilgrimage of Peace," *CCJU Perspective* 7, no. 1 (spring 2000), 17.

Nostra Aetate:
A Catholic Act of Metanoia

PHILIP A. CUNNINGHAM

Introduction

The Second Vatican Council's 1965 *Declaration on the Relationship of the Church to Non-Christian Religions*, known by its opening Latin words, "In our time" or "In our age," *Nostra Aetate*, is rightly called a revolutionary document. Although it was the first authoritative conciliar and magisterial statement in history to address the Catholic Church's relations with the Jewish people and tradition, it nonetheless reversed centuries and centuries of standard Christian presuppositions and teachings about Jews. It launched a trajectory of unprecedented Catholic reform and creativity.

Its impact continues to unfold today as we observe the declaration's fortieth anniversary, even though—in the words of Cardinal Walter Kasper, current president of the Pontifical Commission for Religious Relations with the Jews—we are probably still only at "the beginning of the beginning" of a deep-seated process of reform.[1] Indeed, the renewal catalyzed by *Nostra Aetate* can properly be described by the Greek word *metanoia*, in Hebrew *teshuvah*, a complete "turning," a total reorientation of attitude or action. This can be demonstrated by considering Catholic perspectives before 1965, the story of the composition of the document, and the development of its key points over the past four decades. This essay will focus on the Declaration's importance for Catholic-Jewish relations, the original concern from which eventually emerged the final version that discussed all religions.

The Catholic Theological Stance
Toward Jews and Judaism Before *Nostra Aetate*

The *metanoia*, the turnaround represented by *Nostra Aetate*, becomes strikingly clear if one contrasts pre-Vatican II Catholic understandings with those that began to arise subsequently. In 1938, Pope Pius XI commissioned the preparation of an encyclical letter that ultimately was never promulgated because of his death. To be titled *Humani Generis Unitas* (*The Unity of the Human Race*), this letter was intended to condemn racism in the wake of Hitler's rise to power in Germany. A section of the draft of the encyclical dealing with anti-Semitism provides a convenient synopsis of pre-Vatican II Catholic theological perspectives on Jews and Judaism.[2]

While rebuking circumstances in which "millions of [Jewish] persons are deprived of the most elementary rights and privileges of citizens" (246), the draft goes on to state that there is an "authentic basis of the social separation of the Jews from the rest of humanity" (247). This "authentic" reason for discrimination was not because of race but because of religion: "The Savior . . . was rejected by that people, violently repudiated, and condemned as a criminal by the highest tribunals of the Jewish nation. . . . [However,] the very act by which the Jewish people put to death their Savior and King was . . . the salvation of the world (248-49).

Having asserted that the "Jewish nation" bore a collective responsibility for the death of Jesus, the draft claims that Jews were doomed "to perpetually wander over the face of the earth . . . [and were] never allowed to perish, but have been preserved through the ages into our own time" (249). The draft opined that there exists "a historic enmity of the Jewish people to Christianity, creating a perpetual tension between Jew and Gentile" (251-52). Therefore, the Church has constantly had to be on guard against "the spiritual dangers to which contact with the Jews can expose souls" (252). This danger, which "is not diminished in our own time" (252), was "the authentic basis of the social separation of the Jews from the rest of humanity" (247).

It must be stressed that it is not known whether Pius XI would have approved these words. Clearly, the drafters of this text operated with theological ideas about Jews that undermined their ability to condemn the racist policies of the Nazis. Indeed, the "social separation of the Jews from the rest of humanity" is a goal that Hitler could claim he was merely implementing.

The draft's main theological positions about Jews—that they had killed Christ, that they were doomed to eternal wandering, and that they posed a constant danger to Christian souls—were simply restatements of elements of the perennial Christian "teaching of contempt" that had persisted for over 1,500 years.[3] A third-century teaching by Origen is frequently quoted because it neatly summarizes so many elements of this teaching of contempt:

> One of the facts which show that Jesus was some divine and sacred person is just that on his account such great and fearful calamities have now for a long time befallen the Jews . . . For they committed the most impious crime of all, when they conspired against the Savior of mankind, in the city where they performed to God the customary rites which were symbols of profound mysteries. Therefore that city where Jesus suffered these indignities had to be utterly destroyed. The Jewish nation had to be overthrown, and God's invitation to blessedness transferred to others, I mean the Christians, to whom came the teaching about the simple and pure worship of God. And they received new laws which fit in with the order established everywhere.[4]

Among other possible observations, it is clear that the collective blaming of "the Jews" for the crucifixion of Jesus, together with attendant consequences, has endured down the centuries from the patristic era to the preparation of the encyclical draft in 1938. In the words of Cardinal Edward Cassidy, president of the Pontifical Commission for Religious Relations with the Jews from 1989-2000, "preaching accused the Jews of every age of deicide."[5]

However, another long-standing Christian belief expressed by Origen did not appear in the draft of *Humani Generis Unitas*. This is the notion that God's covenant with the Jewish people, and hence their calling as God's Chosen People, had ended because of the crucifixion and had been transferred to the Church. Notably, the draft asserted:

> Israel remains the chosen people, for its election has never been revoked. Through the ineffable mercy of God, Israel may also share in the redemption that Israel's own rejection has made available to the Gentiles, who had themselves been unbelievers. . . . [St. Paul] holds out still the possibility of salvation to the Jews, once they are converted from their sins, and return to the spiritual tradition of Israel, which is properly theirs by their historic past and calling. (251, 250)

Key to analyzing this comment theologically is the phrase "return to the spiritual tradition of Israel." The authors of the draft apparently believed that their Jewish contemporaries had departed from Israel's heritage. Israel here is understood as biblical Israel, whose traditions are significant to the authors only because they prepared for the coming of Christ and the Church. Thus, their argument is that while Jews remain the Chosen People, they have betrayed their own spiritual heritage because of their rejection of the Christian message. In this wayward state, they stand outside of salvation despite their chosen status.

The Conception and Gestation of *Nostra Aetate*

Such was the Catholic theological landscape when Angelo Roncalli was elected Pope John XXIII on October 20, 1958. As a Vatican diplomat during the Second World War, he had facilitated the escape of thousands of Jews from the Nazis. His experiences surely motivated him when he became pope. On March 21, 1959, only two months after announcing that a great council would be held, he ordered the removal of the word *perfidus* from the Good

Friday prayer for the Jews. The next year, John XXIII greeted a delegation of American Jews with the biblical words, "I am Joseph your brother," suggesting that reconciliation between Catholic and Jews was imaginable, something akin to the Genesis reconciliation between Joseph and the brothers who had subjugated him. Most important, on September 18, 1960, he directed Cardinal Augustin Bea, S.J., president of the Secretariat for Promoting Christian Unity, to prepare a draft declaration for the upcoming council that would address the relations between the Church and the people of Israel.

However, the process of bringing *Nostra Aetate* to birth was a prolonged and difficult labor. Despite John XXIII's desire, it was not clear whether the proposed statement should be a free-standing document, part of the planned constitution on the Church, part of an ecumenical text on Christian unity, or, as ultimately happened, contained within a declaration on the Church's relations with all the other religions of the world. After all the bishops assembled in 1962, it became clear that there was opposition to the endeavor from both inside and outside the Council. Some bishops recoiled at the thought of changing long-standing teachings, while others feared for the safety of Christians in Arab countries. The press offices of various Middle-Eastern countries publicly campaigned against any statement that absolved "the Jews" of the crime of crucifying Jesus. Various procedural maneuvers were employed in an effort to scuttle the document, at one point causing Pope Paul VI to intervene to reinstate the proper process.

The eventual decision to address Judaism within the larger context of all the world's religions was a compromise that weakened the text's stress on the unique relationship between the Church and Israel, but was necessary, in the colorful image of Cardinal Kasper, "in order to save the furniture from the burning house."[6] Despite these travails, on October 28, 1965, the declaration was officially promulgated after a final, overwhelmingly favorable vote of 2,221 bishops for and 88 against.[7] For the first time in its almost two thousand year history, a formal council of the Catholic Church had issued an authoritative declaration on Catholic-Jewish relations.

The Teaching of *Nostra Aetate*

Although chapter 4 of the *Declaration*, the section concerning Jews and Judaism, is fairly brief, each phrase was repeatedly discussed and refined by the Council. The chapter has proven to be tremendously influential. The following seven items summarize its main points. In the subsequent forty years each of them has been expanded upon and intensified in official Catholic documents, as will be noted. Ongoing questions and issues will also be briefly mentioned.

1. *Nostra Aetate repudiated the long-standing "deicide" charge by declaring that "Jews should not be spoken of as rejected or accursed as if this followed from holy scripture."* This refutation of any notion of a divine curse upon Jews was an explicit reversal of a presupposition held universally by Christians for more than a millennium. No longer was it permissible for "preaching [to] accuse the Jews of deicide," as Cardinal Cassidy had put it. This in itself justifies describing the *Declaration* as revolutionary.

2. *Nostra Aetate stressed the religious bond and spiritual legacy shared by Jews and Church.* It acknowledged the Jewishness of Jesus, his mother, and the apostles, and recognized Christianity's debt to biblical Israel. This has become foundational in later Catholic ecclesiastical and theological writings. For example, John Paul II wrote movingly that "Jesus also came humanly to know [Israel's scriptures]; he nourished his mind and heart with them, using them in prayer and as an inspiration for his actions. Thus he became an authentic son of Israel, deeply rooted in his own people's long history."[8]

It remains an open question, though, whether most Christians in their religious imaginations really picture Jesus as "fully a man of his time, and of his environment—the Jewish Palestinian one of the first century, the anxieties and hopes of which he shared," or if they envision of him purely in terms of later Christian concepts.[9] Lingering habits of imagining Jesus as opposed to a supposed heartlessness or legalism of contemporary "Judaism" have not fully grappled with an appreciation of Jesus' Jewishness. Likewise, understanding what could be called the Jewishness of the early Church—in other words, that the Church was for many decades a movement *within* the diverse late-Second Temple period Jewish world—has not really penetrated Christian thinking at large, which is more comfortable thinking of a Church cleanly and distinctively separated, and even opposed to "Judaism" from as early as Pentecost, if not from Jesus' ministry itself.

On the other hand, the spiritual connectedness between the two traditions has been strongly emphasized since *Nostra Aetate*, perhaps most powerfully during John Paul II's historic visit to the Great Synagogue of Rome: "The Jewish religion is not 'extrinsic' to us, but in a certain way is 'intrinsic' to our own religion," he declared. "With Judaism therefore we have a relationship which we do not have with any other religion. You are our dearly beloved brothers and, in a certain way, it could be said that you are our elder brothers."[10] This familial attitude has been widely disseminated.

3. *Nostra Aetate strongly implied that God and Jews abide in covenant.* Citing Romans 11, the Council Fathers observed that "the Jews remain very dear to God, for the sake of the patriarchs, since God does not take back the gifts he bestowed or the choice he made." This was reinforced, as Eugene J. Fisher has pointed out, when *Nostra Aetate* rendered an ambiguous Greek verb in Romans 9:4-5 in the present tense: "They *are* Israelites and it is for them *to be* sons and daughters, to them *belong* the glory, the covenants, the giving of the law, the worship, and the promises; to them *belong* the patriarchs, and of their race according to the flesh, is the Christ."[11]

Nostra Aetate's implicit recognition that Israel abides in a perpetual covenantal relationship with God has subsequently been made fully explicit. John Paul II repeatedly taught that Jews are "the people of God of the Old Covenant, never revoked by God," "the present-day people of the covenant concluded with Moses," and "partners in a covenant of eternal love which was never revoked."[12]

The draft for the unrealized encyclical *Humani Generis Unitas* could also state that Israel's "election has never been revoked," but after the Second Vatican Council it was no longer possible to subordinate this notion to an alleged divine curse on Jews for the death of Jesus (251). Therefore, post-*Nostra Aetate* Catholic teaching has proceeded from a renewed awareness of the perpetuity of the Jewish people's covenant with God to unprecedented expressions of admiration for the post-biblical Jewish religious tradition.

Thus, the Vatican's 1974 *Guidelines and Suggestions for Implementing the Conciliar Declaration, Nostra Aetate No. 4* insisted that Christians "must strive to learn by what essential traits Jews define themselves in the light of their own religious experience."[13] Unlike the 1938 draft, these *Guidelines* could no longer continue the Christian habit of defining the Jewish heritage according to Christian categories or limiting Judaism's value to biblical Israel. Therefore, the *Guidelines* went on to warn that both the "Old Testament and the Jewish tradition must not be set against the New Testament in such a way that the former seems to constitute a religion of only justice, fear and legalism, with no appeal to the love of God and neighbor." This was a stereotypical contrast used by Christians over the centuries to devalue Judaism. In addition, the *Guidelines* pointed out that the "history of Judaism did not end with the destruction of Jerusalem, but rather went on to develop a religious tradition . . . rich in religious values."

The 1985 Vatican *Notes on the Correct Way to Present Jews and Judaism in Preaching and Teaching in the Roman Catholic Church* praised post-biblical Judaism for carrying "to the whole world a witness-often heroic-of its fidelity to the one God and to 'exalt Him in the presence of all the living' (Tobit 13:4)."[14] The *Notes* also cited John Paul II in reminding Catholics that

> the permanence of Israel [was] accompanied by a continuous spiritual fecundity, in the rabbinical period, in the Middle Ages and in modern times, taking its start from a patrimony which we long shared, so much so that 'the faith and religious life of the Jewish people as they are professed and practiced still today, can greatly help us to understand better certain aspects of the life of the Church. (John Paul II, March 6, 1982)

These formal expressions of esteem toward post-biblical Jewish traditions and the official encouragement of Catholics to learn both from these traditions and from the living Jewish community are not to be found in pre-Vatican II Catholic practice, which instead urged avoidance of Jews and occasionally destroyed Talmuds and other Jewish writings. This reversal is the result of *Nostra Aetate*'s repudiation of the deicide charge and its affirmation of the Jewish People's covenant with God. Nonetheless, the full, theological ramifications of this recognition of Israel's covenanting are still being explored.[15]

4. *Nostra Aetate* deplored *"all hatreds, persecutions, displays of antisemitism directed against the Jews at any time or from any source."* While *Nostra Aetate* did not confess *Christian* anti-Semitism or discuss the perennial Christian teaching of contempt for Jews, subsequent documents acknowledged Christian wrongdoing and labeled anti-Semitism as a sin against God and humanity. John Paul II would insist that a confrontation with the horrors of the *Shoah* must lead the Church to repentance: "For Christians the heavy burden of guilt for the murder of the Jewish people [during the *Shoah*] must be an enduring call to repentance; thereby we can overcome every form of anti-Semitism and establish a new relationship with our kindred nation of the Old Covenant."[16] John Paul II related this moral and spiritual challenge to the proper observance of the beginning of the third millennium of Christianity. Thus, on the First Sunday of Lent during the Great Jubilee of 2000, an unprecedented "Mass of Pardon" was offered at St. Peter's Basilica. The highest officials of the Roman Catholic Church joined with the pope in asking God's forgiveness for the sins of Christians during the previous millennium. Among the sins confessed was the teaching of contempt and Christianity's treatment of "the People of Israel."

Christian penitence has perhaps been expressed most iconically to date in Pope John Paul II's prayer at the Western Wall on March 26, 2000. Following the Jewish custom of inserting written prayers into the remains of the foundations of the Second Temple, John Paul II placed these words:

God of our fathers, you chose Abraham and his descendants to bring your Name to the Nations: we are deeply saddened by the behavior of those who in the course of history have caused these children of yours to suffer, and asking your forgiveness we wish to commit ourselves to genuine brotherhood with the people of the Covenant.[17]

The prayer was signed by the pope personally and stamped with the official papal seal, as if to establish without question the seriousness and permanence of the Catholic Church's ongoing commitment to reform and fellowship with the Jewish people. This is yet another manifestation of *metanoia* since such authoritative public expressions of remorse and solidarity were unheard of before *Nostra Aetate*.

5. *Nostra Aetate stressed the need for accurate biblical interpretation and religious education:* "All must take care, lest in catechizing or in preaching the word of God, they teach anything which is not in accord with the truth of the Gospel message or the spirit of Christ." This sentence introduced a hermeneutical principle for Catholic biblical interpretation that has been further intensified in later documents.[18]

Of particular note are the studies issued by the Pontifical Biblical Commission in 1993 and 2001. Especially significant is the instruction in the 1993 text that

Clearly to be rejected also is every attempt [to use] the bible to justify racial segregation, antisemitism, or sexism whether on the part of men or women. Particular attention is necessary, according to the spirit of the Second Vatican Council (*Nostra Aetate*, 4), to avoid absolutely any actualization of certain texts of the New Testament which could provoke or reinforce unfavorable attitudes toward the Jewish people. The tragic events of the past must, on the contrary, impel all to keep unceasing in mind that, according to the New Testament, the Jews remain "beloved" of God, "since the gifts and calling of God are irrevocable" (Rom 11:28-29).[19]

However, the controversy over the 2004 film, *The Passion of the Christ*, vividly established that conscious or unconscious presumptions about the Bible shape people's understandings of those New Testament passages most connected with attitudes toward Jews and Judaism. By combining crucial scenes unique to specific Gospels and importing non-biblical elements from writings attributed to Anne Catherine Emmerich, that film produced a more negative depiction of Jewish characters than any single Gospel conveys.[20] The fact that many Catholics failed to discern the movie's problems in this regard demonstrates that much work remains to be done in promoting Catholic principles of biblical interpretation.

6. *Nostra Aetate called for Catholics and Jews to collaborate in "biblical and theological enquiry and . . . friendly discussions."* This mandate directly contradicted the prior practice of discouraging Catholics from conversing with Jews on religious matters, as expressed by the worry in the draft of *Humani Generis Unitas* about "the spiritual dangers to which contact with the Jews can expose souls" (252). This reversal has contributed to an enormous number of dialogues on all levels around the world, to the establishment in the United States alone of over two dozen academic centers to promote Christian-Jewish studies,[21] and to many joint research initiatives among Jewish and Christian scholars. Such continuing research is bringing to light new evidence of how the Jewish and Christian communities have been interacting—both negatively and positively—for centuries. This ongoing interaction has exerted a major influence on how both traditions live out their covenantal relationship with God.

The past forty years of dialogue and joint activities that *Nostra Aetate* made possible has also shown that Jews and Christians come together with different interests, concerns, historical knowledge, and (mis)conceptions about each other. Christians tend to want to talk "religion," including why don't Jews "believe in Jesus," while Jews are more inclined to discuss social justice issues. Jews, understandably, tend to wonder if the unprecedented Christian overtures to dialogue are only a temporary cessation of the conversionary campaigns of the past, while Christians, usually unfamiliar with the history Christian oppression of Jews, can be shocked and guilt-ridden when learning of it for the first time. Christians may find it difficult to understand the depth of Jewish fears for the survival of the State of Israel or fright over upsurges in antisemitic incidents, while Jews tend to avoid expressing their general mystification over Christian claims that something called "salvation" is the result of the crucifixion of an individual Jew among the thousands of Jews executed under Roman imperial rule.

Sometimes lurking beneath the surface of interreligious encounters is a fear of what the dialogue will lead to. Co-religionists who have not had much experience of Christian-Jewish dialogue will accuse Christians of "watering down the faith" and will charge Jewish participants with inviting "assimilation." However, authentic interreligious dialogue has nothing to do with syncretism, or some sort of melding of two religious traditions. The boundaries between the two related heritages of Christianity and Judaism must be respected and maintained. However, the dialogue may cause those boundaries to be reconfigured or understood differently.

Fortunately, the past four decades have demonstrated that interreligious dialogue actually leads participants to a deeper understanding of their own tradition as a result of being asked new questions or of viewing their own tradition from the Other's perspective. It is the universal experience of everyone I know who has been involved in dialogue beyond a superficial level that their own identities as Jews or Christians have been enhanced by the dialogue. They are not the same Christians or Jews that they were before experiencing dialogue, but they understand themselves to be more committed and discerning Christians or Jews. This transformation in self-understanding can be expected to continue to evolve in the coming century.

7. *Nostra Aetate expressed no interest in further efforts to baptize Jews,* relegating the resolution of the Jewish and Christian disagreement over Jesus' significance and identity until the eschatological dawning of God's kingdom: "Together with the prophets and that same apostle, the church awaits the day, known to God alone, when all peoples will call on God with one voice and

serve him shoulder to shoulder." This phrase was carefully considered during the Council's deliberations, especially after controversy arose in the public media in the summer and fall of 1964 over whether a leaked draft paragraph would encourage Catholics to try to baptize Jews. Famed Rabbi Abraham Joshua Heschel repeatedly and sensationally declared that he was "ready to go to Auschwitz any time, if faced with the alternative of conversion or death."[22]

This was the context for two crucial days of deliberation in the Second Vatican Council on September 28 and 29, 1964. Several cardinals and bishops specifically addressed the topic of conversionary efforts toward Jews. In different ways they urged that the question of a collective Jewish turn to Christianity should be understood as an eschatological matter; in other words, that it was not the task of Catholics in historical time to try to baptize all Jews.[23] Thus, the final wording of *Nostra Aetate*—that the Church awaits a day known to God alone—was intended to convey, in the words of Cardinal Giacomo Lercaro of Bologna, that "only an eschatological turn of events will bring [Jews and Christians] to the common messianic meal of the eternal Pasch."[24]

Today, unlike some other Christian communities, the Catholic Church allocates no financial or personnel resources for the baptism of Jews. However, the theological reasons for this abandonment of previous and persistent Christian efforts have not yet achieved a definitive articulation in Catholic teaching, no doubt because Catholic insight into the nature of Israel's covenanting with God is still emerging.[25] The theological question that lingers is how the universal grace made available by Jesus Christ relates to or is manifested in the covenantal life between God and the Jewish people. There are a number of avenues that are being explored in pursuit of this question, but they have not yet achieved articulation in a Catholic magisterial document.

Conclusion

The above considerations have sought to illustrate the process of *metanoia*, of *teshuvah*, begun by *Nostra Aetate*. Its authoritative reversal of the tenets of the "teaching of contempt" has made possible an ongoing turnaround in relations between Catholics and Jews that will continue to unfold into the future. In my opinion, it is a journey that has gone too far for there to be any possibility of turning back. As Cardinal Cassidy has put it:

> Let us then turn to consider the future. Our first aim must of course be to press forward. To stand still is to risk going backwards—and I feel absolutely confident in stating that there will be no going back on the part of the Catholic Church. At the same time, there can be a lessening of enthusiasm, a growing indifference or even a renewed spirit of suspicion and mistrust among members of the Catholic community should our efforts to keep up the momentum slacken. . . . We remember, but we refuse to be tied down to the past by chains that hold us back from building a new future, a new partnership between Jews and Catholics, a future based on mutual trust and understanding.[26]

Notes

1. Walter Cardinal Kasper, "The Commission for Religious Relations with the Jews: A Crucial Endeavor of the Catholic Church," address delivered at Boston College on November 6, 2002; online at www.bc.edu/research/ cjl/meta-elements/texts/cjrelations/resources/articles/ Kasper_6Nov02.htm

2. See Georges Passelecq and Bernard Suchecky, *The Hidden Encyclical of Pius XI* (New York: Harcourt, Brace, and Co., 1997). All further references to this encyclical are cited in the text of my essay by page number only.

3. The phrase was coined by the French historian Jules Isaac. *The Teaching of Contempt: Christian Roots of Anti-Semitism* (New York: Holt, Rinehart and Winston, 1964).

4. Origen, *Contra Celsum*, IV, 22.

5. Edward Cardinal Idris Cassidy, "Reflections: The Vatican Statement on the *Shoah*," *Origins* 28/2 (May 28, 1998): 31.

6. Kasper, "A Crucial Endeavor."

7. See John M. Oesterreicher, _The New Encounter between Christians and Jews_ (New York: Philosophical Library, 1986) for the story of the development of _Nostra Aetate_.

8. John Paul II, "Address to the Pontifical Biblical Commission," April 11, 1997; online at www.bc.edu/research/cjl/meta-elements/texts/cjrelations/resources/documents/catholic/johnpaulii/pbcapril111999.htm

9. Pontifical Commission for Religious Relations with the Jews, _Notes on the Correct Way to Present Jews and Judaism in Preaching and Teaching in the Roman Catholic Church_ (1985), III, 12; online at www.bc.edu/research/cjl/meta-elements/texts/cjrelations/resources/documents/catholic/Vatican_Notes.htm

10. John Paul II, Address at the Great Synagogue of Rome, April 13, 1986, 4; online at www.bc.edu/research/cjl/meta-elements/texts/cjrelations/resources/documents/catholic/johnpaulii/romesynagogue.htm

11. Eugene J. Fisher, "Official Roman Catholic Teaching on Jews and Judaism: Commentary and Context," in _In Our Time: The Flowering of Jewish-Catholic Dialogue_, ed. Eugene J. Fisher and Leon Klenicki (New York: Paulist Press, 1990), 6.

12. The first two quotations are from John Paul II, "Address to the Jewish Community in Mainz, West Germany," November 17, 1980; online at www.bc.edu/research/cjl/meta-elements/texts/cjrelations/ resources/documents/catholic/johnpaulii/Mainz.htm. The last quotation is from John Paul II, "Address to Jewish Leaders in Miami," September 11, 1987, in Eugene J. Fisher and Leon Klenicki, eds., _Spiritual Pilgrimage: John Paul II—Texts on Jews and Judaism 1979-1995_ (New York: Crossroad, 1995), 105-08.

13. Pontifical Commission for Religious Relations with the Jews: _Guidelines and Suggestions for Implementing the Conciliar Declaration, Nostra Aetate No. 4_ (1974), Prologue; online at www.bc.edu/research/cjl/meta-elements/texts/cjrelations/resources/documents/Catholic/Vatican_Guideline.htm

14. Pontifical Commission for Religious Relations with the Jews, _Notes on the Correct Way to Present Jews and Judaism in Preaching and Teaching in the Roman Catholic Church_ (1985), VI, 25; online at www.bc.edu/research/cjl/meta-elements/texts/cjrelations/resources/documents/catholic/Vatican_Notes.htm

15. Most recently in a collection of essays by members of the Christian Scholars Group on Christian-Jewish Relations: Mary C. Boys, ed,. _Seeing Judaism Anew: Christianity's Sacred Obligation_ (Lanham: Rowman and Littlefield, 2005).

16. John Paul II, "Address to the New Ambassador of the Federal Republic of Germany to the Holy See," November 8, 1990, in Fisher and Klenicki, eds., *Spiritual Pilgrimage*, 138.

17. John Paul II, "Prayer at the Western Wall," March 26, 2000.

18. Eugene J. Fisher, "Official Roman Catholic Teaching," 7.

19. Pontifical Biblical Commission, "The Interpretation of the Bible in the Church" (1993), IV,A,3; online at www.bc.edu/research/cjl/meta-elements/texts/cjrelations/resources/documents/catholic/pbcinterpretation.htm

20. See my analysis, "Gibson's *The Passion of the Christ*: A Challenge to Catholic Teaching"; available at www.bc.edu/research/cjl/meta-elements/texts/cjrelations/resources/reviews/gibson_cunningham.htm

21. Visit the webpages of the Council of Centers for Jewish-Christian Relations (CCJR) at www.ccjr.us.

22. Beatrice Bruteau, ed., *Merton and Judaism, Holiness in Words: Recognition, Repentance, and Renewal* (Louisville, KY: Fons Vitae, 2003), 223-24.

23. This, of course, does not exclude individual Jews who might choose to exercise their freedom of religion and seek baptism.

24. Oesterreicher, *New Encounter*, 204-05.

25. Though see the text and discussion of the 2002 dialogue document of delegates of the U.S. Bishops Committee on Ecumenical and Interreligious Affairs and the National Council of Synagogues, "Reflections on Covenant and Mission"; online at www.bc.edu/research/cjl/cjrelations/resources/articles/#reflections

26. Edward Idris Cardinal Cassidy, "Catholic-Jewish Relations: 1990-2001." Address delivered at the 17th meeting of the International Catholic-Jewish Liaison Committee, New York, May 1, 2001; online at www.bc.edu/research/cjl/meta-elements/texts/cjrelations/resources/articles/cassidy2.htm

Nostra Aetate: *What Difference Is It Making in North America?*

Frans Jozef van Beeck

Preliminary: Introductory Question and Necessary Answer

Vatican II started with an impasse. Its preparatory committees had been out of touch with the Catholic Church at large.[1] Pope John XXIII saw it and responded with a typically Catholic move: he proposed that the reform of the Liturgy be the first business to start work on. Experience virtually all over the world has reconfirmed that the eucharistic Liturgy is the single most important source of the self-experience of the Roman Catholic Church, the very Body of Christ at worship in the Spirit. Hence both the global acceptance of the "New Liturgy" and the continuing frictions around it in some few places.

This book of essays celebrates *Nostra Aetate,* the Catholic Church's long-overdue farewell to habits of open hostility toward non-Christians, and its conversion, at Vatican II, to liberal encounter. "In our lifetime," not only has our common humanity been propelling us in the direction of mutual understanding; even God's Word in writing, revered by Jews and venerated by Muslims, has revealed affinities rarely if ever acknowledged by Catholics before. There is a problem, though. Open hostility to non-Christians is not really part of North American history, unless we wish to plead guilty to charges brought by Native American survivors, a topic left untouched by Vatican II. Why, then, focus on *Nostra Aetate?* This author has concluded that any sound theological answer to this question must wait a bit. So for now, let us focus on

Nostra Aetate's far more radical companion piece, *Dignitatis Humanae* (*Human Dignity*)—Vatican II's *Declaration on Religious Freedom*.

This implies that my essay will be a finger-exercise in cultural-theological discernment.[2] So, let us ask a question that is both theologically and politically legitimate, as follows. Given that the Catholic Church's central teaching that God is present in the Holy Spirit in Jesus Christ, who died and is risen, to what extent and how is the very successful secular culture of North America, in which we Catholics share, likely to empower us or hinder us in being Catholic Christians? Unsurprisingly (and *pace* most North American Protestants and ecumenists), any Catholic answer will have to be: much as North America has been the bringer of freedom of religion and conscience in the modern world, its constitutional principles and practices can only conditionally guarantee the freedoms necessary for fully responsible membership in the Catholic Church. Put differently, our culture cannot positively support (never mind join) the Catholic Church in its commitment, stated in *Nostra Aetate*, to end any open hostility to non-Christians and pursue paths of peace.[3]

Freedom of Religion:
A "Liberal" North American Victory?

In many ways, at Vatican II the notion of religious freedom was the North American import article *par excellence*. No wonder it met with stiff resistance among a vocal, largely Mediterranean minority at the Council, still accustomed to Justinian's implicit thesis, imposed by the imperial decree *Cunctos populos* in 380 A.D., that "error has no rights." Over time, it had been variously adopted by Orthodox Jews, Catholics, and Protestants; only the radical Reformers had proposed to give it up. Thus, was *Dignitatis Humanae* a clear North American victory? Its chief architect, John Courtney Murray, S.J. (1904-67), was well-satisfied with it, but greeted it not with fanfare but prophetic caution:

The notion of development, not the notion of religious freedom, was the real sticking-point for many of those who opposed the Declaration even to the end. The course of the development between the *Syllabus of Errors* (1864) and *Dignitatis Humanae Personae* (1965) remains to be explained by theologians. But the Council formally sanctioned the validity of the development itself; and this was a doctrinal event of high importance for theological thought in many other areas. . . .

Inevitably, a second great argument will be set afoot now on *the theological meaning of Christian freedom.* The children of God, who receive this freedom as a gift from their Father through Christ in the Holy Spirit, assert it within the Church as well as within the world, always for the sake of the world and the Church. The issues are many the dignity of the Christian, the foundations of Christian freedom, its object or content, its limits and their criterion, the measure of its responsible use, its relation to the legitimate reaches of authority and to the saving counsels of prudence, the perils that lurk in it, and the forms of corruption to which it is prone. All these issues must be considered in a spirit of sober and informed reflection.[4]

Murray realized, of course, that freedom from state-sponsored (or "established") religion had been the climate of the Catholic Church's development and growth in the Western hemisphere, and that it implied a secular universalism from which there was no retreating; the New World, and North America in particular, had been riding the wave of the future. Still, Murray was enough of a Catholic theologian to understand that two painfully inadequate theological—non-political issues—remained to be tackled. They can be summarized in two routine Catholic idioms: "the teaching of the Church" and "being a good Catholic." Together, what do they come to? They express a key norm: "good Catholics" have duties to acknowledge, and the first is acceptance of "the teaching of the Church." But since *Dignitatis Humanae Personae*, the Church's teaching is no longer as plump as a pincushion, for it involves, as

Murray well saw, the interpretation of "the development between the *Syllabus of Errors* (1864) and *Dignitatis Humanae* (1965)"; even more ominously, "good Catholic" now raises "the theological meaning of Christian freedom," to be affirmed "within the Church as well as within the world, always for the sake of the world and the Church." A quick comparison helps clarify the sheer novelty of this.

A Basic Example: Second-Century Christians

Let us go back to the second century, specifically the *Letter to Diognetus* (*c.* 130-200 A.D.). First off, it is not a normative statement on what human beings, Christians or non-Christians, should or should not do. Secondly, it states, descriptively, what actual, historic Christians made of themselves in a culture they recognized as alien. Thirdly, it states some of what Christians typically did—what difference they made in practice, and thus, in the eyes of others:

> Christians are distinguished from the rest of people neither by country, nor by language, nor by customs. For nowhere do they live in cities of their own, nor do they use some different form of speech, nor do they practice a peculiar way of life. For that matter, they do not possess anything elaborated by ingenious or intelligent people; nor are they masters of any human rule of life as some people are. They do not champion, like others, a human philosophy of life. Yet . . . they make no secret of the remarkable and admittedly extraordinary nature of their citizenship. . . . Every foreign country is homeland to them, and every homeland is foreign. . . . They marry like everybody and beget children; but they do not expose their newly-born. The table they provide is common, but not the bed. They obey the established laws, and in their own lives they surpass the laws. They love all, and they are persecuted by all. They are off the beaten track, yet they are condemned. They are put to death, and yet they are filled with life. They

live in penury, yet they make many rich. They are in want
of all things, and yet they abound in all things. They are
dishonored, yet in their very dishonor they are glorified. . . .
Jews wage war on them as aliens, and Greeks take potshots at
them, yet none of those who hate them can give reasons for
their hostility. In a word, what the soul is in the body,
Christians are in the world.[5]

The last line of the text, faintly Platonic, is the clincher. It
goes back to a series of allusions in Paul's letters to the Christians
in Corinth (e.g., 2 Cor 6:9-10). Paul wrote them tongue-in-cheek,
to make it clear to Christian communities that his own life as an
apostle of Jesus Christ was unlikely to find any great acclaim in the
world he was living in. The writer of the *Letter to Diognetus* agrees.
He and his fellow Christians have made their peace with
harassment. The Greco-Roman Empire and its elites liked to
depict themselves as free, enlightened, and unprejudiced. The
writer begs to differ: he and his associates do not feel at home, but
then again, they do not expect to feel at home. Yet, there is no
trace of criticism of, or exhortation to, the world. Unmistakable,
too, are the mild references to what we would call "life issues":
typically, Christians make a difference between table and bed,
between welcoming children and doing away with them. They do
not claim perfection, nor do they come with a forceful message;
yet they do live as a body "incorporate." That is to say, they
implicitly take seriously the Real Presence of God's Word in Jesus
Christ—one of our kind, different in only one thing: he could not
get himself to sin.

Taking the Culture Seriously: Early Christian Thinking

This raises a question. Christians *acted* differently from the
culture in which they lived. What did they *think* of it? Brilliant
Origen (*c.* 182-251 A.D.), in the eyes of many the first great
Christian theologian, mentor, and educator, is an early instance of
the Christian approach.

Around 240 A.D., he wrote a letter to a young friend and former student, Gregory, later to be nicknamed Thaumatourgos—"the marvel-maker." Born in *c.* 210-13 A.D. in Neocaesarea in distant Pontus, where his family was a commanding presence, Gregory had ended up in Palestinian Caesarea—modern Haifa—for an education. (By contrast, Origen, born into a fiercely Christian family in the city of Alexandria in Egypt, had become a commanding absence at home; defying his metropolitan's explicit order to teach in his home city, he had traveled to Caesarea, where he accepted a teaching position and, a few years later, presbyteral ordination.) Under Origen's tutelage, Gregory became a Christian. In 237 A.D., he left to return to Neocaesarea, not without giving a mighty graduation address in praise of his mentor. A little later he also accepted ordination as a missionary bishop, to enable him to convert his home town and region to the Christian faith, a religion still apt to attract the Roman emperors' unfriendly attention.

Not long after his departure, Origen wrote Gregory a letter, to remind him of what he had been taught, and how and why:

> But all I have ever desired for you is that you should apply your entire talent to being a Christian. Thus, in practical terms, I had the wish for you to take in the philosophy of the Greeks as well—anything that could shed light on being a Christian or serve as an introduction to it. This would include whatever matters from geometry and astronomy that might have a bearing on the interpretation of Sacred Scripture. The aim would be this. Whatever we know students in philosophical schools are learning in the way of geometry and music, grammar and rhetoric, and astronomy, all in the service of philosophy, we would do the same in regard to philosophy itself: lead you to being a Christian.[6]

In this passage, what is striking to modern ears is the firmness with which the Christian spirit is already taking the measure both of itself and of the current best in Greco-Roman culture. The pursuit is philosophy—i.e., understanding and wisdom as well as habits of eloquent persuasion to win the loyalties of city crowds as well as rural folk—all in the interest of civilized human life together, yet now in Christ. The larger cities, all of them centers of far-flung trade, were proud of their schools and of the famous teachers who had left their mark on them. The sons of landed elites everywhere in the empire had long been fascinated by them; the young bloods went out to learn what it takes to do their duty as respected local leaders, and as often as not, to sow their wild oats at a convenient distance from home, where they must spend their reputable careers. (The memory of his Roman years drove Jerome into lifelong learning, meddling, and exile.)

Christians were getting themselves emancipated pretty much along the same lines. Thus Justin (*c.* 100-165 A.D.), born in Samaria—the modern Nablus—traveled westward in search of true knowledge, and was won over in Asia Minor by Polycarp (*c.* 70-*c.* 155), who had known the Apostle John; from there, he went to Rome to start a school of "true philosophy." We know some of what he taught from the three apologies in defense of the Christian faith come down to us. Eventually, he was made to pay for his move to imperial Rome with his life.

In fact, entire urban Christian communities had gathered this way. Bolting first from inhospitable Jewish Jerusalem, and after 70 A.D. from its ruins, they had settled, under Peter, in Antioch, where they were first nicknamed Christians (Acts 11:26); from Antioch, they had gone *in Urbem*—to Rome, the City *par excellence* of the empire.

Paul, the ever-traveling apostle, a Roman citizen by birth but a Jerusalem-trained Pharisee as well, was on his way there, too. But Paul had to be careful, as his letter to the Romans intimates. He wisely realized that he needed to offer arguments in defense of his apostolic mettle. He must reassure not just any full-blooded Jewish Roman Christians (who had reason to distrust him), but also such gentiles as had been Jewish proselytes before joining their fellow Jews in joining the Christian community in Rome.[7]

By settling in cities, the Christian communities also showed that they had what we would now call a global agenda.[8] They figured they had news—they called it "the Good News"—for the whole world, physically. In this particular regard, they sounded very much like Jesus of Nazareth, whose teaching and individual lifestyle, open, mild, welcoming, and tough as they had been, had been nothing if not radical, eschatological, and encompassing. He had extended to all comers an offer of actual membership in God's universal Kingship, to Israel first of all, but never without the universalist perspective so typical of Second Temple and Hellenistic Judaism, both in and around Jerusalem and in the far-flung diaspora. Jesus, now known as the Christ, had "shown" that God's kingship was here, barely around the corner, and he had enacted it in and around himself. No wonder Origen could call Jesus *autobasileia*: "the kingdom in person."[9]

Oddly, a stylistic conclusion follows at once. From the start, Christians have spoken the language of self-involvement.[10] They were themselves part of their message, and thus, in their own eyes, of universal history. They were prophetic witnesses before they ever became historians, let alone (allegedly) objective historicists; like Jews (or, for that matter, all people of faith privileged enough to possess written sources), they represented a world that was as yet to come to perfection. Thus Christians always implied that they themselves were imperfect, together with their ever-unfinished world groaning for perfection, in their minds and at their hands. They typically have not pleaded their own consciences to justify their actions, nor have have they often called themselves "right," let alone "saved."

A perfect world, they knew, had never properly existed; even Eden remained to be cultivated. Yet in its past and present forms it had always been both the home and the immemorial challenge to the multiple branches of a human family that was plainly broken. Most of humanity, they understood, was barbarian, unintelligible, and thus, at the very least potentially dangerous—i.e., there was little hope for just treatment at the hands of aliens. Justice lay in warfare. Besides, even on the assumption that barbarians were rational, it was plain that none were satisfied with the state they were in. One nation's food was another nation's poison—one had, it appeared, to live with that; in the last resort, there was no relief in sight. Augustine summed up humanity's plight with the Stoic resignation of the wise: "Creatures endowed with reason [*rationalis creatura*] . . . are thus constituted: they are unable to be unto themselves the good by virtue of which they can become happy."[11]

What enabled Augustine to accept this? As a Christian, he had discovered that each and every bit of justice is gift, not performance. Human beings do not have it in them to make themselves perfectly happy. But God, endlessly giving, had definitively shown the Way to the End.

Besides, every kind of Jew (including the Christian kind) understood this from near-personal (or at least near-familial) historic experience. It stretched from Abraham-Isaac-and-Jacob-Israel on, from Moses and Joshua and David and Solomon (acknowledged sinners all of them) on, from the great captivity experience in the barbarian nations' sinful desert on (Ez 20, 35). All of it had everything to do with a Living God who could be trusted to guide as well as transform vulnerable humanity's great aspirations and near-predictable failures. Yet whatever "all of humanity" would turn out to be like, *all* of it could be expected to have in common one, and only one, prospect: death.[12]

In this context, so the Christians announced, humanity's definitive goal (and to that extent, its present course) had been decisively revised by one single human being, Jesus of Nazareth, both dead and alive. A Galilean Jew of obscure origin, accused of blasphemy by the Jewish religious authorities, and put to a criminal's death by the Roman procurator Pontius Pilate, just outside the city of Jerusalem, he was acknowledged (at least by Christians) to be now alive in what they knew was God's Holy Spirit, and thus, called Jesus Messiah (Gk. *Christos*) and worshiped as the Lord (Gk. *ho Kyrios*).

Interlude: A Topic Sentence

The preceding explanations have prepared us for the topic sentence of this essay. Here it is: There is no such thing as an impartial Christian theology. Put differently, the Christian faith is fundamentally a matter of preference or free choice. However, this implies that it can be practiced neither by mere compliance (that would reduce it to heteronomous subjection) nor by mere self-will (that would reduce it to autonomous, theocratic independence (or ditto counterdependence). For Christians, faith in God implies being privileged.[13] That is to say, it is a matter of theonomy—a divine favor thankfully accepted and endorsed, not a human accomplishment. Quite consistently with this, Christian doctrine ends with God's promise of the transformation of the universe.

Human Openness to Otherness: Some Telling Recent Events

When Hans-Georg Gadamer died in March of 2002, Pope John Paul II sent a telegram to the president of the German bishops' conference in praise of Gadamer, whom he had once met at Castel Gandolfo, for his recovery of tradition as the source of sound judgment. In his masterpiece, *Wahrheit und Methode* (1961), ten years in the making, Gadamer had shown that the Enlightenment's claim to objectivity in knowing (i.e., its professed hostility to prejudice) was in and of itself a huge prejudice—one, in fact, that obstructs the very process of understanding. Why? The key characteristic of human understanding is self-understanding, which occurs only by way of discovering whatever is "other." Continuous with understanding there must obviously be freedom, but only freedom of the considerate, thoughtful kind will do. So Gadamer could explain the philosophic vocation he had discovered for the second half of his long life:

> Not so much acknowledging one's limitations in the presence of otherness, as reducing them by a few paces. What became important was this: being capable of being wrong. And where was otherness except everywhere? Who am I, and who are you?—the question is never answered, yet as a question it is its own answer; from then on, I made it my business to keep asking it.[14]

At the Liturgy just before the conclave that was to elect Pope John Paul II's successor, Joseph Ratzinger, the dean of the College of Cardinals, spoke as follows:

> What storms of doctrine we have known in these last decades, what currents of ideology, how many fads of thought . . . The small boat of many Christians' consciousness has often been shaken by these waves— thrown from one extreme to another: from marxism to [*laissez faire*] liberalism verging on libertinism; from collectivism to radical individualism; from atheism to a vague religious mysticism; from agnosticism to syncretism, and so forth. New sectarian groups are born every day, and they illustrate what Saint Paul called the deceit caused by people, the cunning that will lead to error [cf. Eph 4, 14]. A clear faith based on the Church's Creed is regularly labelled fundamentalism. In the meantime, relativism, i.e., allowing oneself to be carried back and forth by whatever teaching blows in the wind, is made to look like the only attitude worthy of these modern days. A dictatorship of relativism that refuses to regard anything as definite is establishing itself; the only standard left is one's own ego and one's own needs.

These are harsh words, and the use of the term "relativism" is questionable for metaphysical reasons—isn't everything created by definition relative?[15] Still, the point of both thinkers—Gadamer, an agnostic with a deep flair for otherness of every kind; Ratzinger, a learned Bavarian cradle-Catholic priest-theologian—is near-identical. Both indicate that in order to have a functional human community we need more than scientific-technological ingenuity and social contracts coercing us to live rationally, i.e., by moral laws and civil duties. Why? Humanity's undeniable power needs ethical or at least legal foundations; yet the precondition for all actual constructive human conduct must be rooted in consideration of otherness, both infra-human and human. Without this native openness—the soul of our "nobility from on high"—the life of ordinary human (self-)communication cannot be conceived.[16] This willing, unenforceable surrender of self depends on the Holy Spirit enabling human beings to respect each other.

Let us elaborate. Finite though we are, we are not the prisoners of finitude. That is, philosophically as well as theologically speaking, we cannot help acknowledging, natively, implicit in whatever positions we adopt, and *a fortiori* in professed religious positions, a reference to all of reality, and thus, in a radical sense, to God; not for nothing does crass sectarianism of any kind strike us as incompatible with mature humanity. Even the Enlightenment understood that.

This native human openness must never be taken for granted, for God is always to be worshiped in and above all, whatever religious commitments human beings live by. This gift of unconditioned openness, Christians say, is definitively incarnate in Jesus, the Christ unjustly executed, yet raised to Life for good. So, wherever the human openness to this gift is publicly treated as impractical or even prejudicial, what we get to see is the sin against the Holy Spirit (Mk 3:29 parr.)—the sin that can lead only to a culture of death (cf. 1 Jn 5:16c).

Global Participation and the Tradition of Christian Faith

From the point of view of contemporary North American religious culture, we are now living in a man-made world of global participation. Participation-by-communication has slowly led us to a world in which the native human aspirations to *liberté*, *égalité*, *fraternité* have taken shape.

As ever, commerce and warfare—"coin and cannon"—have paved the way. We got humanely serious in the Middle Ages, by dint of dynamic commercial exploits by soloists like Marco Polo and allied cities like the Hanseatic League. We became burghers rather than serfs; we began to live by dint of deliberate exploration, by turns imaginative and forceful—the two never quite in the right proportion from the Christian or even moral point of view; the

Crusades, for example, ended up damaging us all. A process of relatively moderate transmigration and colonization followed. At the hands of Spaniards and Portuguese, expansionism turned imperial and Catholic. Justified as missionary, the Spanish *Conquista* turned into savagery, as evidenced by the slave trade and the systemic oppression of the poor by the rich. Eventually, proud Spaniards exported their *limpieza de sangre* as a claim to socio-religious superiority. Iberians ended up practicing the heartless, anti-clerical mercantilism of the Enlightenment spirit, which poisoned the now powerless imperial courts. This spelled the end of all habits of charity; the rule of raw practical law effectively took over. By this time, too, the Protestant Northwest European powers were defeating the Spanish and Portuguese colonists on the coasts and islands of Asia and America. Eventually, only Catholic Quebec was to remain—a monument to Catholic French expansionism (if, in due course, also to its Jansenism).

The eighteenth-century spirit of enterprise rode high; yet the blessings of the Western hemisphere were contested. Thus Charles Ronan can refer to "an influential group of Eurocentric savants," who were

> staunch advocates of their century's doctrine of progress and belief that no development of consequence was possible outside the pale of European civilization. Hence, the picture these "degraders of America" drew of the New World and her inhabitants was most unflattering. Deeply antipathetic toward the theory of the "noble savage" and the "American mirage," they embarked on a pseudo-philosophical conquest that gave the New World a very bad press.[17]

Still, in North America, the spirit of the Enlightenment won out. Atheism was as yet barely thinkable, being considered savage and immoral; but the new "useful" learning had the advantage of being theistic, at least in theory. A gradual cultural changeover from revealed (i.e., Christian) religion occurred; the new aegis became "natural religion," the intellectual perspective favored by Cartesian and Newtonian mechanics and metaphysics, and Carl Linnaeus's *Systema Naturae*.[18]

This perspective, now roughly three centuries old, found itself fashioned in English-speaking North America, and has long spread to include Canada. It has perceptibly remained indebted to the seventeenth-century liberal-Protestant taste for principled tolerance of all types of religious doctrines and its professed indifference to establishments of religion. If anything struck Alexis de Tocqueville as remarkable after only sixty years of the United States of North America, it was the absence of anti-religious animus: the Founding Fathers of the United States had been visibly successful in devising a true republic, with plenty of room for varieties of (Christian) religion. In so doing, they had made something truly new, "under God."[19]

What is more, in the early nineteenth century, North America was gaining respect in Europe to the point of fascination. It was especially admired in France, where, however, the revolutionary spirit was finding itself defeated by successive imperial monarchies; "Lafayette" became a household word. Yet from the 1832 Reform Act on, and with the support of a common language, England and Scotland were moving in the direction of representative democracy, allowing even Catholics to hold public office. Republican Poles, such as the professional freedom fighter Thaddeus Kosciusko, put themselves on the line for the cause of American freedom. And eventually, in 1859, after the skirmish at Harper's Ferry, the Connecticut-born abolitionist John Brown was hanged and in short order canonized by the hymn:

John Brown's body lies a-mouldering in the grave,
But his soul goes marching on.
Glory, glory, hallelujah!

Two years later, Julia Howe needed less than a day to scrawl, "almost without looking at the paper," the verses of the "Battle Hymn of the Republic." The United States had found its Manifest

Destiny—the virtually eschatological freedom destined for all humanity. Unsurprisingly, the new-found freedom could inspire a Catholic bishop like John Ireland to fervor of apocalyptic proportions.[20]

Meanwhile, the Roman Catholic Church in Europe was finding itself in defensive disarray. It was confused enough to side with the *anciens régimes*, often under invocation of the new political myth of the Middle Ages as Catholic Europe's Golden Age under the papacy. One pope, Gregory XVI, embraced the anti-liberal view and rejected freedom of religion and conscience as "insanity" (*Mirari vos* [1831]); another one, much-plagued Pius IX, issued an encyclical (*Quanta cura* [1863]), followed by a checklist ("syllabus") of eighty formulated doctrinal errors which he had personally condemned (DH 2890-2980).[21]

Papal Rome's most immediate concern, though, was a loss of freedom even more worrisome than enlightened rational modernity. Europe as a whole found itself peppered with a new, artistically very productive phenomenon: nationalism. Especially interesting is the fact that in two Catholic countries, nationalists appealed to the Resurrection to proclaim a religious-political agenda. The Italian *Risorgimento* was anti-clerical and anti-papal. Yet in Paris, in 1831, a band of Polish expatriates led by the deeply Catholic Bogdan Janski were writing a constitution for a reborn, unpartitioned Polish Republic, which some twelve years later led to the founding of a well-known religious community: the Congregation of the Resurrection.[22]

In any case, from the Western hemisphere's point of view, the time for distance from "old Europe" had come. In 1822, United States President James Monroe made it official: "The American continents by the free and independent condition which they have assumed and maintain, are henceforth not to be considered as subjects for future colonization by any European Power." The Spanish-American War (1898) was to prove that it also applied to islands.

In Catholic Latin America, the Church remained theoretically beholden to Rome, but two centuries' worth of civil regime changes saw to it that improvisational adaptation to socio-political facts and fortunes became a way of life. What helped was the fact that large numbers of priests and bishops were religious—more flexible than stationary diocesans. By contrast, across the Atlantic, Europe had fallen victim to two centuries of increasingly polarized and violent socio-political and religious-ecclesiastical turmoil, cresting in two World Wars.

It will never be known how many European Catholics were alienated from the Christian faith by Rome's short-sighted dogmatic propositions against all forms of modernity, but a realist like Pope Pius XI saw that the Catholic Church in Europe had effectively lost not only the enlightened rich and famous in Europe but also the unenlightened working-class poor. Accordingly, he called for Catholic Action.

What was still over the horizon was the realization that the Catholic Church in the new world had found itself tacitly caught within the Latin patriarchate of Rome. Not until Blessed Pope John XXIII decided that "Rome" was ailing from what was to be known as triumphalist stuffiness and called the second Vatican Council did this issue get the recognition it deserved, in documents on the Church (*Lumen Gentium*), on the Oriental Churches (*Orientalium Ecclesiarum*), ecumenism (*Unitatis Redintegratio*), and religious freedom (*Dignitatis Humanae*).

The question for theologians is now: Exactly what (if any) elements of truly eschatological and universalist significance had remained at the first Vatican Council? Let us start with the least often mentioned.

A Call from the Sidelines: George Williams on Universalism

Almost forty years ago, in 1970, Harvard professor George Williams, a student of the Radical Reformation, and a Unitarian (yet arguably crypto-Catholic) friend of then Cardinal-Archbishop Karol Józef Wojtyla of Cracow, argued that the first Vatican Council was effectively more interested in the pope's primacy of jurisdiction than in his infallibility in teaching Christian doctrine and conduct. And indeed, papal infallibility, defined with the highest precision, never became a matter of significant theological consequence in the Catholic Church, despite attempts by later Catholic theologians such as Hans Küng and Luis Bermejo to regard it as a doctrine that was either offensive or superfluous.

By contrast, what Vatican I ended up asserting in the most exorbitant terms and on the narrowest scriptural basis was the pope's primacy of jurisdiction. Christ had bestowed upon Peter the power of the keys of the Kingdom (Mt 16:18) and charged Peter three times to be the supreme leader and shepherd of his entire flock (Jn 21:15-17).

In recent decades, many liberal Catholics have regarded this as Rome's worst failure to connect with modernity. George Williams saw the blessing underneath. Familiar as he was with the history of the Polish Brethren,[23] Williams recognized that on a wider, ecumenical and indeed eschatological perspective, nationalism, including Catholic nationalism, was the greater threat to Christian unity:

> We all agree that the personal activity of Pope Paul, and of his successor one day, touches all of us in a key area. And at the same time we realize that whatever will happen without fracturing the Church into national entities, which is exactly what occurred in the sixteenth century, will be due to a large extent to the victory won over nationalism by the Fathers of 1870.
>
> The spontaneous, even enthusiastic loyalty and the disinterested devotion which inspired the bishops of Vatican I in regard to the Pope were to enable Vatican II in its turn to recognize in all freedom the plurality of rites and juridical regulations without having to fear an intra-catholic nationalism, which was a true menace in Pius IX's day.[24]

No wonder Pope John XXIII signed off on the early documents of Vatican II as *Catholicae Ecclesiae Episcopus*—"Bishop of the Universal Church." Paul VI, admired by John Courtney Murray, followed his example.[25]

What may Pope Paul have had in mind? Minimally, it must have occurred to him that according to the Creed all things and all people remain to be judged in the light of a Justice so final that they cannot hope to know it from direct experience, let alone understand or accomplish it.[26] At best we can hope for it, mostly together, but also individually, in the light of "unanticipated experiences of God's real presence."[27] While we are in the world we live in, "this is the way it is." Yet in the Spirit of Christ's Resurrection we are worshipful because expectant, on probation as followers of Jesus Christ all our lives.

In this way, George Williams's insight leads straight into a fully theological matter of great importance, *viz.*, the eschatological universalism implied in the catholic Creed and the natural universalism that undergirds it.[28] Indeed, the object of this essay is nothing but an attempt to discover and recover the Great Tradition;[29] accordingly, we must attempt to practice what Vatican II recognized as a key and perennial vocation of the Catholic Church, *viz.*, "reading the signs of the times."[30] After all, to those who, led by the Spirit, acknowledge God in Jesus Christ Risen, the world history they are part of is the very stuff of the unfinished history of salvation, to the everlasting glory of God.

Being Catholic in North America Today

This raises the theological issue of the signs of the times with a vengeance. What might they be? Let us begin by not indulging in *Kulturpessimismus*, and think appreciatively and positively. After all, the Tradition has insisted that far from being identical with estrangement, alienation "has a positive prognosis."[31]

North American culture is certainly not thematically anti-Christian, even in our own day. Besides, its record of achievement in the park of both technological and humanitarian enhancement of human life-together is so considerable as to be the envy of the globe—quite apart from any strengths or weaknesses of "capitalism" as a comprehensive socio-economic system. Equally clearly, its recognition of one God "from whom all blessings flow"—i.e., its civil religion, based on humanity's natural religiosity—is a source of sound neighborliness and voluntarism. In Europe, Schleiermacher had pointed out that natural religiosity was self-authenticating, even though it could be found alive only in unity with elements of positive religion, which he still thought of as basically Christian. Interestingly, the parallel holds for the (neo-Protestant) civil religion in the United States and Canada: the freedom of conscience which lies at the root of civil religion is self-authenticating, and it is inseparable from culturally appreciated forms of participation in the community and its political organization, from generous philanthropy, and from neighborly decency.

This had consequences which at one point in modern history became near-indubitable "signs of the times." In 1917, the United States took a stand at the portal of a new, global world. At the initiative of Woodrow Wilson, a liberal Presbyterian evangelizer, the lame League of Nations race-horse ventured out of its gate in Paris and Geneva, only to break its legs a few paces later, on the aggressive reluctance of European nationalism. But New York, symbol of the New World, was the scene of the next attempt, prompted by a visionary Universalist couple: Franklin D. and Eleanor Roosevelt. Starting on December 10, 1948, when the United Nations General Assembly ratified and proclaimed the Universal Declaration of Human Rights, the United States and the principles of its Constitution entered the bloodstream of a worldwide movement toward global integration. All human beings are born free and equal in dignity and rights; they are endowed with reason and conscience and should act towards one another in a spirit of brotherhood. Both times, in acts of secular conversion, the Holy See, under Pope Pius XI, a mountain-climbing scholar of international renown, and Pius XII, a friend of pre-Nazi Germany and a Roman diplomat of high integrity, became active participants in the movement. And eventually, the campaign for universal human dignity and catholic civilization became nothing if not global, as John Paul II, penitent and forceful, proclaimed human rights wherever he went.

It is no exaggeration to say that the twentieth century witnessed the gradual loosening and loss of the affinity between Catholicity and nationality in Mediterranean, Western, and even Central Europe. This phenomenon has eschatological potential. The Irish or the Poles are not quasi-naturally Catholic any more than the Swedes are Lutherans; the Moscow Patriarchate's nervous insistence on the removal of Latin Catholics and Baptists from Russia points in the same direction. The phenomenon is known in the New World, too; neither the Irish nor the Poles are now dutifully Catholic, and "Protestants" (especially of the militant political and sectarian kind) are no longer strangers to Latin America. At the same time we Catholics should recall Karl Rahner's observation that the Catholic Church is now empirically present in every country of the globe.[32] Clearly, concordats are a thing of the past. Equally clearly, an independent Vatican State is not.

All this is not to say that catholicity in North America never harbored any seeds of intellectual and emotional conflict. How so? Leaving aside the Maryland colony, North America has been, right from the start, a largely liberal-Christian revolutionary socio-political experiment, with freedom and human equality as its foundational principles, both of them fruits of Enlightened Neo-Protestant mercantilism, set forth by the great Max Weber. So far so good—i.e., a wonderful start! Again, alienation, understood as the defining human interest in otherness, has a positive prognosis!

A Critical Question for Liberal Catholics

Yet this leaves a deeper, because more universal, question unasked. Can secular North America, and the United States in particular, continue as the world's pioneer of universal freedom, peace, and justice? Christians have a religious right (and perhaps even a patriotic duty) to hope or even expect so. Still, just how common is the common good? Not even the fairest constitutional order is competent to hold it out unconditionally. For one thing, each branch of North American (self-)government—legislative, executive, and judicial—settles matters of freedom, peace, and justice by free votes cast individually. Thus, in principle, a one-vote majority can settle (and has frequently settled) the law of the land.

In this context, on what terms can the Great Tradition of Catholic faith and doctrine find itself at peace and in broad enough sympathy with North American freedom of religion and conscience?

Radical Universalism: Christ's Life, Death, and Resurrection

The answer has to be universalist. In practice it comes down to a common willingness to suffer. For only to the degree in which we North Americans, as bodies politic, find ourselves politically willing to suffer with and on behalf of the disadvantaged everywhere in the world will the United States and Canada be dedicated to participation in the growth and development of the whole world toward Final Justice—i.e., the messianic hope of Jews and Christians. The problem is that the United States and Canada, while enjoying the authority to compel their citizens as a matter of civil law, have as a matter of constitutional self-definition decided not to govern their citizens' consciences, and thus, their freely undertaken religious associations.

From a Catholic standpoint, this is as fair as it was for the man who wrote the *Letter to Diognetus*, and as loaded with consequence. Jewish and Christian worship, conduct, and teaching are unenforceable by civil law, but Jews, Catholics, and other Christians do have bodies of religious law to follow: "in their own lives they surpass the laws."[33] For the Great Tradition has a guiding idea, in the form of the call to *imitatio Christi*.[34] That is to say, Catholic Christianity at its truest, like Judaism at its truest, is committed to the portrayal of God's Creative Word in history. We both await and seek the transformation of the world as a whole, in a history of change that involves daily transformation of ourselves-in-community. Set on our way by God's immemorial promises to mythic "Adam and Eve" and fertile Noah and his boatload, embodied in Abraham's departure into the unknown, specified in the Exodus and the Law of Moses, in the fragile kingdoms of Saul, David, and Solomon, in Israel's Prophets, its Exile, its Second Temple and its Diaspora, and in Jesus' life, ministry, execution, and

Resurrection, Christians and Jews travel toward the Living God beyond each and all socio-political or cultural establishments—a galaxy of missionary witnesses picking up long-suffering associates as it travels (cf. Heb 11:1-12, 2).

Once again, being a Jew or a Christian amounts to more than ideal freedom of conscience or devotion to impressive past example: Judaism and Christianity are dynamically related shapes of the active hope for the Revelation of the Lord's Day—something not even the United States can fancy representing any more, at least not the way it could once seem to be able to.

Being Caught and Conflicted: The Catholic Experience

Now it is not the first time that the Christian Church (or for that matter, Judaism) have gotten themselves caught between cultures. The fourth gospel and the other Johannine writings bristle with the theme, often under the Christological rubric of being "in the world" but not "of the world." Every single Christian establishment, starting at least as early as the Constantinian one, has driven the Christian conscience into tight corners. Luther sought the safety of the Wartburg. Under Generalissimo Francisco Franco, numerous Spanish Catholics chose exile. Throughout the Communist era, the Russian Orthodox Church remained the Soviet Union's established church, only to be gagged, pinioned, and infiltrated by atheists and other rats. In the German nineteen-thirties and forties, Evangelical theologians such as Karl Barth and Dietrich Bonhoeffer found themselves pushed into prophetic exile or retirement—much as Athanasius, Gregory Nazianzen, and John Chrysostom had been in the fourth and fifth centuries in the Mediterranean. Unsurprisingly, we Catholics, being part of North American Christianity, have had our share of enemies in the past, but they were local and untypical. Know-Nothings are strangers in this part of the world.

Still, North America is not miraculously preserved from repeats of this kind of trouble; still, given our traditions of principled tolerance in matters of freedom of religion and individual conscience, it is unlikely to happen. American citizens, self-consciously happy with the United States and its accomplishments as they are, do not make martyrs, certainly not at home. In fact, the shoe may be on the other foot: are we North American Catholics sufficiently discerning about the dubious, downright misleading aspects of the welcome shown to us here in the land of the free? Flannery O'Connor, a Catholic of Irish extraction and a tough-minded American author, was not so sure: "Unfortunately," she wrote, "the word Christian is no longer reliable. It has come to mean anybody with a golden heart."[35]

So the question becomes: are we Catholics now so acculturated to the American way that we fail to notice that it does not really encourage us to be Catholics beyond its own liberal-Protestant and happiness-seeking, financially upward-bound terms? Where is our growth in Christ, as the Mystical Body of Christ? Let us see.

The Open Church: How Are We Free, or, How Free Are We?

Catholics, like everyone else, are at least partly the product of our culture. Thus, we do not usually worry about our use of means and tools; we arguably pay insufficient attention to ends and goals. Along with millions of others we are interested in arms, tools, and quick fixes—at great cost to world peace and to the poor, who depend on sound infrastructures. We do not trouble ourselves overmuch with the possibility that the profit motive and the American dream may well have desensitized us to global concerns typical of catholicity; could it be that both traditional American thankfulness for natural blessings and American generosity in sharing the wealth might require that we change our minds and alter our habits?

We prefer convenience to discipline; like most people in North America, we are in a hurry much of the time, and thus, inconsiderate instead of slowly, maturely discerning. Like most North Americans, we are (quite properly) reluctant to simply subject our minds to the (alleged) teaching of the Church, but we are reluctant to find out by common, open inquiry what our obligations as responsible, democratic Catholics may be; we still count on clergy to tell us, even if we know they may be dead wrong, at least occasionally. Allowing for the lag of our Black and Hispanic fellow-Catholics, we have become loyal, successful, open-minded, fairly prosperous North American citizens. No wonder we are loath to deal with the obvious fact that when it comes to things Catholic, the media, from newspapers all the way to radio and television, show only a slight interest in understanding us as we wish to be understood, let alone in forgiving us.[36] After all, in the media, the constitutional right to freedom from establishments of religion is now made to shade into a right to freedom from all religion.

The key reason behind this is that the media are uninterested in the sacramental nature of the Catholic Church, a feature we leave implicit all too often. In typically Enlightenment fashion, our common culture acknowledges only one guide to life together, *viz.,* "the Law," impartial by definition.[37] In principle, therefore, we Christians will advertise all we want, but the "one-body experience" (which we Catholics deeply associate with the corporate Christian faith made tangible in the Eucharist) has no public rights in North America any more than in second-century Greco-Roman culture. When North Americans say happily that "most Christians attend the church of their choice," the reference is mainly to buildings owned and operated by a local Christian congregation remotely associated with other voluntary communities of more or less the same socio-religious flavor. Also, the common culture and its media cannot be counted on to defer to any supposedly higher (i.e., moral) authority. Politically, this may well be a blessing; theologically, this is a formidable gamble, for simply by being the Catholic Church, we open ourselves to the suspicion of hiding secrets, being corporately prejudiced, and moved by hidden agendas.

Add to this that United States Catholic bishops tend to be dependent on "Rome" and "Romans," and it will look as if we Catholics are begging to be unmasked. We live in a culture that is constitutionally authorized to allow a deliberate investigation and misinformation industry to function, and to call this the fruit of freedom of conscience and self-expression. Put differently, in North

American culture, muckraking may not be a sign of good taste, but it is legal on account of "the public's right to know." As a result, in our prevailing secular culture, for Catholics to try to hide anything in the Church at all is apt to put the media on the scent, and to end up eliciting public exposés as painful as martyrdom—yet without being spiritually productive, as true martyrdom will invariably be. Is Jesus' warning about the revelation of all that is kept secret (Mt 10:26-28 par. Lk 12:2-5) coming into a fresh relevance in our day? Like the writer of the *Letter to Diognetus,* do we not need and indeed want a Church that has nothing to hide?

Interestingly, the culture we are part of, tends to think that openness is all—at least theoretically. Well, let us Catholics join it, for eschatological reasons! Three blessings might follow. First, bishops might stop finding fault with "dissent," for both dissent and its denunciation are grist for the media mill, at the expense of respect for the ordinary Catholic faithful.[38] Second, our bishops might stop sitting tight, hiding their apostolic authority behind the Pope's any and every word, and drawing canonical judgments from it as if it were "the teaching of the Church." Third, their hinting the existence of widespread dissent in the Catholic Church might cease; so would the insults offered to many Catholic laity, who clearly desire active participation in both Church and Ministry; and since motivated Catholics need more, not less care, especially of the collegial, shared kind, it might open the promise of a truly open church.[39] First intuited by a bright Catholic seminarian at the American College, Rome, in 1964, it was seriously started only in 1996, by the late Cardinal Joseph Bernardin, under the title of the Common Ground Initiative.[40]

A Suggestion: Following Christ in Today's Culture

Ever since Justin Martyr's *Apologies,* the Christian Church has professed to be, by divine grace, the fulfillment of all that is positive in the world. This must enable the Church to recognize and welcome, with discriminating love, Christ in the features of the great souls of all times, to admire their wisdom, let themselves be freed by it, and even to adopt it. This would also help the Church return the favor, by accepting economic, social, political, as well as artistic and literary responsibility, and to make its appeal to all men and women of good will, in order to share its moral wisdom with society at large.[41]

Yet throughout, the Christian faith must incorporate an abiding determination to be different. What is the nature of this difference?

Being Different: Aquinas's Implicit Challenge

Cultures shape us, mostly implicitly, but quite often by explicit judgments. The United States Constitution and its amendments attached over time, remains a fine example of an explicit, freedom-shaping document.[42] Yet its implicit judgments are much harder to bring to awareness; witness the loss of public consensus in regard to the existence of an unspecified "right to privacy," in the wake of *Roe v. Wade* (January 22, 1973). Ideologies lurk everywhere.

Here, Thomas Aquinas's teaching on the relationship between nature and grace comes to mind. He developed it in the interest of the encounter between Catholic faith and culture: the Church's witness to the world must integrate grace and nature. That is to say, it must freely combine its own specific profession of faith with the demonstration, by way of an appropriate apologetic, that its principles and practices are also naturally attractive, imbued with reason and good taste. Yet Christians do not live by laws of nature alone; "in their own lives they surpass the laws." For all his thirteenth-century reasonableness, Aquinas knew he was formulating an ideal he could not count on everywhere; he was writing his *Summa contra Gentiles* for young, bright Dominican missionaries training for service in North Africa, a place from which not all came away alive.

Analogously, numerous North American priests, pastoral associates, and parishioners join hands and rub shoulders with dozens of North American Catholics—young and old, married, unmarried, divorced, and widowed, poor, relatively well-off, wealthy, and extremely wealthy, sinners all of them, yet generous, wise, and forgiving, to whom the words of the *Letter to Diognetus* justly apply. They are the true witnesses—quite a few pistics, many charismatics, many more mystics than we know.[43]

Why are the bishops so silent in their regard? Are they unimpressed by Christian laity, unless they are unproblematic "good Catholics"—members of the "church" as only bishops appear to know it? For that matter, why are the bishops so vocal in the laity's regard around election time? Are the laity unable to make up their minds in elections? From what judgment seat came the bishop who said out loud in front of a large group of Catholic chaplains at state universities that he expected vowed religious and priests to be "at least ordinary good Catholics"? For that matter, from what judgment seat came the bishops who declared certain named Catholics to be denying "the teaching of the Catholic Church," implying that they were public sinners? All Catholics are sinners, recognizably so, for quite a few sins—published and unpublished— are noticeable outside the Sacrament of Reconciliation. Yet from the beginning, and equally uncomfortably, lives explicitly aimed at the pursuit of holiness, too, have been an integral part of the *imitatio Christi*. Typically, these lives have taken place at a distance from local communities that have become excessively comfortable with life in the big city and their politically interested bishops. Yet if the best data are to be trusted, Athanasius wrote his *Life of Anthony* between 357 and 362 A.D.—the years just before he made his peace with the Antiochenes, which was to lead to the Church's concord on the faith of Nicaea. Was he hinting that Anthony the Hermit in the desert was the personification of the life for God alone, for the benefit of the Church in the secular city?

In this context it would be irresponsible to pass over the life of Dorothy Day (1897-1980), a quintessential North American woman revolutionary, a journalist and seeker for justice and freedom for all, an activist decrying the material and spiritual poverty of the marginalized. She found herself drawn into the Catholic Church by prayer, and became a witness to the urban poor—underpaid, undervalued as human beings, tools in a merciless production process in whose fruit they never get to share fairly. Her autobiography, *The Long Loneliness*, covers the first half of her life. Surrounded by stubbornly hard-headed men (from some of whom she learned), she describes a life of ever-questioning presence, embodied in the Catholic Worker Movement and the people in and behind it, shown in action in *Loaves and Fishes*. Without her, the Catholic Church at large here in North America would be harmless and effectively incomplete. Thank heaven, her beatification cause is in process.

Being Different: Is North American Ecumenism "Good Enough"?

Yet we North American Christians are typically not forward-looking, let alone consistently eschatological. We are used to interpret Christ's Resurrection in a largely exemplarist fashion, along the following lines.

Jesus lived a simple, exemplary, attractive life, yet "underneath it all," he was a force for goodness on behalf of God, his Father, especially against the hypocritical Pharisees and scribes. Sometimes gentle, sometimes forceful, he was all along giving proof of the fact that he was right in everything he did; in some real sense "He was God." He confirmed this by performing at least a number of "miracles"; he also uttered many memorable sayings reported in the New Testament—even if these reports are perhaps not in every case *historically* true. Still, at least one, viz., "John 3:16" sums it up: God has saved the world because he loves it. How? The main thing Jesus Christ did was this: he offered himself to be our substitute in God's eyes; so he died the horrible death which an angry God had ready for us sinners. God raised him to life and so Jesus became our advocate with God. So the message (i.e., the "Good Word," which all true Christians must help to "get out") is: "Jesus Saves." Professing Jesus Christ "at least for me" as the Savior means "salvation." And salvation is victory (and victory is "not the most important thing; it is the only thing"). So each American Christian agrees that Jesus Christ is the "way to go, in my book."

All Christians pretty much believe this. The problem is that innumerable Catholics tacitly find all of this "true enough." So they will agree that ecumenism is naturally at home in North America. In other words, Christian faith in North America is apt to be a matter of a shared message, not a community. Unsurprisingly, the North American type of Christianity at its best is apt to be soulful, dynamic, effusive, tolerant, and ecumenical on easy terms, yet at a safe distance from "the Catholic thing." Traditionally suspicious of "theological tradition," North American Christianity will resist sober thought, and mistake intellectual integrity for "lack of faith." Yet, being human, even North American Christianity will look for visibility and stability of image; this makes it vulnerable to dependence on surprisingly aggressive right-wing political means, belying its professed love of separation of church and state.[44] While hospitable, it has difficulty serving interests other than North American. Apparently spontaneous, it can harden into repetitiousness, and thus, into lack of understanding *vis-à-vis* whatever is *other*. But don't we know that even trust in "experience" rather than firm teaching can turn implicit, and harden into dull moral monotony supported by tolerant cant?

By contrast, the Great Tradition, as Wilken puts it, "enters history."[45] For Catholics, there is no sound reason to doubt either the faith or the integrity (or the entrepreneurial spirit) of Rev. Billy Graham and his many colleagues-evangelizers. Yet in the end, their appeal stops at individuals ready to turn their lives around and make their peace with their God now. Noble as it is, it stops short of the corporate hope held out by Christ Risen, notably in the Eucharist, the Living God's pledge of Final Justice for all of humanity and the world. That is to say, Catholicity will enter not as a cultural message borrowed from the Scriptures, but as a call to actual Life Together, of which the Scriptures as a whole are both the product and the evidence.[46]

So, when all is said and done, participating in the Great Tradition of Catholic faith has very little in common with the "freedom of religion" as a central feature of North American culture; it shares only a thin slice with most typical Protestant denominations. At the verbal level, North America as a freely-made socio-political artifact is undoubtedly a "Christian culture," as the editors of *First Things* keep reminding us; but this is where the ecumenical consolation must yield to embarrassment. At its best, typical North American Protestantism, like many things made by human hearts and hands and minds, is a moderately well-established mixed blessing.

Why mixed? The religious freedom held by the typical North American kind of Christian can encourage the healthy secular freedom that allows citizens to live conscientiously while actively pursuing lives of holiness, whether Christian, Jewish, Muslim, Hindu, Buddhist, or religious-beyond-words. These blessings, held out in *Nostra Aetate*, Catholics have now joined North American Protestants to hold out to all believers. But that same freedom of religion, being man-made, is also capable of degeneracy. In that case, it will turn into the phony freedom endorsed by a mentality and a culture whose standard of human decency is convenience and sharp contrivance. Such freedom of opinion will encourage and make plausible a wide assortment of ways and means of falling short of deep human decency, all too well known, all too well glossed over, all too well excused by associated influential citizens and the media they control. In this way, in practice, and even in the guise of humaneness, the secularist view of life will be in control; the way of least resistance will win out over temperance and fortitude, law over justice and especially prudence. Religious convictions will be widely found charming but distrusted lest they should prove inconvenient in practice. Religious disagreements will be seen as proof of the need for further license. Religious defections and divisions will be appreciated as signs of sincerity.

This is where a problem arises for Catholic Christianity and Catholic theology. For as a matter of principle, any call to faith in Jesus Christ, while admirable, is theologically insufficient. It obscures the mystery ("sacrament") of Jesus Christ's Presence in the Holy Spirit. For, by the mercy of God, Christian faith is incorporate. Being in Christ is being part of an actual, imperfect community, a visible communal presence in secular society, worshiping, living, and learning in the Spirit of Christ Risen. It is already at work, as a leavening agent in and for the world as a whole, transforming it. Jesus Christ is a very good idea indeed, and God bless all who call upon his name; yet Christian faith is faith together, in Christ's "Body." In Wilken's words, it is "a society or city, whose inner discipline and practices, rituals and creeds, and institutions and traditions are the setting for Christian thinking." If God is God of all at the expense of none, then there is no Christian faith without an actual life with living, imperfect brothers and sisters, ready to forgive and be forgiven.

The Letter to the Hebrews (Heb 12:2-3) expresses this by encouraging—the point of the whole letter—the Christian community. We are to go on looking to (*aphorountes*) Christ as the "trailblazer" (*archgon*) and "consummate runner" (*teleits*) of our faith race. And we are to do so together. First of all, we are not alone; "a galaxy of witnesses" in Israel's long history of endurance surrounds us and spurs us on. Secondly, we are to free ourselves from the cloying burden of sin that keeps slowing us down. Thirdly, this course is not for children, except God's and in companionship with others who have suffered. Fourthly, look at how the Son let himself be treated by sinners!

Epilogue: Paul's Radical Call to Eschatological Faith

Before we conclude this essay, we do well to reread one of the earliest radical Christian writings, Paul's first letter to the Corinthians. Paul knows how to use the stylistic figure known as *hyperbole* ("piling it on") to make his point. If his Corinthians, unable to settle everyday issues (*bitika*) among themselves, take each other to pagan courts, how can they think of themselves as perfect in Christ? Does not the anticipation of Jesus Christ's coming in glory put literally everything in perspective? If judgment on the world is God's, and God's alone, then (so Paul suggests) you are excluding yourselves from any association with God by keeping on judging and blaming others, including even the "angels" (i.e., the invisible powers in creation).

This enables Paul to put the issue of cultural compromise as starkly as possible:

> Don't you know that the holy ones are to sit in judgment on the universe? And if God means to have you sit in judgment on the universe, are you unequal to handling the most trivial cases? Don't you know that we will sit in judgment on the angelic powers, never mind everyday issues? So if you have your differences on everyday issues, will you really settle for judges who have no standing whatever in the community? I say, shame on you! So there is really no one wise enough among you to fairly settle a conflict between brothers or sisters?

"The holy ones sit in judgment on the universe." Paul's point is that despite his making himself available as God (Phil 2:6), Jesus Christ let himself be defeated by both human justice and cosmic courses of events, so as to become in person the saving grace of the universe. He carried off his Father's healing work by not availing himself of the powers that be (cf. Mt 26:53-54; Jn 3:17; 18:36), let alone by victimizing anybody (Lk 23:41c). No wonder Jesus tells us, "Make a point of not judging" (Mt 7:1 parr.; cf. 1 Cor 4:1-16).

We Catholics are to find life in the Body of Christ, and only in that taxing context, by canon law, which must never be taken for the primary vehicle of pastoral care. That would be a departure from Christian freedom. But far more important, as long as we Catholic Christians take any others to civil courts, we are forcing our brothers and sisters to live, as a matter of routine, by the ever-imperfect justice of our mixed culture, justified (but by what standards?) by rationality of the socio-political kind. Accordingly, we repeat the mistake of mythical Adam and Eve: we agree to sit in judgment on each other and on ourselves. What a way to be free!

Today, in North America, if we wish to commit to a firmly Catholic Church, we must attempt what the Great Tradition has attempted from the beginning. It begins with the Resurrection of Jesus Christ. Thus we are to be an unequivocally eschatological community—a matter, not of virtual claims to sinlessness, but of unconditional hope for Final Justice. Put differently, the Church Catholic we profess in the Creed is not a passable interim arrangement for good Catholics prepared to hold enforced truths and obey rational rules—the kind of folk whom young T.S. Eliot, inspired, no doubt, by Ezekiel 37, had in mind when he wrote

But our lot crawls between dry ribs
To keep our metaphysics warm.[47]

Notes

1. Xavier Rynne [Francis X. Murphy], *Vatican Council II: An Authoritative One-Volume Version of the Four Historic Books* (New York: Farrar Straus and Giroux, 1968), 23–56.

2. See Frans Jozef van Beeck, *God Encountered: A Contemporary Catholic Systematic Theology* (henceforth *GE*), vol. 1 (Collegeville, MN: The Liturgical Press, 1997), §§9–11; §14, 2.

3. Much as the United States President spoke like a true American when he accused the perpetrators of the terrorist attacks on September 11, 2001, of "hijacking a great religion."

4. *The Documents of Vatican II,* ed. Walter M. Abbott (New York: America Press and Geoffrey Chapman, 1966), 673–74 (italics added).

5. *The Epistle to Diognetus*, V, 1–4. 6–7. 10 (*SC* 33, pp. 62–65; italics added).

6. Both the address and Origen's letter are in *Sources chrétiennes*, 148.

7. See Thomas H. Tobin, *Paul's Rhetoric in its Contexts* (Peabody, MA: Hendrickson, 2004), 16–78.

8. See Robert Louis Wilken, *The Christians as the Romans Saw Them* (New Haven: Yale University Press, 1984); and Wayne A. Meeks, *The First Urban Christians: The Social World of the Apostle Paul* (New Haven: Yale University Press, 2003).

9. Origen, *Comm. in Mt.,* 14, 7; *MG* 13, 1197.

10. Amos Wilder's *Early Christian Rhetoric* (New York: Harper and Row, 1964) is dead right in pointing out the freshness of New Testament language use, sign of a new start in capacity for life experience. See also Donald D. Evans, *The Logic of Self-Involvement* (New York: Herder and Herder, 1963).

11. *Ep.* 140 (*Liber de gratia Novi Testamenti ad Honoratum*) XXIII, 56 (*CSEL* 44, p. 202; *PL* 33, 561).

12. All those living in the early Jewish-Christian tradition would easily have intuited the twentieth-century anthropologists' thesis: evidence of *intentional burial* is evidence of "civilized humanity."

13. See Frans Jozef van Beeck, "One God: And Other Revelations": *Commonweal* 123 (1996): 15–19.

14. "Am Anderm die eigenen Grenzen nicht so sehr zu erkennen als ein Paar Schritte weit zu überwinden. Was es galt, war, Unrecht haben zu können. Und was war nicht überall das Andere? Wer bin ich, und wer bist du?—daß diese Frage sich nie beantwortet und doch als Frage ihre eigene Antwort ist, das war es was ich fortan zu bewältigen suchte." (Note. I have irretrievably mislaid my reference to this passage.)

15. Many European Catholics would recognize the *facts* enumerated here, yet question the *diagnosis* "dictatorship of relativism." In my judgment, "deep communal desolation" might be an alternative description of the symptoms in Catholic Europe today; if my judgment should fit, other diagnoses and remedies might be appropriate.

16. *"memn menoits an then eugeneias"*: Gregory Nazianzen, *Oration* XXVII (= *Or. theol.* I), 7, 16–17 (*SC* 250, pp. 88–89; *PG* 36, 20C [49–50]); see esp. *GE*, vol.II/1, §95.

17. Charles E. Ronan, *Juan Ignacio Molina: The World's Window on Chile* (New York: Peter Lang, 2002), 143. Ronan refers to the work of Gilbert Chinard for this quotation, but his entire sixth chapter ("America's Detractors and American Myths," 143–63) is an eloquent account of eighteenth-century Eurocentrism.

18. See E.J. Dijksterhuis, *The Mechanization of the World Picture* (Oxford: Clarendon Press, 1961).

19. As individuals, the Founding Fathers considered Christianity morally unnecessary. Free citizens, they theorized, could be trusted to live by individual conscience.

20. See Thomas E. Wangler, "The Birth of Americanism: 'Westward the Apocalyptic Candlestick,' " *The Harvard Theological Review* 65 (1972): 415–36.

21. Oddly, error nr. 80 read: "The Roman Pontiff can and should reconcile himself with progress, liberalism, and contemporary culture, and befriend them" (DH 2980).

22. See Frans Jozef van Beeck, "Christ's Resurrection and the Vowed Life," in *Jubilee: A Commemorative Meditation Presented by the U.S.A.*

Province of the Congregation of the Resurrection in Joyful Observance of its Sesquicentennial (Chicago, 1987), 25–38.

23. Needless to say, sixteenth-century Catholics and Protestants were united in warfare against anti-Trinitarians. Its first victim was Spanish: Michael Servet (Servetus) (1511–53), was a Catholic theologian critical of the doctrine of the Trinity and a physician who had early intuitions about the circulation of the blood in the cardiac-pulmonary system. Pursued by the Inquisition, he went to Geneva looking for safety. Calvin wanted him beheaded; the city council wanted him burned at the stake. The latter prevailed. As Servet was dying, the crowd heard him praying an implicitly Arian profession of faith: "O Jesus, Son of the eternal God, have pity on me." The anti-Trinitarian cause, picked up in Italy by Fausto Sozzini (1539–1604), was later taken to faraway Poland. These Antitrinitarians (known as the Polish Brethren, Arians, or Socinians) settled near the city of Kielce around 1562, and made a point of keeping themselves out of the doctrinal debates of the various Protestant churches looking for a doctrinal consensus. Their purposes were oddly comparable to those of contemporary Jesuits in the region, being mainly intellectual and educational. Not till the year 1658 did they find themselves expelled from Poland, at last branded as Arians.

24. George Hunston Williams, "Omnium christianorum pastor et doctor: Vatican I et l'Angleterre victorienne," *Nouvelle revue théologique* 96 (1974): 113–46, 337–65; quotation at p. 365: "Nous sommes d'accord pour reconnaître que l'action du Pape Paul seul et de celui qui lui succPdera un jour nous concerne tous dans le domaine le plus central. Et en même temps nous nous rendons compte que ce qui se passera sans fragmenter l'Église en entités nationales, comme ce fut le cas au XVIᵉ siècle, on le devra dans une large mesure à la victoire remportée sur le nationalisme par les Pères du Concile en 1870. Le loyalisme spontané et même ouvertement enthousiaste ainsi que le dévouement désintéressé qui inspira si constamment les évêques de Vatican I à l'égard du Pape firent qu'à son tour Vatican II pu en pleine liberté reconnaître la pluralité des rites et des formes juridiques sans plus avoir à redouter un nationalisme intra-catholique qui menaçait à l'époque de Pie IX. Cependant les mêmes forces sont toujours à l'œuvre et disposent d'instruments de plus en plus puissants. Fasse le Ciel que grâce à la fidelité comme au zèle prophétique des catholiques, un Pape du XXᵉ siècle soit effectivement «omnium christianorum pastor et doctor». — Years before, in 1970, in a thoughtful article in *America* magazine titled "Loyalty and Dissent: Perspectives from

History," Williams had elaborated the high *theological* significance of a properly unified Roman Catholic Church, both toward a global ecumenism and as a way to global, civilized peace.

25. John Courtney Murray thought highly of Pope Paul VI's support of *Dignitatis Humanae*. He concluded the essay quoted above (note 1): "The issue of religious freedom was in itself minor. But Pope Paul VI was looking deep and far when he called the Declaration on Religious Freedom 'one of the major texts of the Council.' "

26. See Frans Jozef van Beeck, "What Can We Hope For, Really? Towards a Theological Anthropology of Hope," *Gregorianum* 80 (1999): 489–524.

27. See Frans Jozef van Beeck, "Unanticipated Inner Experiences: Three Cases and a Reflection on Discernment," *Toronto Journal of Theology* 19 (2003): 7–23.

28. See van Beeck, *GE*, vol. Two/1, §59.

29. See van Beeck, *GE*, vol I, §4.

30. Cf. *Gaudium et Spes* 4.

31. On this theme, see van Beeck, *GE* vol. II/3, §122, 1, e, [*f*].

32. See Karl Rahner, "Towards a Fundamental Theological Interpretation of Vatican II," *Theological Studies* 40 (1979): 716–27.

33. So, presumably, have those participating in all kinds of non-Christian "religions." The difference is that in North America such laws have no standing in civil courts, nor do attempts on the part of religious authorities to enforce them.

34. This invites an explanation. Residual Christians like John Toland, the Cambridge Platonists, the German Neologians, Immanuel Kant, and Georg Wilhelm Friedrich Hegel have shown themselves inspired by Jesus' example of deep humanity. So have great souls like Mahatma Gandhi, Dag Hammarskjöld, and many modern agnostics. This is fine from the Catholic point of view. After all, Jesus Christ preached misguidedly is better than not preached at all (see Phil 1:18).

35. Flannery O'Connor, *Mystery and Manners: Occasional Prose* (New York: Farrar, Straus and Giroux, 1969), 192.

36. In North America, we are free to broadcast what we wish to say. Madison Avenue knows only line: "Try it, you'll like it." But once you "buy" the message, you are on your own, unless you can show in a court of law that you have been purposely misled. American Protestantism is mainly *message*, not *community*. Nice Catholics may tell a priest after Mass, "Father, I liked your message," but the sentiment is not Catholic.

37. This raises the issue of the apparent pride of place of Canon Law in the Catholic Churches of North America.

38. Elsewhere, I have elaborated this in the case of the encyclical *Humanae vitae;* see *GE,* vol. Two/4b, §§170, 172.

39. See van Beeck, *GE* vol. I, §54, 4, and also my *Catholic Identity after Vatican II: Three Types of Faith in the One Church* (Chicago: Loyola University Press, 1985), 39.

40. Michael Novak, *The Open Church: Vatican II, Act II* (New York: Macmillan, 1964).

41. Twenty years ago, the American bishops gave us illuminating samples of this by their letters on War and Peace and on Economic Justice for All—documents unnecessarily politicized (mainly in the media, of course) by socio-political nigglings by Catholics on the so-called left and right, and in the end turned to the great and unfortunate gains of the Republican Party and its well-trumpeted "message" of righteousness.

42. See Karl Rahner, "Towards a Fundamental Theological Interpretation of Vatican II," *Theological Studies* 40 (1979): 716–27.

43. See van Beeck, *Catholic Identity after Vatican II.*

44. Were there ever times when the CIA embraced Evangelical Protestantism in Latin America?

45. Robert Wilken, *The Spirit of Early Christian Thought: Seeking the Face of God* (New Haven: Yale University Press, 2003), xv.

46. In the nineteen-thirties, a time of acute crisis, Dietrich Bonhoeffer concluded that *communio* was essential if Christ's purposely peaceful Church was ever to succeed in not becoming a mere function of political expediency, held hostage by public culture and state; see his book, *Life Together* (New York: Harper and Row, 1954). See also Frans Jozef van Beeck, *Sanctorum Communio: Eine dogmatische Untersuchung zur Soziologie der Kirche* (München: Chr. Kaiser Verlag, 1969); translated into English as *The Communion of Saints* (New York: Harper and Row, 1963).

47. T.S. Eliot, *Collected Poems 1909–1962* (London: Faber and Faber, 1963).

Contributors

JUDITH HERSHCOPF BANKI is one of the pioneers of organized interreligious dialogue. She is an award-winning author (Graymoor Prize) whose articles have appeared in *Commonweal, Religious Education,* the *Journal of Ecumenical Affairs,* and *The American Jewish Year Book,* where her coverage of the struggle over *Nostra Aetate* at the Second Vatican Council constituted the major Year in Religion article for two consecutive years. More recently, she co-edited an anthology of the writings of Rabbi Marc Tanenbaum, and two volumes emerging from conferences at Catholic Theological Union and Cambridge University which she helped coordinate. She was awarded an honorary doctorate by Seton Hall University for her work in promoting Jewish-Christian understanding, and received the "Peace through Dialogue" Interfaith Gold Medallion from the International Council of Christians and Jews.

FRANS JOZEF VAN BEECK, S.J., Ph.D., was born in Helmond, the Netherlands, on June 1, 1930, became a Jesuit in 1948, and was ordained a priest on July 31, 1963. He started teaching at Boston College in 1968. In 1985, he accepted the John Cardinal Cody Chair of Sacred Theology at Loyola University, Chicago, where he soon wrote two books on ecclesiology and the Catholic Church's relationship with contemporary Judaism. He continues to work on his multi-volume project, *God Encountered: A Contemporary Catholic Systematic Theology,* and has recently published *Driven Under the Influence: Essays in Theology, 1974-2004.*

EDWARD IDRIS CARDINAL CASSIDY, a native of Australia, is the President Emeritus of the Pontifical Council for Promoting Christian Unity within the Vatican and headed the Commission of the Holy See for Religious Relations with the Jews. He was elevated to a Cardinal in June 1991, and returned to Australia upon his retirement in 2001. His book *Rediscovering Vatican II: Ecumenism and Interreligious Dialogue* (2005), marking the fortieth anniversary of *Nostra Aetate,* made a significant contribution to ongoing international interreligious dialogue. In 2004, he created controversy with his comment that *Dominus Iesus*, a declaration issued by the Vatican's Congregation for the Doctrine of the Faith, did not completely represent the Catholic Church's position on ecumenism and interreligious dialogue.

ANTHONY J. CERNERA, Ph.D., is President of Sacred Heart University in Fairfield, Connecticut. The holder of a Doctorate of Philosophy in Systematic Theology from Fordham University, he continues to teach undergraduate and graduate students in related disciplines. He is president of the International Federation of Catholic Universities and is on the Board of Directors of the Association of Catholic Colleges and Universities. Dr. Cernera is the editor of *Toward Greater Understanding, Vatican II: The Continuing Agenda, Continuity and Plurality in Catholic Theology, Lay Leaders in Catholic Higher Education*, and, with Oliver J. Morgan, two volumes *of Examining the Catholic Intellectual Tradition.*

PHILIP A. CUNNINGHAM, Ph.D., is Executive Director of the Center for Christian-Jewish Learning and Adjunct Professor of Theology at Boston College. The author of several articles and books, his academic interests include biblical studies, religious education, and theologies of Christian-Jewish relations. The author of numerous articles on Christian-Jewish relations, his most recent books are *A Story of Shalom: The Calling of Christians and Jews by a Covenanting God* and *Sharing the Scriptures*, both published by the Paulist Press.

EUGENE FISHER, Ph.D., recently retired as Associate Director of the Secretariat for Ecumenical and Interreligious Affairs of the U.S. Conference of Catholic Bishops, in charge of Catholic-Jewish relations, a position he held since 1977. His doctoral degree, from New York University (1976), is in Hebrew Culture and Education. He has published some twenty books and over 300 articles in major religious and scholarly journals, many of them translated into several languages. Since 1981, he has chaired the National Workshops for Christian-Jewish Relations, held in cities throughout the U.S. In April of 1985, Dr. Fisher was appointed by Pope John Paul II to be Consultor to the Vatican Commission for Religious Relations with the Jews, receiving his fifth quinquennial appointment in 2003. In May of 2007, he was awarded the Anti-Defamation League's Dr. Joseph L. Lichten Award and was honored by the National Council of Synagogues for his work in Catholic-Jewish relations. In June, he was honored by the American Jewish Committee and given their Cardinal Joseph Bernadine "Common Ground" Award.

REV. LAWRENCE E. FRIZZELL, D.Phil., is Department Chair of Jewish-Christian Studies and the Director of the Institute of Judaeo-Christian Studies at Seton Hall University. He pursued graduate work at the University of Ottawa and the Pontifical Biblical Institute in Rome, and received a Doctorate of Philosophy from the University of Oxford, where he specialized in the Qumran Scrolls.

REV. JOHN T. PAWLIKOWSKI, O.S.M., Ph.D., a Servite priest, is Professor of Social Ethics and the Director of Catholic-Jewish Studies at the Cardinal Bernardin Center at the Catholic Theological Union in Chicago. He is also President of the International Council of Christians and Jews, centered at Heppenheim, Germany, and is a member, by presidential appointment, of the U.S. Holocaust Memorial Council. Father Pawlikowski is the author and editor of more than fifteen books, including *Jesus and the Theology of Israel, Reinterpreting Revelation and Tradition: Jews and Christians in Conversation,* and, most recently, *Ethics in the Shadow of the Holocaust.* He is currently at work on a book on non-Jewish victims of the Nazis.

RABBI MORDECAI WAXMAN (deceased August 2002) was the spiritual leader of Temple Israel in Great Neck, New York, for fifty-five years. He was instrumental in shaping the character of Vatican-Jewish relations and the Catholic-Jewish dialogue in the U.S. Among other numerous affiliations with various interreligious dialogue organizations, he was the chairman of the International Jewish Committee on Interreligious Consultations, recognized by the Vatican as the official Jewish representative in international Christian-Jewish relations.

Index

A Guest in the House of Israel, 71

A Sacred Obligation, 68, 73

'abhodah, 38

"Abraham's Heritage–A Christmas Gift," 23

adversos Judaeos, 63

Ambrose, Saint, 104

American Jewish Committee, 5, 79, 85, 92, 95

American Jewish Congress, 85

Annual Institute for Seminarians and Rabbinical Students, 155

Anthony the Hermit, 202

Anti-Judaism, 9, 10, 12, 22, 24, 103, 131-36, 147

Anti-Semitism, 6, 9, 10, 20, 30, 49, 81, 83, 86, 88, 89, 91, 95, 98, 99, 103, 104, 117, 123, 131, 132, 135, 136, 161, 168

aphorountes, 206

Apologies, 172, 200

Aquinas, Saint Thomas, 127, 201

Arafat, Yassir, 104, 124

archgon, 206

Athanasius, 197, 202

Augustine, Saint, 48, 67, 115, 127, 133, 134, 184

Auschwitz, 8, 14, 90-93, 103, 104, 124, 138, 153, 156, 172

autobasileia, 183

Barak, Eliud, 154

Barbie, Klaus, 101

Barth, Karl, 197

Baum, Gregory, 57

Bea, Augustine Cardinal, 67, 113, 164

Ben-Hure, Oded, 156

Benedict XVI, Pope, 1, 16, 23, 25, 27, 66, 69, 73, 74, 89, 186

Bermejo, Luis, 192

Bernard of Clairvaux, Saint, 116

Bernardin, Joseph Cardinal, 62, 70, 73, 200

Bernstein, Leonard, 13

Bishop, Claire Huchet, 97

bitika, 206

Bonhoeffer, Dietrich, 197

Boyarin, Daniel, 71, 72

Boys, Mary, 71

Brown, John, 189

Brown, Raymond, 61, 64
Buber, Martin, 140
Bultmann, Rudolf, 62
B'nai B'rith Anti-Defamation
  League, 6

Carmina Burana, 118
Casseroli, Cardinal, 86, 87
Catechism of the Catholic
  Church, 149
Catholic Bishops' Committee
  on the Liturgy, 61
Catholic Commission on
  Religious Relations with the
  Jews, 79
Catholic Theological Society of
  America, 57
Catholic Worker Movement,
  203
Catholic-Jewish dialogue, 3, 8,
  59, 66
Catholic-Jewish relations, 1,
  5, 6, 8, 12-14, 25, 30, 35,
  42, 50, 51, 57, 59, 60, 86,
  92, 99, 124, 125, 137, 160,
  164
Catholicae Ecclesiae Episcopus,
  192
Center for Christian-Jewish
  Understanding of Sacred
  Heart University (CCJU),
  143-59
Centre for the Study of Jewish-
  Christian Relations
  (Cambridge), 68
Chamberlain, Neville, 120, 135
Charlesworth, James, 62
Chazan, Robert, 116
Chief Rabbis of Israel, 18

*Christ in the Light of the
  Christian-Jewish Dialogue*, 73
Christendom, 96, 101, 106,
  115, 135, 136
Christian Scholars Group on
  Christian-Jewish Relations,
  73
christology, 73, 74
Chrysostom, Saint John, 197
Cohen, Shar Yishuv, 18
Colleagues in Dialogue, 156
Commission for Religious
  Relations with the Jews
  (CRRJ), 4, 9, 15, 18, 19, 66,
  68, 99, 100, 126, 148, 156,
  160, 162
Committee on Church and the
  Jewish People, 4
compline, 39
Conciliar Declaration, 5, 31,
  146, 167
Congregation for the Doctrine
  of the Faith, 16, 23
Congregation of the
  Resurrection, 190
*Constitution on Divine
  Revelation (Dei Verbum)*, 45-
  49, 144
*Constitution on the Sacred
  Liturgy (Sacrosanctum
  Concilium)*, 36
contra-Judaeos, 139
conversion, 13, 26, 29, 50, 80,
  102, 115, 119, 124, 133,
  172, 176, 194
Council Fathers, 2, 40, 48, 51,
  58, 125, 166
Council of Trent, 133, 149
Councils of the Church, 121

Cullmann, Oscar, 36
Cunctos populos, 177
Cushing, Richard Cardinal, 145

dabhar, 46
Danielou, Jean, 67
Davies, W.D., 62
Day, Dorothy, 202-03
Declaration on Religious Freedom (Dignitatis Humanae), 177
Decree on Ecumenism and Religious Liberty, 44, 50, 51
"Day of Pardon," 13
Decree on the Church's Missionary Activity, 51
Decree on the Ministry and Life of Priests, 48
Dialogue with Trypho, 102
Divine Office of Lauds and Vespers, 39, 40
Divino Afflante Spiritu, 36, 45
"Dominica," 100
Dominus Jesus, 23, 73
Dreyfuss, Richard, 13
Dulles, Avery Cardinal, 58, 66, 69
Duprey, Pierre, 88

Ecumenical and Interreligious Affairs Committee, 25
Ecumenical Council of the Church, 111
Eichmann, Adolf, 101
Emmerich, Anne Catherine, 170
eschaton, 43
eschatology, 102
Eucharist, 97, 98, 131, 199, 204
evangelization, 26, 66

Fathers of the Second Vatican Council, 1
Federice, Tomaso, 26, 80
First Vatican Council. *See* Vatican I
Flannery, Edward, 103
Franco, Francisco, 197
French Bishops' Committee for Relations with Jews, 99
Fumagalli, Francesco, 82, 92

Gadamer, Hans-Georg, 185, 186
Gaudium et Spes, 48-50, 145, 146
Geiger, Abraham, 140
genocide, 10, 49, 131, 135
gentile, 2, 27, 29, 41-43, 49, 63, 64, 67, 71, 80, 99, 122, 123, 132, 161, 163, 182, 201
German Society for Christian-Jewish Collaboration, 152
Gibson, Mel, 60
Glemp, Józef Cardinal, 91-93
Gobineau, Joseph Arthur, Comte de, 135
God's Mercy Endures Forever, 61
Graham, Billy, 204
Great Rabbinate of Jerusalem, 18
Great Tradition, 193, 196, 204, 207
Gregory the Great, Saint, 115, 133
Gregory XVI, Pope, 190
Guidelines and Suggestions for Implementing the Conciliar Declaration Nostra Aetate, 5, 143, 146, 167
Guidelines for Catholic-Jewish Relations, 99

Harrington, Daniel, 62
Hegel, Georg Wilhelm Friedrich, 140
Hertzberg, Arthur, 119
Heschel, Abraham Joshua, 84, 127, 172
Higgins, George G., 125
Holocaust, 14, 59, 74, 79, 81, 83, 84, 86-88, 92, 93, 95, 104, 120, 126, 127, 130, 136, 141, 149, 150, 151, 154, 155, 158. *See also Shoah*
Holocaust (television miniseries), 126
Holy See, 4, 9, 35, 66, 68, 69, 86-88, 104, 124, 126, 127, 130, 132, 136, 137, 141, 154, 156, 194
Howe, Julia, 189
Hruby, Kurt, 67
Humani Generis Unitas, 161, 163, 166, 170

International Jewish Committee for Interreligious Consultations (IJCIC), 5, 6, 15, 78, 83-86, 88
Institute for Judeo-Christian Studies at Seton Hall University (IJCS), 143, 147, 149, 151
International Catholic Liaison Committee (ILC), 4-9, 15, 16, 30
Image of God, 19, 22, 28
imitatio Christi, 196, 202
Institute for Judeo-Christian Studies at Seton Hall University, 143, 147, 157

Institute of Contemporary Jewry, 30
International Catholic-Jewish Liaison Committee, 4, 5
International Council of Christians and Jews, 59
International Jewish Committee for Interreligious Consultations, 5, 141
Interreligious Assembly for Peace, 153
Ireland, John, 190
Isaac, Jules, 97, 112, 113, 132, 143
Israel Interfaith Committee, 79
Israel Jewish Council for Interreligious Dialogue, 6

Janski, Bogdan, 190
Jerome, Saint, 48, 182
Jewish Scriptures, 17, 37, 39, 47, 71, 97, 132
Jewish-Christian Relations, 18, 35, 69, 74, 95, 103, 113, 107, 116, 130, 133, 139, 154
The Jewish People and Their Scriptures in the Christian Bible, 16
Jews for Jesus, 118, 140
John, Saint, 103, 110, 172, 193
John Paul I, Pope, 80
John Paul II, Pope, 1, 6-9, 11-14, 18, 29, 31, 35, 60, 61, 66, 69, 81, 83, 87, 103, 104, 121, 123, 125, 126, 129, 147-49, 153, 154, 158, 165-68, 181, 185, 186, 191, 194

John XXIII, Pope, 13, 40, 78,
113, 132, 143, 163, 164,
176, 191, 192
Jubilee Year 2000, 13, 141
Judaism, 3-5, 9, 10, 12, 18,
19, 21, 22, 24, 26, 28, 31,
35, 48, 60-74, 78-80, 82-
85, 92, 96-100, 102, 103,
108-111, 113-16, 121, 126,
127, 131-39, 142-44, 146,
147, 149, 150, 155, 161,
164-67, 170, 171, 183,
196, 197
"Judensau," 134

Kaddish (symphony by Leonard
Bernstein), 13
Kasemann, Ernst, 62
Kasper, Walter Cardinal, 18,
26, 31, 66, 68, 69, 73, 148,
160, 164
Keeler, William Henry
Cardinal, 86, 87, 89-91
Kelman, Wolfe, 86
Kennedy, John F., 129
Kittel, Gerhard, 62
Klapperman, Gilbert, 85, 88
Klenicki, Leon, 83, 96
Kosciusko, Thaddeus, 189
Kulturpessimismus, 193
Küng, Hans, 192

Lateran Council, 88, 117, 121
"Law of Love," 138
League of Nations, 194
Lercaro, Giacomo Cardinal,
172
Letter to Diognetus, 179, 180,
196, 200, 202

Letter to the Hebrews, 43, 58,
206
lex talionis, 101
Lieberman, Joseph, 153
Life of Anthony, 202
limpieza de sangre, 188
Linnaeus, Carl, 189
Loaves and Fishes, 203
The Long Loneliness, 203
Lopez, Aharon, 154
Lumen Gentium, 40, 42-46,
121, 122, 191
Lustiger, Jean-Marie Cardinal,
20

Macharski, Franciszek Cardinal,
92
Mahoney, Archbishop Roger
Michael, 90
Marcion of Pontus, 103
Maritain, Jacques, 67
Martini, Carlo Cardinal, 62, 65
Martyr, Saint Justin, 102, 182,
200
"Mass of Pardon," 168
Mbiti, John, 58
Mediator Dei, 36
Meeks, Wayne, 64
Meier, John, 62
Mejia, Jorge Cardinal, 19, 79,
83
Messiah, 25, 28, 44, 60, 67,
68, 74, 96, 97, 133, 146,
184
metanoia, 160, 161, 169, 172
Metz, Johannes-Baptist, 59, 65
mezuzah, 139
Michelman, Henry, 86
mirari vos, 190

The Mission of the Jews and the Perfection of the World, 27
mitzvoth, 108
Monroe, James, 190
Murray, John Courtney, 177-79, 192
Muszynski, Henryk, 92
mystici corporis, 36

National Catholic Commission for Relations with the Jews, 99
National Conference of Catholic Bishops, 90, 99
National Conference of Catholic Bishops' Subcommittee for Catholic-Jewish Relations, 99
National Conference of Christians and Jews, 89
National Council of Synagogues USA, 25
Nazianzen, Saint Gregory, 197
Nazism, 8, 15, 22, 23, 120, 124
Neusner, Jacob, 69
New Catechism Conferences, 151
"New Liturgy," 176
New Testament, 10, 16, 17, 37, 39, 43-45, 47, 61-63, 66, 67, 83, 108, 111-14, 132, 134, 138, 139, 144, 167, 169, 170, 203
Notes on the Correct Way to Present the Jews and Judaism in Preaching and Catechesis in the Roman Catholic Church, 5, 83, 100, 133, 136, 157

Noth, Martin, 62
Nuremberg Trials, 101

Oesterreicher, John, 40, 147
Old Testament, 2, 16, 36, 39, 41, 43, 47, 60, 61, 79, 124, 122, 138, 144, 167
Orientalium Ecclesiarum, 191
Origen, 162, 163, 180, 181, 183
O'Connor, Flannery, 198
O'Connor, John Cardinal, 86, 90, 93, 153

papal nuncio, 86
Paschal, 36, 37, 43, 100
The Passion of Sister Rose, 59
The Passion of the Christ, 60, 170
Passover, 37, 10, 110, 111, 113, 146
Paul, Saint, 2, 41, 42, 43, 44, 58, 60, 62-64, 67, 80, 109, 110, 111, 113, 122-23, 163, 180, 182, 186, 206, 207
Paul VI, Pope, 1-4, 82, 164, 192
Perelmuter, Hayim, 69, 71
perfidus, 163
Peter, Saint 78, 182, 192
Phan, Peter, 58
Pharisees, 60, 83, 111, 112, 203
Pilate, Pontius, 132, 184
Pius IX, Pope, 190, 192
Pius XI, Pope, 47, 161, 162, 191, 194
Pius XII, Pope, 36, 45, 125, 129, 194
Polish Brethren, 192

Pontifical Biblical Commission, 16, 17, 66, 67, 73, 169
Pontifical Commission for Religious Relations, 156, 160, 162
Proclaim the Truth (Dabru Emet), 21, 23, 25, 59, 61, 66, 74, 150
Protestant Reformation, 135
Psalms, 37, 39, 47, 108

Qahal, 43
Quanta cura, 190

Rad, Gerhard von, 36
Radical Reformation, 191
Rahner, Karl, 195
rationalis creatura, 184
Ratzinger, Joseph Cardinal. *See* Pope Benedict XVI
Reagan, Ronald, 101
Regimini Ecclesiae, 3
Religion and Violence, Religion and Peace, 153, 155
Religion, Violence and Peace: Continuing Conversations and Study Guide, 155
Resurrection, 36, 37, 58, 93, 107, 110, 118, 190, 193, 196, 197, 203, 207
Riegner, Gerhardt, 79, 83, 87
Risorgimento, 190
Rivkin, Ellis, 69
Roman Curia, 4
Roncalli, Angelo. *See* John XXIII, Pope
Roosevelt, Eleanor, 194
Roosevelt, Franklin D., 194
Rudin, James, 92

Sacred Scriptures, 17, 36, 47
Saldarini, Anthony J., 64, 70
"Salvation History," 36
Sanders, E.P., 62, 99
schism, 65
Schleiermacher, Friedrich, 194
Scroggs, Robin, 62-64
Second Vatican Council. *See* Vatican II
Segal, Alan, 64, 71
Shema, 39, 139
Shoah, 8-11, 13, 14, 24, 79, 106, 124, 126, 130, 131, 136, 143, 145, 148-50, 154, 156, 158, 168. *See also* Holocaust
Shuemli, Efraim, 69
Siegman, Henry, 79
Sinai Covenant, 37
Solveitchik, J.B., 81
Stein, Edith, 7, 124
Stepinac, Aloysius Cardinal, 125
Strober, Gerhard, 97
Summa contra Gentiles, 201
Syllabus of Errors, 178, 179
Synagogue Council of America, 5, 78, 79, 81, 85, 88, 90, 141
Systema Naturae, 189

Talmud, 29, 82, 127
Tanakh, 79
Tanenbaum, Mark, 79, 86
teaching of contempt, 97, 112, 113, 122, 132, 133, 135, 137, 138, 162, 168, 762
Teleits, 206
Thaumatourgos, 181

Thering, Rose, 59, 137, 147
Thoma, Clemens, 62
Tikun ha-olam, 28
Tocqueville, Alexis de, 189
Torah, 11, 22, 64, 108, 109, 111, 139
Towards Greater Understanding, 155
Two Types of Faith, 140
Typical Jewish Misunderstandings of Christianity, 139

U.S. Bishops Study Tour, 156
Unitatis Redintegratio, 191
United Nations General Assembly, 194
United States Bishops' Commission for Catholic-Jewish Relations, 25
United States Conference of Catholic Bishops, 25, 57
Universal Declaration on Human Rights, 51

Vatican, 5, 12, 13, 23, 57, 59, 60, 68, 69, 78, 85, 87, 92, 93, 99, 100, 114, 127, 130, 131, 133, 135, 136, 137, 148, 156, 163, 167, 195
Vatican I, 191, 192
Vatican II, 1, 4, 8, 17, 26, 35, 36, 57, 59, 60, 74, 78, 95, 98, 105, 106, 108, 109, 113, 121, 124, 127, 132, 137, 144, 145, 147, 152, 157, 160, 161, 166, 168, 169, 172, 176, 177, 191, 192, 193

Vatican Congregation for the Doctrine of the Faith, 23
Vatican-Jewish International Dialogue, 57
Voltaire, Francois Marie Arouet de, 119, 135

Wagner, Richard, 120
Wahrheit und Methode, 185
Waldheim, Kurt, 7, 85, 86, 88, 101, 104, 124
We Remember: A Reflection on the Shoah, 9, 130, 143, 148
Weber, Max, 195
Weiss, Avi, 91
What Do We Want the Other to Teach About Us?, 154, 155
Wigoder, Geoffrey, 30, 83
Wilken, Robert, 64, 204, 206
Willebrands, Johannes Cardinal, 3, 6, 7, 30, 79, 81, 83, 84, 86-88
Williams, George, 191-93
Williamson, Clark, 71
Wilson, Woodrow, 194
Wissenschafte des Judentuums, 99, 140
Wojtyla, Karol Jozef, 191. *See* John Paul II, Pope
World Council of Churches, 4, 59
World Jewish Congress, 5, 20, 78, 79

Yad Vashem, 14, 154
Yerushalmi, Yosef, 135, 136

Zunz, Leopold, 140